The
Theology
of

H. RICHARD NIEBUHR

by

Libertus A. Hoedemaker

The Pilgrim Press
New York City

The author wishes to thank the individuals, journals, and publishers who have graciously granted permission to quote from their copyrighted material. A list of acknowledgments appears on pages xi-xii. Other brief quotations are acknowledged in Notes.

ISBN 0-8298-0186-3
Library of Congress Catalog Card Number 78-139271

Copyright © 1970 United Church Press
The Pilgrim Press, 132 West 31st Street
New York, N.Y. 10001

CONTENTS

Foreword   v

Acknowledgments   xi

Preface   xiii

Introduction   xv
    1. Niebuhr the Theologian   xv
    2. Variety and Consistency   xvi
    3. Purpose of the Present Study   xviii

CHAPTER 1: Choice of Direction   1
    A. Persistent Patterns   1
        1. Sovereignty and Pluralism in American Religion   1
        2. The Liberal Heritage   7
        3. The Problem of Troeltsch   11
    B. Post-liberal Consciousness   17
        1. The End of an Era   17
        2. Influences from European Crisis-theology   21
        3. The Deity of God and the Conversion of the Church   27

CHAPTER 2: Development of Position   33
    A. The Structure of Niebuhr's Theology   33
        1. The Rediscovery of Jonathan Edwards   33
        2. Radical Monotheism   38
        3. The Major Themes in Retrospect   45
    B. The Temper of Niebuhr's Theology   51
        1. The Nature of God   51
        2. The Possibility of Faith   56
        3. The Interpretation of Moral Existence   60

CHAPTER 3: The Scope of Responsibility   65
    A. The Triad of Faith   65
        1. Self, Community, and Cause   65
        2. Social Selfhood and Absolute Dependence   71
        3. Speaking of God   77
    B. The Moral Life   80
        1. The Sovereign God and the Moral Life   80
        2. Shaping the Response   85
        3. The Dethronement of the Gods   89

CHAPTER 4: The Revelation of God in Christ   93
  A. The Possibility of Historical Revelation   93
    1. The Problem of History   93
    2. Revelation and the Duality of Internal and External History   98
    3. The Community and the Interpretation of History   105
  B. The Unity of God and the Work of Christ   108
    1. Trinity   108
    2. Reconciliation and Christology   115
    3. History, God, and Christ   120

CHAPTER 5: The Church   127
  A. The Christian Community   127
    1. The Confessional Attitude   127
    2. The Authority of Scripture   131
    3. The Symbols of the Christian Faith   135
  B. The Church in the World   138
    1. Purpose and Perspective   138
    2. The Institutional Pole   142
    3. The Vision of Unity   145

Concluding Remarks   149
  1. The Significance of Niebuhr's Theology   149
  2. The Problem of Niebuhr's Theology   153
  3. Ways Ahead   158
    a. The Moral Life   158
    b. Christ and the Church   160
    c. God   163

Notes   167

Bibliography of the Writings of H. Richard Niebuhr   196

FOREWORD

Among the major theologians who are widely recognized to have made important contributions to the theological and ethical thinking of the Christian community in the thirties, forties, and fifties, Helmut Richard Niebuhr is one of a very few who are not the subject of a published full-scale study. Libertus A. Hoedemaker's book is the first to undertake such a task. A few articles on Niebuhr have appeared in scholarly journals, and a number of dissertations have been written on various aspects of his work. The festschrift presented to him in 1957, *Faith and Ethics*, contains very important essays for understanding Niebuhr's theology, but by its very nature does not serve as a comprehensive introduction. His influence is readily detected in books and articles that have been published in recent years; two examples are Van A. Harvey's *The Historian and the Believer* and Gordon D. Kaufman's *Systematic Theology: A Historicist Perspective*. Seven years after his death, it is clear that Niebuhr's work continues to stimulate theological and ethical reflection.

It will never be easy for a single critical study to be wrapped around the circumference of Niebuhr's various contributions to Christian thought. The obvious reason for this is the breadth of interest which he had. He made contributions that are recognized by sociologists of religion, historians of American Christianity, historians of ethics, systematic theologians, systematic ethicists, and perhaps even moral philosophers. Intensive critical work would require mastery of the background materials out of which these various contributions have come, and such is not easy to develop. A second reason is that some of Niebuhr's major constructive contributions were never completed in his lifetime; *The Responsible Self: An Essay in Christian Moral Philosophy*, for example, was the only development of his systematic ethics that had been written in publishable form by the time of his death. There are subjects on which he lectured that never received extensive published treatment by him, such as Jonathan Edwards, Martin Luther, nineteenth- and twentieth-century theological developments, sin and forgiveness, and language theory.

A third reason is indicated by the theme of Hoedemaker's study; namely, the style of Niebuhr's thinking. It is easier to write a study of a theologian whose style is polemic rather than irenic; such a theologian draws the battle lines with his opponent, cites the precise texts which he is disputing, and engages in explicit counterargument. On the whole, however, this was not Niebuhr's style of thinking. Or a less creative systematic mind might indicate very precisely the texts on which he is dependent in developing a point farther, and thus it is not too difficult for the critic to indicate with some exactness what the influence of one and another writer was on the subject under study. But Niebuhr absorbed currents of thought from his wide reading and study, and drew them into his own developing pattern of thinking in such a way that it is not easy to measure the degree in influence which Ernst Troeltsch or Karl Barth, Edwards or Frederick Denison Maurice, George Herbert Mead or Martin Buber, Wilhelm Dilthey or Josiah Royce, W. David Ross or Immanuel Kant had on his work. If one knows well the sources that influenced Niebuhr one can detect both major and minor consequences of them in books, chapters, paragraphs, sentences, and even phrases. But it is not easy to conclude from such observations, "Ah! it's Dilthey that is the clue to understanding this." It may or may not be, but any mechanical effort to establish the point might be wrecked on the shoals of oversimplification, for in Niebuhr's own context of thought what Dilthey contributed might be transformed or converted, and be combined with insights equally transformed or converted from Royce and others.

Another difficulty that critics will have in writing about Niebuhr is also indicated in Hoedemaker's theme; it is often a sense of direction that one learns, rather than logically rigorous or exegetically rigorous ways of exploring themes. Niebuhr was gifted with creative imagination that discerned relations between things, or probed out alternative approaches to problems, or formulated typologies in such a way that the reader senses a thrust in a direction. Some of the finer points of exposition or development are, in a sense, left for more prosaic minds to examine and reformulate. For example, the typology of ethics found in the first chapter of *The Responsible Self: An Essay in Christian Moral Philosophy*—man the maker, man the citizen, and man the responder or answerer—has met with gratitude on the part of many persons because of the fundamental clarifying insight that is expressed in it. It stimulates further reflection, and seems to set alternatives in order. But the critic, by his calling, probes more prosaically and rigorously with a whole range of questions. If Aristotle and Thomas Aquinas are the historical sources of the "maker," does Niebuhr's type represent them accurately, or is there something askew? If Kant is a primary historical source of the "citizen," or law-obeyer, is justice done to Kant? Or do these types represent a creative venture that poses ideal alternatives? In the "responder" with its ethics of the "fitting," is Niebuhr working with an intuitionist model of ethics like Ross's or Maurice Mandelbaum's? How does it differ from these? Is the concept of responsibility developed carefully? How does it compare with the work of moral philosophers such as Herbert L. A. Hart and Kurt Baier on the one hand, and John Wild on the other? Is Niebuhr describing how people seem to determine their actions? If it is a description, what makes it normative? To what extent does "God is acting in all actions upon you" entail a rigorous determinism?

And so the critical questions add up. It would be unfair to Niebuhr to cast him in an intellectual role he did not intend to play; the critic must do justice to his author's intentions, frame of reference, style, and direction. And he can readily appreciate the special kind of clarity that comes from the exercise of a creative imagination. Yet he quite fairly is called upon to probe from a frame of reference different from Niebuhr's. But he will radically misjudge Niebuhr's intention and contribution if he does not have an empathic understanding of the issues with which Niebuhr is dealing, and with Niebuhr's style and direction of thought.

Hoedemaker's book is the first, but by no means the last, effort to set before the public a comprehensive interpretation of H. Richard Niebuhr's theology. It is the most ambitious and extensive effort among the various dissertation manuscripts, article manuscripts, and published articles and sections of books that I have examined. Hoedemaker has explored widely the range of materials that Niebuhr himself had read and thought about, and the range of issues that Niebuhr dealt with. Thus the comprehensive scope of this book is one of its principal merits. It does not fulfill the need for more narrowly and sharply defined studies of particular aspects of its subject; these are being done, and will continue to be done. But it does function in the best sense of a "critical introduction" to Niebuhr. Thus the scope of the book constitutes one of its merits.

Hoedemaker's theme, style and direction, enables him to draw a great deal of the Niebuhr material together in a way that some other themes do not. To be sure, the exploration of Niebuhr's Christology, or his view of memory, require a movement beyond the texts that deal with those particular notions into the range of things covered by Hoedemaker's theme. But they do not free the critic to cover the range of the subject in a way that style and direction do. The appropriateness of style and direction as a focus rests on more than its convenience. It probably comes as close to finding a unifying theme as any other possibility would. For other purposes, other themes, subordinated in this study, would do as well. For one example: a case could be made for Niebuhr's preoccupation with Troeltsch's *Fragestellung* from the time of his dissertation to the publication of *Radical Monotheism and Western*

Culture. Hoedemaker's choice of a theme has the particular merit of suggesting that style and content have a peculiarly intimate relationship in Niebuhr's thought, and thus a great deal of his subject's diverse reflections can be broken open through the use of this theme.

Hoedemaker is deeply sympathetic with his subject, but he does not make the book an apologetic for Niebuhr. Indeed, Hoedemaker has the advantage of coming to a study of Niebuhr not as an American but as a Dutchman, whose basic theological training took place under a faculty whose outlook was more sharply influenced by the contemporary currents of continental theology than most American schools have been. Yet, more than most Europeans who study American theology, or who have studied under American theological faculties, Hoedemaker has the capacity to identify with the intention of his subject. His wide reading in theology provides a critical focus that he uses in his comparisons of Niebuhr with other theologians, but does not distort him by the kind of lack of appreciation that has characterized a number of other Europeans who also studied at Yale during Niebuhr's prime. Hoedemaker's own studies with Niebuhr during his first stay in the United States, and his warm personal relation with him, add to the quality of empathy which this book portrays, and aid in the author's understanding of his subject's mood and intention in his writing.

The book has a thesis. The theological reading public has been offered "introductions" to theologians that are not much more than summary compilations of major texts of their subjects, with a few general observations appended. Hoedemaker's is of a different quality from such efforts, for he seeks to work at his theme while he is working at his exposition, and he sets materials in a wider theological context throughout. Thus it is a book with which subsequent writers will be able to quarrel. But the thesis is not extrinsic to the materials and is not imposed upon them in a high-handed and oversimplified way. The quarrels with it will have to be equally well researched and documented, and thoroughly argued.

Hoedemaker's own interests and professional activities perhaps account for some of the appreciation that he has for Niebuhr. From my conversations with him, he strikes me as a person who is appreciative of the Christian tradition while bringing it under the kinds of questions which are being raised in a period of radical secularization. He is a person whose interests in theology are not purely academic, but those of a person who is deeply concerned about and committed to the mission of the Christian community in the modern world. His talents and accomplishments extend beyond the narrowly academic; to hear him play Mozart on a grand piano is sheer joy. His present service as a theologian in Indonesia not only continues a history of representatives of his church, but provides a laboratory in which his theological, cultural, and practical reflections on the mission of the church are being forged. and tested. One hopes for the appearance of constructive work by Hoedemaker from which to discern the impact of his studies of Niebuhr as they are shaped also by his Dutch theological training, and his service in the mission of the church.

James M. Gustafson

ACKNOWLEDGMENTS

The Christian Century:
 Virgil C. Aldrich and H. Richard Niebuhr, "Is God in the War?"
  Copyright 1942 Christian Century Foundation. Reprinted by permission
  from the August 5, 1942 issue of *The Christian Century.*
 H. Richard Niebuhr, "Can German and American Christians Understand Each
  Other?"
  Copyright 1930 Christian Century Foundation. Reprinted by permission
  from the July 23, 1930 issue of *The Christian Century.*
 H. Richard Niebuhr, "The Grace of Doing Nothing"
  Copyright 1932 Christian Century Foundation. Reprinted by permission
  from the March 23, 1932 issue of *The Christian Century.*
 H. Richard Niebuhr, "The Only Way into the Kingdom of God"
  Copyright 1932 Christian Century Foundation. Reprinted by permission
  from the April 6, 1932 issue of *The Christian Century.*
 Reinhold Niebuhr, "Must We Do Nothing?"
  Copyright 1932 Christian Century Foundation. Reprinted by permission
  from the March 30, 1932 issue of *The Christian Century.*

Harper & Row, Publishers, Inc.:
 H. Richard Niebuhr, *Radical Monotheism and Western Culture*
  From *Radical Monotheism and Western Culture by H. Richard Niebuhr.*
  Copyright 1943, 1952, 1955, 1960 by H. Richard Niebuhr. Reprinted by
  permission of Harper & Row, Publishers, Inc.
 H. Richard Niebuhr, *The Responsible Self: An Essay in Christian Moral
  Philosophy*
  From *The Responsible Self* by H. Richard Niebuhr. Copyright © 1963 by
  Florence M. Niebuhr. Reprinted by permission of Harper & Row, Publishers,
  Inc.

Hill & Wang, Inc.:
 Jonathan Edwards, *Representative Selections,* ed. C. H. Faust and T. H. Johnson

The Macmillan Company:
 H. Richard Niebuhr, *The Meaning of Revelation*
  Reprinted with permission of The Macmillan Company from *The Meaning of
  Revelation* by H. Richard Niebuhr. Copyright 1941 by The Macmillan
  Company, renewed 1969 by Florence Niebuhr, Cynthia M. Niebuhr, and
  Richard R. Niebuhr.

Florence M. Niebuhr and Richard R. Niebuhr:
 H. Richard Niebuhr, *The Social Sources of Denominationalism*
  Copyright, 1929, by Henry Holt and Company, Inc.; renewed, 1957, by H.
  Richard Niebuhr.
 Quotations from the unpublished works of H. Richard Niebuhr.

The Open Court Publishing Company:
 G H. Mead. "The Genesis of the Self and Social Control." *The Philosophy of the
  Present,* ed. Arthur E. Murphy
  The Open Court Publishing Co., La Salle, Illinois. First published in
  1932; reprinted 1959.

Charles Scribner's Sons, Publishers:
 D.C. Macintosh, *The Reasonableness of Christianity*

PREFACE

The present book is a slightly revised edition of a doctoral dissertation which was defended at the University of Utrecht, the Netherlands, in March 1966. Method and scheme used for the interpretation of Niebuhr's thought, and the viewpoints expressed in the course of that interpretation, have not undergone substantial change. The major differences between this book and the dissertation lie in the fact that the number of footnotes and references has been reduced, and that many passages have been rewritten for the sake of clarity.

It has been tempting to include more references to recent developments on the theological scene, and to relate the significance of Niebuhr's thought more explicitly to these. I have resisted this temptation in order to keep the book within reasonable limits and to stick to its main purpose: to give an interpretation of H. Richard Niebuhr's theology as it developed against the background of the theological world between 1920 and 1960.

The beginnings of this study go back as far as 1959, when I received a World Council of Churches scholarship to study at Yale Divinity School; and it received its major impetus toward completion in 1964, when I visited Yale Divinity School again with the aid of a research grant of the Netherlands Organization for the Advancement of Pure Research (Z.W.O.). I gratefully recall the guidance of Profs. Claude Welch, James M. Gustafson, and Hans W. Frei in the development of my understanding of Niebuhr's thought; and, in the Netherlands, of Profs. Johannes C. Hoekendijk (now at Union Theological Seminary, New York), and Johannes de Graaf, my promoter at Utrecht. In addition, I gained major insight and inspiration from conversations with my friend and fellow student at Yale, Robert A. Rickard.

I wish to express my sincerely felt gratitude to Mrs. Florence M. Niebuhr and Richard R. Niebuhr for giving me permission to use and to quote hitherto unpublished material, consisting mainly of papers, lectures, and notes of H. Richard Niebuhr. My own understanding of Niebuhr has been considerably enriched by these sources, and I trust that the use of them has been to the advantage of the interpretation set forth here. Finally, I wish to express my appreciation to Miss Jane E. McFarland, reference librarian of Yale Divinity School, who has been a great help, not only by compiling a bibliography for this book, but also by solving many bibliographical problems too difficult for one who works in Indonesia.

The book is divided into two parts. The first two chapters outline the development and structure of Niebuhr's theology as a whole; the last three chapters treat three specific areas in which the style and direction, described in chapters 1 and 2, receive further elaboration and illustration. The name Niebuhr will be used throughout to designate H. Richard Niebuhr. When reference is made to Reinhold Niebuhr or Richard R. Niebuhr, the first name or initials will be mentioned.

Libertus A. Hoedemaker

Djakarta, Indonesia

INTRODUCTION

1. Niebuhr the Theologian

Helmut Richard Niebuhr was born on September 3, 1894 in Wright City, Missouri, the son of a minister of the Evangelical Synod of North America (in 1934 to merge with the Reformed Church of the United States in the Evangelical and Reformed Church). He graduated from Elmhurst College in 1912, from Eden Theological Seminary in 1915, and was ordained as a minister of his denomination in 1916, after which he held a pastorate in St. Louis until 1918. Meanwhile, he received the M.A. degree from Washington University. In 1919 he returned to Eden Theological Seminary to teach, a career which he interrupted in 1922 to continue his theological education at the Yale University Divinity School in New Haven, where he received a B.D. in 1923 and a Ph.D. in 1924 (with a dissertation on Ernst Troeltsch's philosophy of religion). In the same year he was called to the presidency of Elmhurst College, a position which he exchanged again for a professorship at Eden in 1927. In 1931 he went to Yale as associate professor of Christian ethics. In 1932 he spent a year of study in Germany.

In 1938 Niebuhr became full professor at Yale Divinity School. Later, in 1953, he added to this the position of director of graduate studies in religion at Yale University. He directed a survey of the situation of theological education in the United States and Canada during the years 1954-55.

At the time of his death, on July 5, 1962, he held honorary doctorates from the University of Chicago (1954), Franklin and Marshall College (1956), Wesleyan University (1956), and the University of Bonn (1960).

Niebuhr's writings include seven books and a number of articles, essays, and contributions to other books. They are not writings of a "leading" theologian, in the sense that they do not present a clear and forceful theology such as would be expected of a school-forming pioneer. This is especially clear when we compare them to the works of his brother Reinhold. Nevertheless, when Niebuhr died, many felt that they had lost a man whose influence on contemporary theological thought in America through lectures, seminars, and personal contacts could not easily be overestimated. There are those who hold that his thought is more profound and more representative of contemporary America than that of his brother.

To do theology and to be a theologian did not mean for Niebuhr the construction of a consistent system. It meant rather to engage in a continuous living dialogue with other thinkers about God, man, and men in their complex interrelations. Theology is a "highly contemporary exercise" as he often said in the classroom, and his method illustrates this. It is the method of a teacher whose main purpose is to draw men into the dialogical struggle of question and answer, rather than to give answers or to criticize given answers, and who insists that theological views have to be creative views rooted in the needs of our own day.

Throughout Niebuhr's theological work there is the suggestion of a crucial personal involvement. The central theme in his work is a theme of personal religious anxiety: it is the movement between lostness and fear of a hostile God, and the rare moments of vision in which the source of being is seen as gracious and trustworthy. Is faith in God genuinely possible? It is mainly this haunting question which gives to his theology a highly personal and extremely restless character.

2. Variety and Consistency

In one of his lectures Niebuhr describes himself as "one who, as a Protestant Christian of a perhaps rather nondescript sort, is deeply concerned about the condition of man in our time, and as a scholar, equally nondescript and unspecialized, looks to the past to discern there the broad outlines of those great movements which have imparted to men—not less beset by doubts than moderns are—new force and courage for life's strange journey." Such a framework can include practically all fields and themes of theology, and indeed we find a great variety of topics in Niebuhr's writings. He is engaged in a constant observation and analysis of the many phenomena of faith and community in which the Christian tradition is present among us. Greatly indebted to Ernst Troeltsch, he works largely inductively, fascinated by the complex ways in which faith and church express themselves in the history of social structures. Yet this "observation" is not neutral; it takes place, confessedly, from the standpoint of the particular faith of the Christian community.

Niebuhr undertakes to understand "human life in general from the Christian point of view." At one place he calls himself a *Christian moral philosopher*. By this designation he intends to avoid labels like philosopher of religion, phenomenologist of religion, and dogmatic theologian, though he wishes to combine elements of all three, and to combine these, in addition, with elements of sociological and psychological observation. Hunting, as it seems, for something like a comprehensive science of man, which cannot bypass reflection about "man before God" and "God before man," he refuses to commit himself prematurely to any particular discipline.

Yet in all Niebuhr's themes there is a fundamental consistency. They all figure around what he sees as the essential problem of Christianity: *the relation between the gospel and the culture to which it belongs and in which it functions.* This is the "unity of place" in his thought. "The Christian life moves between the poles of God in Christ as known through faith and Bible and God in nature as known through reason in culture," and it cannot be understood or guided by exclusive attention to either pole. Something of the double interest of Ernst Troeltsch can be found in Niebuhr: on the one hand the presence of "religion," of a relation with the Absolute, in all relative givenness of cultural and social structures; on the other hand, the social phenomenon of Christianity as a "redeeming factor" in culture. In other words, social involvement of faith is not only a fact, it is also a calling. Between these two points lies the full problem of faith: faith misunderstood, warped, distorted, redirected, transformed. Man and his society have to be delivered from a pluralism which is demonic; this has to happen through faith, not through retreat into an arbitrarily absolutized structure. To become an isolated island in this world is the greatest sin the church can ever commit.

For Niebuhr, the only way to solve the basic problem of Christianity, to redirect its language, its attitudes, and its movement in our time, is a rediscovery of *the greatness of God.* In the spirituality of Niebuhr's theology there is much similarity and indebtedness to Revivalism. Something like a new revival of human faith and hope is anticipated as the only answer to a situation in which the church has lost much of its relevance. There is, in the social and cultural life of our century, a great need for reconciliation and transformation of the many warped and twisted forms of faith which, if anything, reveal an unconquerable lostness and defensiveness of man. It will not do to chide so-called secularism unless we seek to revive the concern with God *for his sake alone.* We live on the eve of a new reformation, which ought to be coupled to a radical renaissance of living theological language and to a *resymbolization* of the Christian message. The concern for such a revival necessarily includes a concern for the church. No reformation of cultural or political life will be lasting and successful unless the church itself is revived.

All this indicates that the varied and detailed observation of the many ways in which human faith manifests itself, is combined in Niebuhr's thought with what to him is the basic religious question: the relation of man to the source of being on whom he is absolutely dependent. The way in which Niebuhr seeks to combine this fundamental problem with an honest appreciation of an endlessly complex pluralism, determines as it were the structure of his theological questioning.

3. Purpose of the Present Study

A study in comtemporary theology has its obvious limits. The picture one tries to paint is necessarily blurred and incomplete, for there is no possibility of getting the whole network of relations and influences involved into focus. Only too easily does one exaggerate minor details or overlook important ones. The assessment of the historical significance of the object of study can therefore hardly be adequate. Nevertheless, it also has its specific advantages. A study in contemporary theology can be an effort to bring to consciousness some of the important problems with which any theologian in our day finds himself confronted—or should find himself confronted—and to do this coherently, as far as the thought of the theologian under discussion shows coherence. Niebuhr's theology, which is often described as a movement between Ernst Troeltsch and Karl Barth, who may well be regarded as two opposite poles in the theology of the twentieth century, seems to be well suited for such an undertaking. This is precisely the purpose of the present book: to give a description and an interpretation of the style and direction of Niebuhr's theology against the background of, and with a view toward, the larger problems of twentieth-century theology. It is definitely *not* a book about twentieth-century theology; it focuses on Niebuhr and intends *only in that way* to contribute a little to an understanding of some of the issues which occupy theologians in our time.

Among those issues the relation between church and world—in the largest possible sense, including for instance not only problems of social ethics or missionary conviction but also problems of theological language and church structures—stands out as one of the most pressing. There is no longer a self-evident or generally accepted relation, even though the Christian community continues to exist as part of social and cultural history and entangled in its structures. More than ever, therefore, are church and theology occupied with very basic questions concerning their legitimacy and purpose.

Already our century has witnessed a widespread recovery of the identity of the church. The specific message that its *kerygma* carries for the world, the distinct nature of its mission to the world, the special character of its communal life, have been widely emphasized and discussed. The popularity of Barth's theology and the growth of the ecumenical movement, both stimulated by the events around World War II, testify to this. But for some time we have witnessed the beginnings of a reaction against these emphases—a reaction which is often described by both its advocates and its opponents as a "return to the nineteenth century." Its advocates mean that many questions of the nineteenth century with regard to man, his history and his religion, have not been answered but dodged in the twentieth century. Its opponents feel that long-exposed and refuted positions, already proved to be dead-end streets, are sought again as basis for an ill-advised and superficial call for "relevance" and "involvement." However this may be, the reaction that we mean, in all its baffling diversity, intends to focus again on the complicated and fragmentary nature of theology, and on the immediate demands of the situation.

Niebuhr's theology brings to the indicated field of problems first of all a specific American history, then a consistent Troeltschean questioning, and finally an attitude toward the theology of Barth which is at once appreciative and suspicious. These elements might make his theology an interesting focal point for many problems. We will try to investigate this in the following pages by concentrating on the *style* of his theology. This automatically entails limitation to basic issues, rather, to *prolegomena;* and it makes some superficiality inevitable, especially with regard to the thought of those who influenced Niebuhr.

In all this we will continually have in mind the question of the identity of American theology. From a European point of view, American religious history still manifests specific characteristics, and it would be most challenging to test this assumption with regard to the most recent developments. An analysis of Niebuhr's theology might be a first step in this direction. For although one gains the impression that the movement called neoorthodoxy is often considered a deviation from the mainstream of American thought, it might be worthwhile to focus attention once more both on its specific American roots and on its specific message for contemporary theology.

Chapter 1
Choice of Direction

A. PERSISTENT PATTERNS

1. *Sovereignty and pluralism in American religion.* Niebuhr is an American theologian. He thinks and writes in a specific history, responding to specific problems, inspired by specific convictions; and he does this consciously as an American. Time and again he directs his students to the history of his country; guidance for today, he believes can be found by retracing the steps of those men who once guided their contemporaries, and by uncovering the movements which once created and sustained the convictions of church and nation. Theology today is, to a large extent, critical dialogue with the past.

This implies that we have to begin with a glance at the history of church and theology in the United States. Such a glance tells us, first of all, that "church" and "theology" cannot very well be isolated from the complex movement in which both the American nation and American religion developed. Actually, the proper object of the history of American religion is not theology or the church, but rather-human life as it shaped itself between order and disorder, movement and stability, expansion and conservation, faith and unbelief. Whether this is true only for America, is not a question to be discussed here. It remains a striking characteristic of American theology that it is entangled in the movement of social and cultural history as such. In addition, theological reflection seems to be subordinated to the concrete demands of the situation. This humble role of theology is underscored by the effects of the revivals with their stress on individual decision. Theology, we are told, is of no use unless it is *preachable.*[1] At worst, this leads to extreme pragmatism and an antitheological bias. At best, it connects the history of theology firmly with the common life.

In view of these considerations, we will need categories for the description of American religious history which can also be applied to wider fields. For our brief survey we turn to the concepts *sovereignty* and *pluralism.* Both reflect realities in American history which are always there: in tension, in harmony, or in simple coexistence. The notion of sovereignty reminds us of the pervasive, hardly questioned faith in the overarching concerns of a providential deity, which remains a binding element in all expansion and diversity.[2] And pluralism, of course, points to this expansion and diversity itself, as well as to the emphasis on freedom and human possibilities.

In terms of the general history of theology it is perhaps legitimate to say that the tension between the two elements mentioned is a major characteristic of the Calvinistic-Reformed tradition. Here the emphasis on the sovereignty of God, coupled with that on the objective church and the covenant, is accompanied by a typical concern for the religious act, for regeneration and sanctification; thus both establishment and sectarianism can grow on its soil. But it is in America that we find clear historical manifestations of this; and the first of these is the Puritan theocracy. Originally, the Puritan system provided a balance between divine Providence and human activity,[3] as well as between establishment and regenerate church membership. But when several factors began to threaten its coherence in the course of the seventeenth century, balance was replaced by tension; and thus one of the major problems of American Christianity made itself felt.

In the case of the struggle with separatism this is, of course, obvious. Other striking examples are offered in the adoption of the Half Way Covenant (1662), which provided for the baptism of the children of those church members who had not given visible evidence of their regeneration; and in the views of Solomon Stoddard (1643-1729), who advocated the admission of nonregenerate members to the Lord's Supper, treating them as "visible saints." On the one hand these instances show a respect for the objectivity of the church, though perhaps also a concession to the "doctrine of inability" according to which man can do nothing but wait passively for the event of conversion.[4] On the other hand they precisely reveal how much significance was attributed to individual regeneration.

In the process of disintegration the more rationalistic aspects of the Puritan system, which themselves were a fertile soil for the influence of the Enlightenment, came under successful attack from the revivals of the Great Awakening. A renewed emphasis on individuality, experience, and decision infused the traditional conceptions of Christianity with new life and greatly influenced the development of the indicated tension. It was Jonathan Edwards (1703-58) who in this new situation rephrased the concept of God's sovereignty and thus gave to the problem its essentially post-Puritan form.[5]

Edwards' central significance lies in his restatement of Calvinism in the framework of Lockean psychology and Neoplatonic metaphysics,[6] by which he delivered God, as it were, from the restrictions of rationalistic covenant-thinking and restored him as "the present, omnificent power on whom the self and all the world immediately depended for existence."[7] On this basis he retained the emphasis on individual conversion yet fought vigorously against all shortsighted rationalism, particularly Arminianism. One of the major problems of the subsequent New England theology was that it could not in the end successfully combine these two interests.

The growth of Enlightenment and Revivalism on the soil of Puritanism was an important factor in the acceptance and establishment of *religious liberty*. Religious liberty and separation of church and state are dominant phenomena of American history. Already in the "Old Calvinism" of the Founding Fathers we find contributing elements, particularly the profound distrust of all human government. Yet these elements could not have developed without the pressures of Revivalism (with its tendencies toward voluntarism),[8] the Enlightenment, and the demands of the situation during and after the Revolutionary War. This is to say that diverse influences were at work here; and from the purely religious point of view there were reasons to counteract some of them, especially the "French infidelity": the pervasive deism and general skepticism which had crept into American religion, even in its rapid movement toward liberty and differentiation.

It is telling that the so-called Second Great Awakening, initiated by Edwards' grandson Timothy Dwight (1752-1817), began as a defense of the remaining bulwark of church establishment, as if religious liberty and infidelity were two fruits of the same tree! It was soon apparent that an effective restoration of the element of sovereignty had to begin with the acceptance of expansion and pluralism. This insight was forced upon the churches by the situation of the western frontier. It was this situation which created the specific climate of American religion,[9] and gave it its decisive shape through the development of the voluntary humanitarian and missionary organizations, which in turn served as models for the denominations.[10]

The phenomenon of *denominationalism* reflects the inner problem of this expansive period. On the one hand it was an inevitable and natural consequence of religious liberty and of the expansive force of Revivalism; on the other hand it is a clear illustration of a pluralism that had become static because it had lost the comprehensive movement which held it together:

> With the cessation of the movement and the turn to institutionalism the aggressive societies became denominations, for that peculiar institution, the American denomination, may be

described as a missionary order which has turned to the defensive and lost its consciousness of the invisible catholic church.[11]

The dynamic view of the divine sovereignty, which was characteristic of the early revivals, was gradually replaced by a general belief in Providence that resulted in institutional complacency.[12] It seems that the forces which sent American Christianity on its way in the beginning of the nineteenth century, could not remain together in a living synthesis. Once in mutual tension or isolation, both sovereignty and pluralism were in permanent danger of being replaced by less worthy and more superficial substitutes.

The development of the New England theology is partially illustrative of this problem. Its work was determined—and handicapped—by a split between the Edwardeans, or Revivalists, and the Old Calvinists, but also by the necessity to cope with the challenge of Unitarianism. The ideas of this movement reach back to early days when ideas of arbitrary predestination and stern sovereignty were combatted by emphasizing the benevolent nature of God and the capability of all men to attain salvation and perfection.

The basic issue for the New England theology in its efforts to restate orthodoxy in view of the new challenges became *the freedom of man*. As soon as this became the focus of rational scrutiny, the acknowledgment of the sovereignty of God turned into *the problem of divine determination*. This development was facilitated by a slight change in the doctrine of the atonement; the emphasis no longer lay on the need to satisfy for sins but on the permission of sin in the whole moral order. This meant practically that the mainstream of New England theology retained the rationalist Old Calvinist rather than the Edwardean climate, and, along this road, found room for extensive reflection on the abilities of human reason and moral agency.[13]

Revivalism thus survived in a framework which was tilted toward rationalism and subjectivism. It is not surprising, therefore, that movements developed to counterbalance these trends. That most of these movements were colored with a romanticism typical of the age should not keep us from regarding them as legitimate efforts to recapture the original dynamism of "American religion." Among them we might list the Mercersburg theology, which sought to repair the negative effects of Revivalism by returning to an understanding of the church as an organic whole, and a view of Christianity as a life which feeds upon the objective significance of the sacraments. Experience, including the preoccupation with the individual man that it entails, is set over against faith as a relation to something which *is*. Even the Transcendentalism of men like Ralph W. Emerson (1803-82) and Theodore Parker (1810-60), though it may not seem to be more than an infusion of Unitarianism with romantic and mystical elements, is in some sense a revival of the idea of the sovereignty of God.[14]

The most creative reaction at this point is clearly the thought of Horace Bushnell (1802-76), the Schleiermacher and the Ritschl of America.[15] His work is of central importance in American religious history because of its reasonable romanticism, its axiom of the contextual nature of the human situation, and its emphasis on education. In all three elements Bushnell wanted to combat the excesses of, and the overconfidence in, Revivalism. We find here a genuine effort of a modern theologian to transcend Revivalism while retaining its indispensable contributions; an effort, in other words, to recast the problem of sovereignty and pluralism.

Renewal of the Christian faith meant, for Bushnell, the rediscovery of its reality and function in the flow of daily life. "Let us have the divine, the deific itself—the very feeling of God, God's own beauty, truth, and love. Then we shall have both the pure ideal of a life, and a power flowing out from God to ingenerate that life in us."[16] Concentration on doctrine leads us away from the place where life can be transformed; it prevents us from seeing that truth is given to us in "forms or images naturally expressive" without being identical with these. Confidence in doctrine must be mitigated by a "knowledge of the Christian truth which is of the heart."[17]

Bushnell undergirded his basic interest by a significant analysis of *language* and by insisting upon the central importance of the *social texture of personality* for knowledge and faith. Is it not "the very character and mark of all unchristian education, that it brings up the child for future conversion?"[18] Does the method of Revivalism not ignore that the Christian truth is "wrapped up in the life of every Christian parent,"[19] that it is incarnated in the processes of individual and social life, rather than in a single experience? Bushnell's plea for education, which was to become highly influential, had its roots in these concerns. It does not reflect an effort to assimilate and relativize the Christian faith, but rather a fervent desire to rediscover the living reality of the divine truth which no single formula can adequately express. Any one who speaks about sovereignty and pluralism in American religion cannot easily overestimate the significance of this motif.

At this point, we might mention briefly the thought of a British theologian who influenced Niebuhr in somewhat the same way as Bushnell did: Frederick Denison Maurice (1805-72). Like Bushnell, Maurice underscored the contrast between *God* and *a system of truths;* and here, too, the newly gained insights had their origin and consequences in specific views on education and social life. Unlike Bushnell, however, Maurice based his thought on the key concept of the universal kingship of Christ and on the significance of the church as a witness to the universal society of all men in Christ.[20] According to Maurice, Christianity defeats itself when it persists in the error of substituting an expression of its faith for the object of faith itself. The true task of the church is to witness to the *true constitution of humanity:* "The church is . . . human society in its normal state; the world, that same society irregular and abnormal."[21]

Truth is not the formulated possession of one group by which it distinguishes itself from other groups, it is rather "that which lies at the bottom of all men's trowings,"[22] that in which the relational structure of human life has its basis and fulfillment. Universal truth is a religious necessity of all men[23]; and it is *mocked* by the defensive constitution of any group or church, by the substitution of a religion for God. Of course, systems have their valid and complementary contributions, but the "sect tendency" tends ever again to take possession of them. " 'Let all thine enemies perish, O Lord'; all systems, schools, parties which have hindered men from seeing the largeness, and freedom, and glory of thy kingdom; 'but let them that love thee,' in whatever earthly mists they may at present be involved, 'be as the sun when he goeth forth in his strength.' "[24]

The thought of men like Bushnell inaugurated in America the era of Liberalism. This is not to say that those specific liberal elements as an optimistic view of human nature, an emphasis on moralism and education rather than on doctrine and church, had not been present before. Time and again they have served as correctives of an institutionalized orthodoxy. But in the Liberalism of the second half of the nineteenth century the correctives themselves became the basis for a theological thinking which in addition allied itself with conceptions and ideologies contingent upon the rise of science. It is precisely the misfortune of this particular period of American history, that the conservative and liberal movements gradually stabilized themselves over against each other. On the one side the tension between sovereignty and pluralism was solved by a rigid system of doctrine, on the other by a smooth evolutionary optimism. This situation accounts for a lack of creative movement in American theological thinking during that period and is one of the reasons why even the Social Gospel movement, despite its effort to apply basic convictions of American Protestantism to the unexpected problems of industrial society, failed to become a significant step forward.

The intention of the Social Gospel relates it to the permanent tension of American religion that we have sought to describe; but it remained too shallow to be of revolutionary impact. It did in a sense revive the old dynamic fervor of the expansive movement; it also made a genuine effort to bring the kingdom of the sovereign God into relationship with the problems of social life—but in all this the basic scheme of Liberalism remained unquestioned. Social problems were indeed approached from the standpoint of the Christian gospel and with the aid of sociology, but they were not allowed to challenge the current formulations of the Christian faith.

Although in the later development of the Social Gospel a distinction began to appear between the application of the "law of love" for social problems and the use of certain sociological techniques,[25] it remained for Reinhold Niebuhr to draw out the full implications of this distinction; and it remained for his brother to show that the problem of faith and culture is more complicated and more fundamental than is apparent in the Social Gospel theology. Not till after the end of World War I, when the alliance of the social sciences with a general optimistic ideology began to fade, did the basic problem of Christian faith and society, of sovereignty and pluralism, come to the surface again.

This problem is part and parcel of the context in which Niebuhr's thought developed its style and direction. To mention only one example: the concept of relativism, which occupies an important place in Niebuhr's theology, can only be understood adequately against the background of the specifically American tensions between sovereignty and pluralism. A theologian like Niebuhr, who takes this particular history seriously, faces the task to recover the binding and driving vision of the sovereign source of being within the experience of an endlessly diverse social reality, and to interpret and guide man's religious and moral aspirations in such a way that once more they are seen to stand in a living relation to the ultimate truth present in them.

2. The liberal heritage. Niebuhr spent his formative years in an atmosphere in which the major problems of theology were solved along the lines of religious Liberalism. Though it is difficult, if not impossible, to say that Niebuhr has ever been a full-fledged liberal theologian, it is evident that the patterns of the liberal heritage with which he worked, and the problems that were present in it, stayed with him throughout his life. It is imperative, therefore, that we look briefly at a few aspects of American religious Liberalism as it presented itself in the beginning of the twentieth century. We think here especially of the confidence in science and the attention to religious experience. With this we do not mean to suggest that Niebuhr knew Liberalism only in its American form. In fact, the German liberal tradition had been present in his life from the beginning. At home, the Niebuhr brothers were trained by their father in the thought of Harnack,[26] and this definitely left its stamp on Niebuhr's theology. In some respects, Niebuhr even stands closer to

German than to American Liberalism. He does not share, for instance, the pervasive deistic concept of religion and the unreserved emphasis on the autonomy of science and reason, which are characteristic of the American tradition; and over against American liberal Christology, which tends to emphasize the dynamic influence of Jesus' character and teaching on social and moral issues, he retains Adolf Harnack's attention to Jesus' inner relation to God, which reveals the saving possibilities of a like submission.

"The idea of a dynamic, unitary world in which Spirit is *gradually* permeating nature with meaning and value is fundamental to the modern understanding of reality."[27] In other words, not only is meaning and value regarded as immanent to the factual reality which the human mind observes and interprets, but also the world of men is seen as gradually becoming more meaningful and more valuable. These convictions determine the relation of science and religion in American Liberalism. There is a general unshaken confidence that empirical research will lead to religious and moral progress, and a firm conviction that religion and theology should not remain aloof from it.[28] This is true not only for natural science but for sociology as well. The use of sociology in America has to a certain extent always been regarded as auxiliary to practical reform, and was often rooted in a concern for the moral welfare of man[29]; or, in other words, situational analysis was never wholly separated from a belief in the positive outcome of the process operative in society. The Social Gospel is a case in point; here sociology was often regarded as an adequate tool to shape the future of America, and as such as a necessary supplement to the ethics of the New Testament.

The typical combination of science and value which is present in this approach[30] was never uncritically accepted by Niebuhr, yet he never relinquished it entirely either. His "continental" learning which in this respect fed upon the thought of men like Immanuel Kant and Max Weber never led him to abandon the basic structure of the liberal search, though it did lead him to serious questions about the superficial and confident way in which this search was often carried out. This is perhaps an important reason why Niebuhr was attracted to Ernst Troeltsch; the latter's approach to the problem of history and value may have seemed to him more profound and more adequate to the American situation than "simpler" solutions which separate the realms of value and observation. However this may be, the conviction that sociological analysis will lead to theological clarity remains one of the pillars of Niebuhr's approach.

The second aspect of American religious Liberalism that we have mentioned is its concentration on religious experience. We do not intend to draw attention to Pragmatism here, since this is a distinct movement which never colored Liberalism as a whole. Rather, we are interested in a type of empirical theology which is built on confidence in metaphysics, and which, in the study of experience, concentrates on the nature and existence of the religious *object*. We think especially of D. C. Macintosh (1877-1948) and Henry N. Wieman (1884-). Though it cannot be said that Niebuhr was influenced specifically by either one of these men,[31] they are mentioned here because they discussed problems which also concerned Niebuhr, and because they clearly represent a typically liberal approach to these problems which, though rejected by Niebuhr, left its traces on his thinking. The problems are the reality of God as implied in religious experience, and the possibility of choosing the right values in the context of the total moral development of mankind.

Macintosh's concern is to treat theology as a full-fledged science, and to ground its affirmations in empirically verifiable fact rather than in the relativities of history. Religious experience becomes the major object of study; from here inferences can be made about the objective reality of God. The major proof for God's existence lies in experience, provided there is the "right religious adjustment."[32] Moral optimism—a "normal and necessary" attitude of life—is precisely the essence of Christianity. Why, then, should we not believe the *reality* of what is implied in this attitude and eliminate "unsuccessful adjustments" on the basis of this belief?[33] ("We have a right to believe as we must in order to live as we ought.")

Wieman presents a metaphysical solution for the problem of the relation between social process and religious meaning. According to Wieman, who drops all theological terminology but retains a certain theistic structure in his thought, the center of being is creative power. God is the behavior of the universe, which increases toward human good when man gives his values and ideals into its keeping. Like Macintosh, Wieman opposes the Kantian restrictions of theological reason ("the transcendental must be ignored"[34]): reason can and must reach the reality of the divine source, which is the creative good. Thus, "the human problem is to shape human conduct and all other conditions so that the creative event can be released to produce maximum good,"[35] which means the subordination of the good *as we discern it*. The problem of our age is a false order of domination, in which human power blocks the work and the service of the creative event.

Thus far we have reviewed the liberal heritage mainly because of the specific nature of some of its problems and the specific structure of its thinking, and we have refrained from mentioning men who influenced Niebuhr directly. Yet for Niebuhr, the liberal heritage also included the thought of two men who did influence him directly. Though he ultimately rejected the total atmosphere of Liberalism to which they also belonged, these men did hand him tools and concepts which came to be important in his theology, and which in an often unexpected way kept functioning as a last but firm link with the whole heritage of Liberalism. We think of George Herbert Mead (1886-1931), the University of Chicago behaviorist with whom Niebuhr studied for some time in the early 1920's, and of the philosopher Josiah Royce (1855-1916).

Mead has no use for the concept of the subjective inner world. All human behavior, including the behavior of the mind, can be observed and analyzed objectively. Mead presents his behavioristic psychology as a practical science which states "as far as possible the conditions under which the experience of the individual arises"[36]; in other words, he deliberately leaves all metaphysical implications out of consideration. The conditions for the existence of a self, then, are of a functional nature; through the interchange of "vocal gestures," later to become symbols,[37] a pattern of social responses is developed which is the basis of thought and meaning. Mind is not some kind of substance, but simply "a process in which the conversation of gestures has been internalized,"[38] or the functioning of significant symbols. What makes the self a *social* self is the fact that in the process of response *it takes on the role of others.* Language is essential in this process; its "gestures" are meant to arouse the same response in speaker and listener. The social response pattern is thus prior to and determinative of the encounter of physical objects and the shaping of selfhood. The quality of social life, with its more and more complex social acts and patterns, depends upon "the degree to which the individual does assume the attitudes of those in the group who are involved with him in his social activities."[39]

Josiah Royce has been said to mark a transition between absolute Idealism and Existentialism[40]; but aside, perhaps, from his emphasis on individual decision and choice, he remains essentially an idealist who posits the existence of a world-consciousness with which man's thinking is in "a significant unity."[41] The eternal is not so much creator as seer or *thought.* All emphasis falls on the encompassing whole and the infinite variety it comprehends—the reason why Royce has his doubts about the religious significance of words like "progress" and "evolution."[42] Elaborating on the problem of the unity between individual and eternal thought, Royce develops a theory of knowledge in which *interpretation* is posited as a third cognitive process after perception and conception. *Interpretation has a triadic structure*[43]—it always involves self, other, and object; in other words, it involves three selves, since the "object" is present to us only as previous interpretation. The element of *time* is essential here: "We can define the present as, potentially, the interpretation of the past to the future."[44] The "will to interpret," then, brings about *a community of interpretation.*[45] Both interpretation and community are present at the very heart of existence.

From here Royce goes on to define man's basic *moral problem* as the conflict between individual self-will and the realization of a more and more inclusive and universal community of interpretation. Saving faith—this has been the essential message of Christianity, according to Royce—is the hopeful and practical devotion "to the cause of the still invisible but perfectly real and divine Universal Community."[46]

The core of Royce's thought lies in the concept of *loyalty;* and it is through this concept that he exercised his main influence on Niebuhr.

> A man is loyal when, first, he has some *cause* to which he is loyal; when, second, he *willingly* and *thoroughly* devotes himself to this cause; and when, third, he expresses his devotion in some *sustained and practical way,* by acting steadily in the service of his cause.[47]

The cause lies at the basis of a community; though the act of loyalty is individual and personal, it links various selves into higher social unity.[48] *Right loyalty,* then (we are reminded of Wieman here!), brings about that unity of consciousness "which individual human persons fragmentarily get," but which exists "upon a higher level than that of our ordinary human individuality."[49] "Loyalty is the will to manifest, so far as is possible, the Eternal—that is, the conscious and superhuman unity of life—in the form of the acts of an individual self."[50] The true cause, the true object of loyalty, is ultimately no other than *loyalty itself.* In acts of loyalty to loyalty the universal human community is realized.

Here we are at the point of Royce's "existentialism." Acts of loyalty are not primarily carried out on the basis of insight and knowledge, but they consist of decision, of the choice of a cause, *as such:* "We are fallible, but we can be decisive and faithful; and this is loyalty."[51]

Throughout our study we will have abundant occasion to point out the specific contribution of men like Mead and Royce to Niebuhr's thought. Here we only mention the recurring themes of the self as a "system of relations and responses" (Mead), and of the conflict between universal loyalty and lesser loyalties, rather, between the universal community of interpretation and all partial visions of reality (Royce)—themes which, as we shall see, remain central to Niebuhr, just like most of the general concerns present in the liberal heritage.

3. The problem of Troeltsch. Ernst Troeltsch is one of the few thinkers to whom Niebuhr keeps referring explicitly and emphatically when acknowledging influence and guidance; and the interpreters of

Niebuhr's thought largely agree that his position "between Troeltsch and Barth," suggested in the Preface of *The Meaning of Revelation*, is an adequate starting point for a description of his thought. Even for the superficial observer the presence of Troeltsch in Niebuhr's work is obvious. His widely known analysis of *The Social Sources of Denominationalism* (1929), evidently inspired by Troeltsch's *Social Teachings*,[52] and the consistent emphasis on historical relativism in his other works, provide the most conspicuous proof for it.

The most elaborate passage in which Niebuhr acknowledges his indebtedness to Troeltsch can be found in the Preface of *Christ and Culture:*

> I am most conscious of my debt to that theologian and historian who was occupied throughout his life by the problem of church and culture—Ernst Troeltsch. The present book in one sense undertakes to do no more than to supplement and in part to correct his work on *The Social Teachings of the Christian Churches.* Troeltsch has taught me to respect the multiformity and individuality of men and movements in Christian history, to be loath to force this rich variety into prefashioned, conceptual molds, and yet to seek *logos* in *mythos*, reason in history, essence in existence. He has helped me to accept and to profit by the acceptance of the relativity not only of historical objects but, more, of the historical subject, the observer and interpreter.[53]

This particular quotation refers us to a penetrating German philosopher and theologian who will continue to live in theology by the questions he raised rather than by the answers he sought to give. Ernst Troeltsch refuses to side with any theology that treats Christianity and Christian faith as something isolated, something a priori superior. He refers Christianity, without remainder, to history, and wishes to treat it as an ordinary object of historical investigation. He does not undertake this as a skeptic with a malicious hobby, but out of necessity in view of what historical science is and has become.

> The wall of miracle which has been erected by the theologians between Christianity and the other religions as well as between religion and the remainder of historical life, has been destroyed by historical criticism and investigation, not by opinions but by documents and sources.[54]

Reflection about Christianity needs a much broader base in the philosophy of history and the philosophy of culture. Troeltsch attempts to establish this base by approaching religion as a socio-historical phenomenon, and by approaching culture as a religious phenomenon. In this attempt he finds a partner in Niebuhr.

This means a delivery from liberalistic tendencies to compartmentalize and provincialize theology, but it also fully exposes theological thinking to the dangers of relativism. If relativism is the necessary and inherent consequence of historism, the problem is how to avoid skeptical consequences of the former while accepting the latter: to keep unique content and meaning for the Christian faith without giving in to the anxious question of whether the substance of Christianity allows such rigorous historical treatment.

Troeltsch himself teaches us how the concept of "Christianity" *(Christentum)* is a relatively young phenomenon. It is, in fact, an abstraction from concrete expressions to a general "idea," or "essence," peculiar to the Enlightenment. Later Idealism and Romanticism rediscovered, as it were, the manifoldness of the individual historical creations. Our typically modern problem is that the rediscovery of this manifoldness takes place with the aid of a historical method which slowly but surely emancipates itself from all preconceived concepts of Christianity.[55]

Troeltsch's efforts to deal with Christianity and history in the context of the problem indicated are bound to be misunderstood if we do not see him as a thinker who intends to contribute to the solution of concrete political and social questions. The problem of "historism" is ultimately a *practical-ethical problem* for Troeltsch, and "relativity" is a concept without which man as moral agent cannot be understood.[56] Troeltsch is a relativist *because* he insists on the imperative obligation for man to live an integral and constructive life in his culture; this is the reason why history must be taken seriously. And relativism is not skepticism, though it has to be shielded against it constantly; it is a tool to grasp the richness of the individual expression. Here lies Troeltsch's problem: to maintain the immanent worth of the individual forms and yet to construct an imperative system of values capable of guiding man through his confusing world. This is the source of his struggle with the neo-Kantian philosophers who influenced him so much; this system of values cannot be a foreign body hovering over the actual reality of history, it must originate in historical life itself. How can this be done, when historical judgment is caught inescapably in a relativism of values?[57]

Of course, the transcendental presuppositions of human thought warrant the connection of knowledge and value; but this connection cannot be an arbitrary deed of dogmatism within relativity. It must be grounded firmly in history *itself*; the particularity and individuality of the event must be an integral part in the universal direction of history. One who seeks to describe absolute norms cannot go beyond "systematizing fragments,"[58] and yet it must be possible to retain the possibility of genuine absoluteness.

This is the problem of Troeltsch. It has two inseparable components: the problem of the philosophy of religion (the nature of the religious a priori, the relation between religion and social life, the absoluteness of Christianity), and the practical-ethical problem (the ethical a priori, the cultural synthesis, the inevitability of compromise). Troeltsch's treatment of Christianity as a social and historical phenomenon must be seen in the context of this problem. It is not his intention to deliver the Christian tradition into the hands of a destructive and relativizing analysis, but rather to save it from impotence and irrelevance.

Troeltsch's main objection to the neo-Kantian treatment of history is that it reduces history to a piece of nature, because the a priori category of causality—basically connected with natural science!—still plays too crucial a role. This must lead to tyranny of the moral ideal and to denial of significance to the historical reality itself. A formalism without relation to actual historical life is just as serious a temptation for the philosophy of history as is naturalism or determinism. The a prioris of thought are not disconnected with empirical history; they come into being in the activity of dealing with objects, consist largely of confidence of memory, and prove themselves in their fruits.[59] There is, of course, a primary, a priori activity of reason, consisting in the fact that it "works," that it keeps forcing its way through empirical reality; but the material with which it works is always historical. Purely as a formal structure the a priori is unknown to the historian; it is known only in connection with historical individuality (synthesis).

In every a priori, then, there is an element of venture, of risk. It is the venture to grasp the absolute and the relative in one act of thought, without prior justification. It is, ultimately, the act of will that dares to regard an act of thought as *emanation of the divine life.*[60] We reach here an important point in Troeltsch's thought: the religious a priori and the metaphysical framework for the manifold relativities of history. From here, Troeltsch is able to recognize an absolute value or end of existence as the key to all being, and at the same time to maintain room for genuine particularity and individuality. It means that all historical judgments are connected with *faith*—faith in the broadest and deepest possible sense. Only by an act of faith can validity of a certain individual synthesis be established, and in no other way. This entails a profound restlessness: a synthesis must always be renewed in acts of decision; it bears the permanent marks of battle and compromise, but it is confirmed by practical fruits and sustained by a conception of individuality of metaphysical proportions. With regard to the validity of Christianity we can say no more. As a historical phenomenon it has validity because it has made us into what we are.[61]

It is clear that the ultimate solution is a metaphysical one. Individuality and development of the whole can only be brought together in a system which views both as ultimately connected. In the book on the absoluteness of Christianity, Troeltsch places the emphasis on the end, the goal of history, which always transcends the particular historical situation yet is grasped in it; in his work on historism he leans toward a Leibnizian monadology,[62] in which the perfection and the harmony of the whole find their expression in the widest possible manifoldness and individuality. This is true universality: the ever new, ever individual appearance of the direction of the divine life.[63]

Before we turn to look more closely at the impact of Troeltsch's thought on Niebuhr, we must briefly consider the question of why the problem of Troeltsch came to Niebuhr as an unsolved and complicated problem. Two points may clarify this.

First of all it may be legitimate to ask whether Troeltsch's conception of individuality is *historical enough*, whether it is not, after all, too reminiscent of the "naturalizing of history" or even of the positivism for which Troeltsch criticizes others. We can think of R. G. Collingwood's insistence that the proper subject matter of history is not individuality as such, but individuality as a "vehicle of thought" which must be reenacted,[64] and further remind ourselves that Troeltsch consistently treats the problem of history as the problem of *historical science* without considering the problems of historicity and timefulness *as such*. Attention to problems such as these brings Niebuhr closer to men like Martin Heidegger, who regard the concept of history as secondary to the specific historicity of human existence and thus seem to radicalize Troeltsch's consistency.

Second, there is in Troeltsch a rather conspicuous divorce between theology and Christology on the one hand and the philosophy of history and religion on the other. The problem of history is not conceived as a christological problem; nowhere is Christ as a point in history brought in in connection with the totality of history. Christianity as social entity, as historical phenomenon, is, of course, part of the total development; but this Christianity is largely conceived as a religious and moral ideal, only formally, not materially connected with God and history, and ultimately no more than an illustration of the philosophical problem. Niebuhr, in accepting Troeltsch's basic presuppositions and yet predestined to be a much more Christocentric thinker, thus inherited the problem of Troeltsch as a much more difficult problem than it perhaps was for Troeltsch himself.

After these preliminary remarks we can now attempt to sketch briefly Troeltsch's influence on Niebuhr.

There are obvious similarities between the two men in their

method of analyzing Christianity as a social entity. Especially in *The Social Sources of Denominationalism*, but also in *The Kingdom of God in America* and *Christ and Culture*, the problems of compromise in the cultural synthesis, of historical relativity and absolute value, are permanently in the background.[65] In the Troeltschean pattern Niebuhr evidently finds a way to cope with the problem of American pluralism and with the threat of a sterile petrifaction of the relation between church and culture. At the same time, however, it should be recognized that Niebuhr bends the moral problem of the church in a different direction than Troeltsch does. The latter's main concern is with the social relevance of the church and its responsibility for actual everyday questions of life and culture. It would be foolish to deny that Niebuhr shares this concern; in a sense the focus of attention in *The Social Sources* is not even the church, but the "disinherited in culture." But the root of the difficulty with the church's relevance, according to Niebuhr, lies in its failure to distinguish between higher and lesser *loyalties*. It is the problem of *compromise*, in Troeltsch more or less treated as an inevitable phenomenon, that is the main issue for Niebuhr. Cultural relativism is ultimately a problem of loyalty. It points to the human predicament of decision and choice of values.

We can raise the question here as to whether this does not point to a decisive difference in climate of thought between Niebuhr and Troeltsch. Niebuhr's reflections are in a peculiar sense focused on *man;* the human moral situation of loyalty and decision is his permanent starting point. Is this true for Troeltsch? Or is Troeltsch's thought in the last analysis more occupied with the neutral concept of the *individual (Das Individuelle)*? Troeltsch's emphasis is on the historicity of things, of individual forms, of the objects of historical investigation—reason perhaps why his ultimate solution has to be metaphysical. He does, of course, give attention to the actual significance of individuals, but since the actual situation of man in history is not his starting point, the amount of real individuality and unpredictableness that he can allow is in fact prescribed by his overall view of history as reconciliation of the universal and the particular. This prevents him from becoming as concretely "anthropocentric" as Niebuhr. Crucial for Niebuhr remains the historicity of man, of the self, in both a subjective and an objective sense—reason perhaps why his interest in metaphysics is practically nil.

Essentially connected with the anthropocentric bias in Niebuhr's thinking,[66] though it may seem paradoxical at first, is his effort to correct Troeltsch's relativism by *theocentrism*. Niebuhr's own acknowledgment of Troeltsch's influence, quoted in the beginning of this section, continues as follows:

If I think of my essay as an effort to correct Troeltsch's

analyses of the encounters of church and world, it is mostly because I try to understand this historical relativism in the light of theological and theocentric relativism. I believe that it is an aberration *of faith* as well as of reason to absolutize the finite, but that all this relative history of finite men and movements is under the governance of the absolute God.[67]

The question as to what extent theocentric thinking with its inclinations to connect history with eschatology and predestination only builds on tendencies already present in Troeltsch himself, can be left aside here. In any case it is evident that the problem of Troeltsch, when passed on to Niebuhr, is modified and complicated both by anthropocentrism and theocentrism. But the *structure* of the problem of Troeltsch remains. With this we mean the persistent tendency to approach religion *culturally* with an emphasis on *relativity*, and to approach culture *religiously* with a quest for the *absolute*. Connected with this is the tendency to treat culture—any culture—as a phenomenon admirable in itself, not to be vulgarized by apologetic defense or to be pressed in a preconceived theological framework, and also the refusal to find sense and meaning in history anywhere except in the individual synthesis of faith. Ultimately—perhaps we might even say eschatologically—it is the cultural synthesis that matters, not the preservation and the history of church and religion.

Niebuhr's commitment to the structure of the problem of Troeltsch singles him out as a profound analyzer of the problems peculiar to American religious history. From Troeltsch, Niebuhr learns to regard the problem of multiplicity and unity, of sovereignty and pluralism, as a problem of the historical relativity of both faith and culture. The application of this insight to the American situation and tradition marks Niebuhr's thought from beginning to end.

B. POST-LIBERAL CONSCIOUSNESS

1. The end of an era. It has become customary in the history of theology to regard the nineteenth century as an ideological unit that found its end during and after the years of World War I. In Europe, it was the second edition of Karl Barth's *Epistle to the Romans* that underlined the decisive and radical nature of the break with the past; but there were, of course, many more factors which contributed to a general, more or less radical and consistent, reaction to the age of Liberalism. From the beginning, Niebuhr was aware of those forces. We have reviewed the context of Liberalism in which his thought was shaped; now we must look more closely at his early thought in which the forces of change are already at work in the midst of the last flowerings of a bygone age. One who reads Niebuhr's works in chronological order will look in vain for a

dramatic and sudden turning point; one sees, rather, a gradual groping for answers and a gradual change of temper. The early 1930's were of crucial significance in this process, but they were more like rapids than like a new source. Therefore, it does not seem to be correct to point to a *liberal period* in Niebuhr's thinking. At most, one can say that there is a period in which his attack upon Liberalism is not yet so explicit and so sharp as in the 1930's.

The persistent patterns in Niebuhr's thinking that we have sought to describe determine his questions throughout the years of his activity as a theologian. We drew attention to his use of sociology for theological data and his concern with religious experience; to his emphasis on the social character of selfhood and the notions of community and loyalty (Mead and Royce); and to his Troeltschean way of approaching religion culturally and culture religiously, with the inherent problem of historicity and value. We have suggested that Niebuhr brings a combination of these patterns to bear on the problems of the American religious tradition with its tension between sovereignty and pluralism—a tension which, in a sense, dies with Liberalism, and is revived temporarily in the Social Gospel.

In Niebuhr's early work, especially in *The Social Sources of Denominationalism*, we find an approach to the problem of the Social Gospel in which the presence of men like Ernst Troeltsch, Max Weber, and Richard H. Tawney can be easily recognized, and in which the moral question of *loyalty* is placed in the center. We find here *both* the clear and analyzable fact of the cultural entanglement of church and religion *and* the question of whether this is "a good thing," whether the nature of church and religion does not demand something different. "Religious life is so interwoven with social circumstances that the formulation of theology is necessarily conditioned by these."[1] "Doctrines and practice change with the mutations of social structure, not vice versa; the ideological interpretation of such changes quite misses the point."[2] In the later analyses of church and culture, this approach is never abandoned.

Niebuhr's refusal to treat religion and culture as two separate phenomena[3] constitutes his fundamental problem. Faith cannot exist or be expressed apart from the believer's mind, which is shaped by philosophy, science, and culture.[4] The relativism which thus forcefully presents itself is primarily a moral problem; it is impossible to find an absolute starting point for any ethics or theory of value. Yet relativism cannot be the last word, for precisely the Christian message calls men to a loyalty which is in necessary and essential tension with the more obvious loyalties of daily life.[5] How can this "call" be made valid? Does not cultural entanglement of church and religion inevitably mean confusion of values? Does it not mean that it is hardly *possible* to avoid compromise and betrayal of the true nature of the church? "Are not the churches the church's worst enemy?"[6]

The dilemma is clearly presented in Niebuhr's article "Back to Benedict?"[7] Here Niebuhr considers the possibility that the church retreat completely from the world for a while, to regain its integrity and to restore the boundary line between the kingdom of God and the world. But this, he says, is not the ultimate answer; eventually the church will have to face the choice again, the choice between "Calvary" and "uneasy compromise," between self-sacrifice and prolonged yet inauthentic existence. Jesus, Niebuhr says on another occasion,[8] was able to make this choice for the highest good because he was not afraid of sacrifice. *"He looked upon life from the point of view of the Father"*—and so "we must teach men to think like God, not like men." If man does not allow himself to live and think according to a standard greater than himself, and courageously face the consequent possibility of sacrifice, he betrays his true nature.

This is the problem of *The Social Sources of Denominationalism.* Not the multiplicity and pluralism of the churches as such is offensive to Niebuhr, but rather the failure of the churches to transcend the social conditions "which fashion them into caste organizations."[9] Compromise may be inevitable, but it is no less an evil,[10] and denominationalism "is the church's confession of defeat and the symbol of its surrender."[11] Is the road of retreat and sacrifice the only alternative to the moral problem of cultural entanglement? In any case, the church, too, must learn "to live and think according to a standard greater than itself"; in other words, the least that can be asked of the denominations is to retrace the line of distinction between mere adjustment to culture and compromise with a social ethics which does not meet the standards of the Christian gospel.[12] This is the solution of Niebuhr's first book. An honest and careful retracing of this line of distinction will enhance the effectiveness of "a common Christian system of values,"[13] in which the leading ideal is the center of all subordinate purposes.[14] This leading ideal is the "eternal harmony of love," revealed in the life of Christ: "His sonship and his brotherhood, as delineated in the gospel, are not the example which men are asked to follow if they will, but rather the demonstration of that character of ultimate reality which they can ignore only at the cost of their souls."[15]

The solution is uneasy, but not insignificant. The uneasiness lies, first of all, in the fact that the *given* situation of cultural entanglement of church and religion appears as *in itself* deplorable, as something on which the Christian ideal of brotherhood must be brought to bear with wisdom and care to save the church from total irrelevance: in other words, the disjunction between *ideal* and *situation* can be bridged only by an appeal to goodwill and wise leadership.[16] The uneasiness lies, second, in a certain weakening of the presuppositions of moral relativism and relativity as social conditioning, by the assumption that "the Christian values" *can* be universal and *can* serve to keep cultural entanglement within the limits of "mere adjustment." The significance of the solution, however, should not be overlooked. The problem of religion and culture is, in *The Social Sources*, definitely designed as a problem of *human commitment*; in other words, it is an anthropological affair. This is an axiom which Niebuhr never relinquishes. Moreover, what is ultimately at stake in this commitment is *the character of ultimate reality*—and although this term clearly does not receive the emphasis and the connotation of later years, it does point in the direction of a more stringent and radical view of the whole problem.

Such a view developed in the 1930's; for it was precisely in the 1930's that the "nineteenth century" in American religious thought was publicly relieved of its duties by a sober realism. On the one hand this realism was only a phase in the process of fragmentation which had started in the 1890's and which gradually created the awareness that the problems of the emancipation of science could not be met with old answers—that, for instance, the newly discovered "irrationality of man" was incompatible with the convictions of Liberalism.[17] On the other hand, the realism was a direct response to social circumstances, among which the 1929 crisis played a much more crucial role than, for instance, World War I.[18] Theology shared in this development. This is one of the main reasons why we should not overestimate the similarities between the theological revolt in Europe—which was essentially a *theological* revolt—and the realistic developments in America. In America it was *primarily* social experience that forced men like Reinhold Niebuhr to challenge the adequacy of several liberal doctrines.

This is significantly illustrated by the fact that the book which played a role comparable to Barth's *Epistle to the Romans* was Reinhold Niebuhr's *Moral Man and Immoral Society*.[19] Reinhold Niebuhr's attack on Liberalism is largely characterized by a renewed concentration on man—in the case of the book cited, man's ambiguous place in the interplay of power-groups and class-structures; in his later works, man's ambiguous place as a being both *in* history and *transcending* history.[20] Barth's attack, on the other hand, is characterized by a renewed concentration on the priority and transcendence of God. This is much more than a difference in dogmatic preoccupation; it is a difference in situation and background, and in the assignment derived from them.

Although it was not exactly the same experience as his brother had that accelerated the change in Niebuhr's thinking, it was comparable.

Typical for Niebuhr's thought, and of crucial significance for the understanding and interpretation of it, is the fact that the change develops around his reactions and responses to the major historical events of the day. In the beginning of the 1930's he occupied himself not only with the European theological development—to these influences we must turn presently—but also with the rise of Nazism and with the development of Marxist Russia. The necessity to look differently at human nature and to engage in more profound reflection on its evil possibilities, its perplexities, its despairs and hopes, was forced upon him mainly in these involvements.[21]

With these brief indications we have actually started to describe a movement which is often called "neoorthodoxy." The term neoorthodoxy is unfortunate. It is "an arbitrary name devoid of internal significance, which was foisted on an only vaguely identifiable movement."[22] Not only does it generate associations of "restoration"; it also suggests the possibility that the diverse ways of thinking indicated by it can be brought under one meaningful heading. This is even difficult in the case of the Niebuhr brothers. A general characteristic, however, is that neoorthodoxy contains an attack on Liberalism without being a denial of all the liberal assumptions. It presents a development of the profitable insights and gains of Liberalism in a realistic way, rather than an apostasy.[23]

Against the background of this general change of climate we will have to view Niebuhr's development of the 1930's. But in order to do this effectively, we must first step aside to assess the importance of European theological influences in these years.

2. **Influences from European crisis-theology.** The term crisis-theology cannot serve as an adequate definition of any one school of thought; it is meant, rather, to designate the theological *temper* of several diverse movements in the European theology of the 1920's. Crisis-theology is all theological thought that starts with the rediscovery of the critical distance between God and man; crisis means that man learns how little reason there is to speak of God and man in the same breath, and yet how impossible it is for man to depend upon his own resources. Crisis means: I am on earth and God is in heaven, yet I am thrown on God's mercy for existence. The names that immediately come to mind are those of Sören Kierkegaard and Karl Barth. Both men are concerned to reemphasize the "quality" of God and to stress the meaning of "truth" as "subject-ivity."[24] Yet their influences do not necessarily coincide; in American post-liberal thought, for instance, there are Kierkegaardian influences at work which do not carry the seeds of Barthianism.[25] One might even venture the guess that the difference in the ways in which

Niebuhr and Barth are affected by Kierkegaard partly accounts for Niebuhr's complicated attitude toward Barth.

Main elements in American post-Liberalism that can be regarded as Kierkegaardian are the emphasis on existential freedom rather than on permanent principles in ethics, and the insight that Christianity is essentially a subjective commitment rather than an objective state of affairs. Kierkegaard's chief concern, writes Niebuhr, was "to dispel the illusion that Christianity can exist in an objective form or that anything objective can be Christianity."[26] As a provisional generalization we might suggest that Niebuhr is primarily attracted by Kierkegaard's stress on the irrationality of the act of faith and on the complexity of religious experience and Christianity as a whole; whereas Barth focuses on the "qualitative otherness" of God as the only determinative of faith and knowledge.

Niebuhr's implicit and explicit reactions to the theology of Karl Barth form an aspect of his thought that is fascinating, complex, difficult, and of central significance. It cannot be treated exhaustively in this section; only a few lines will be drawn, and further references to the Niebuhr-Barth relation will be made at appropriate places in the course of the study.

Barth's *Epistle to the Romans* is a radical denunciation of all efforts to assimilate God into human thinking. God encounters us in the No that we experience in the limitation of all human reality; and *only* because this No is God's No, it is also his Yes. Faith is: to let this God be God, to stake one's life on this open question, to give oneself to the paradox of salvation by this negation; faith is, therefore, no significant human act—it is the venture to leave open space where normally "religion" takes over, and even this cannot become a method but remains a divine initiative. God is in no sense at man's disposal, and yet this is precisely man's salvation. This is the principle which Barth endeavors to make the exclusive basis for speaking about God, both for the language of faith and for theological discourse. Anything short of this principle means a prostration to "religion," for man. Theology can only approach its object dialectically: only thus can it make the best of a situation in which the necessity to speak about God is counteracted by the impossibility to do so legitimately.[27] God as an object of speech and reflection is an idol, is "not God."

Barth's strong advocation of a permanent living *suspension* of all objectified speaking of God in these years introduces force and excitement into his thought, and it is certainly safe to say that Niebuhr has felt a lasting affinity to this radical and living restoration of God's otherness and nearness. The acute sense of crisis which the early Barth is able to convey in his vivid, highly dialectical language, made a profound impression on Niebuhr, especially when—and because—it concurred with his own experience. And yet we should not speak too quickly. For it seems equally true that the basic *interest* in the early works of Barth, notably in the *Epistle to the Romans*, is a proper restoration of theo-logy, the discovery of the way back to the biblical idea of God. It will not do to exaggerate the difference between the young Barth and the "Barth of the Dogmatics"; already in the *Epistle to the Romans* a *Dogmatik* lurks in the background. The fact that Niebuhr does not share this basic interest determines his attitude; he follows sympathetically, he is even influenced profoundly, but he never becomes a Barthian.

This becomes even clearer when we follow Barth's road in the direction of the *Church Dogmatics*. His main concern here is to give theology its own independent method; in other words, to make the qualitative difference of the *object* of theology into a qualitatively different *epistemology*, so that theology can distinguish itself fundamentally and permanently from all philosophy.[28] Theology comes from a place that philosophy is trying to reach. Knowledge in a philosophical sense must necessarily presuppose something like a common plane between subject and object; theological knowledge, however, can only be recognition of divine giving prior to knowledge, which means that both nature and reason are inadequate as starting points for reflection on God. Theological reasoning, therefore, can only travel from actuality to possibility; the *noetic* relation with the object is based on its *ontic* priority: that it is true is *presupposition* rather than the *aim* of thought. We arrive here at the concept of the analogy of faith: the starting point and possibility of the *Church Dogmatics*.[29] The epistemological significance of justification by grace is converted into the indispensability of Christology as the basis of theological knowledge. The *ethical* distance between God and man in the *Epistle to the Romans* becomes the *epistemological* principle of the *Dogmatik*. This has profound consequences. We believe that it is one of the reasons why Niebuhr eventually rejects the Barthian road.

Barth's reflections start in the anxiety of the pastorate in the struggle with the stubborn biblical material. (His first major work is a commentary!) Niebuhr does not exhibit the same anxious preoccupation with the Bible. His concern, like Barth's is to restore the sovereignty and priority of God, yet not primarily as an object of preaching but rather as a way to cope with daily reality. He remains concerned with human faith, its possibilities and its practical results. When Barth speaks of Jesus Christ as the place where God reveals himself as the Hidden One, or of the fact that our only *hope* lies in the knowledge that it is God who "negates" us, Niebuhr speaks of the quality and the dialectical movement of human *faith*; his concern is precisely with the transition that *man* has to make between a simple awareness of the negation and the trust that it is *God* who negates. For Niebuhr, the object of theology can never be simply God in his self-giving—it is always God in his self-giving *as trusted and distrusted* in the movement of human faith.

It should not surprise us, therefore, when, in the beginning of the 1930's, we see how Niebuhr is attracted to Paul Tillich.[30]

The crisis theme is for Tillich, too, central in these years, albeit in a different thought-setting than we find in the early Barth. Unlike Barth, Tillich is from the start interested in an analysis of culture, its autonomy and heteronomy, and in the combination of theological and philosophical insights into one coherent system of thought.[31] This does not keep him, however, from stressing revelation as a *critical principle* which directs itself against all human religious efforts to use it as a judgment on others.[32] Revelation of the Eternal, the Unconditioned, does not mean that things hitherto hidden become evident and visible; it means, rather, the realization in history of what is *essentially* hidden and inaccessible. Revelation is not something natural or supernatural; one should think of it in terms of *shaking* and *shocking* the natural and *altering* its course. It contains simultaneously moments of judgment and of grace—genuine crisis occurs only in combination with grace. This occurrence Tillich calls *kairos*. Living in "kairos-consciousness" means heeding the invasion of the Eternal and giving shape to the limitation of all culture by the Eternal without trying to enclose the Eternal itself in temporal form. Living in kairos-consciousness means living in "a new theonomy."

At the heart of these reflections there is, clearly, a drive toward concrete expression. Indicating an absolute tension between the temporal and the Eternal is only half the story; this absolute tension must be made visible in the relative tensions of history and culture. This Tillich calls giving shape to one's cultural existence in "beliefful realism,"[33] or—in shorthand—"protestant shaping": cultural expression in which both limitation and grace are made manifest, in which prophetic criticism is embodied in rational criticism. This is one of the distinctive characteristics of Tillich's thought of the 1920's: even if defective, constructive Protestantism is far better than mere theological criticism, which does not lead to cultural construction. From here we can understand his positive emphasis on the *church*, not as an isolated island of special insights, but as a visible carrier of the transcendent significance of *all* human endeavor.

The most concise statement of the cultural attitude which is the consequence of these reflections can be found in the book that Niebuhr translated and introduced to the American readers: *The Religious Situation.*[34] Much of the thrust of Niebuhr's thinking in the 1930's can be associated with this book. The basic combination of sovereignty and construction, and the attack on all forms of cultural expression—all "isms"—that have come to rest in themselves without a critical and corrective relation to the Transcendent,[35] are examples of this. His revision of the relation of the absolute to the particular is deeply conditioned by these insights.

Summarizing the main points of contact we find: first of all, the conviction that no form of culture, religion, or political life carries within itself a guarantee against demonization or loss of relation to the Unconditioned; second, the anxiety over the inner paradox of Protestantism (it has to deny all cultural realization that wants to be something in itself, yet needs such realization to make this denial heard); and third, the method, or rather, the *attitude* of beliefful realism. This attitude takes seriously the stubborn facts of the situation, of man and of God; and it combines radical criticism with appreciation of the relative values involved. It means a renewed attention to the objective givenness of the object and its participation in the Unconditioned.[36] For Niebuhr it entails a special reinforcement of the relativism with which we have found him occupied in so many ways.

And yet, here, too, we must caution against too easy an association of Tillich and Niebuhr. Niebuhr will not have failed to see that Tillich's interest behind his beliefful realism is primarily the *metaphysical system*, in the framework of which Tillich seeks the possibility for and the road to a religious socialism. Tillich's fight against the heteronomy of culture ("The Great Inquisitor") must be understood against the background of his systematic theology that he started in 1925[37]—and on central points of this system Niebuhr departs from him. But the interest of both men in social ethics brings them close together, even though, seen from the Tillichian standpoint, Niebuhr seeks as it were a shortcut to it. It may well be that what unites Niebuhr and Tillich at this point, separates them both from Barth.

Tillich accuses the early dialectical theology of lack of constructive power. With this he seems to mean both the lack of interest in a system in which God, man, Jesus Christ, and culture are put in their proper places[38]; and the lack of concrete criticism and construction in the actual situation. This gives the movement a conservative character: all its forceful theological criticism results in support of the status quo. Very similar, yet more hostile, reactions to early Barthianism can be found in Reinhold Niebuhr:

> All moral striving on the level of history is reduced to insignificance. . . . It is becoming increasingly apparent that the emphases of the new theological conservatism are being exploited in the interest of political reaction to a greater degree than in the interest of social liberalism and radicalism. . . . Perhaps this

theology is constructed too much for the great crises of history. It seems to have no guidance for a Christian statesman for our day. It can fight the devil if he shows both horns and both cloven feet. But it refuses to make discriminating judgments about good and evil if the evil shows only one horn or the half of a cloven foot.[39]

Niebuhr himself voices similar dissatisfaction in *The Social Sources of Denominationalism.*[40]

The digression on Tillich's thought can enable us to take a second look at Niebuhr's attitude toward Barth. Though the evidence thus far compiled might point to the contrary, we must maintain that as a theologian Niebuhr is closer to Barth than to Tillich. Only temporarily, and precisely in the formative 1930's, is there more attraction to Tillich, because of the latter's emphasis on cultural construction. Underneath there is the constant presence of Barth, though more "religious and ethical" than "epistemological"—indeed the major interest of Barthianism as Niebuhr conceived it.[41] Like Barth, Niebuhr would say that the relation of crisis between man's constant search for God and God's revelation in Jesus Christ is the fundamental theme of theology. Like Barth, Niebuhr would say that God's self-revelation in Jesus Christ confronts us with something qualitatively different from any cultural ideology. But he refuses to structure his theological method according to these insights; for this would in fact imply a weakening of the basic theological concern for the situation of natural man, his faith and experience, and the situation of the church in the midst of its cultural loyalties.

Niebuhr's problem is the relation between theocentrism and anthropocentricism, not the relation between theology and philosophy. Therefore, though Niebuhr stands closer to Barth than to Tillich, it was the Tillichian emphasis which contributed to his decision not to choose the Barthian road, in addition, of course, to the inherited problems of American religious history, which determined his criticism of Barth's theology.[42]

This criticism has basically two aspects. Barth's theology is socially impotent, it has no word for the complicated problems of social ethics; and it leads in the end to an authoritarian Christocentric dogmatism.[43] Is it really necessary to develop a theocentric theology in this way and in no other? Does *this* theocentric development not weaken the crisis element? Is it not precisely the crisis element in the theocentric revelation which forbids us to concentrate everything in the Christ-event? Can we, in a Christocentric theology, still take the Christ-event itself seriously enough in its significance for the movement of human faith?

It is quite possible to argue that this criticism reflects a misunderstanding of Barth's theology. It seems that important concerns of Barth are completely overlooked. One of these concerns is, for instance, to define as exactly as possible what we mean by "crisis." For Barth, the crisis element in the God-man relation is not weakened or eliminated but *revealed* in the Christ-event. For it is not crisis as such that is important—not crisis as a general awareness, however profound it may be—but this particular crisis and this particular God. Christological concentration does not, in Barth's intention, jeopardize the sovereignty of God, nor does it isolate the Christ-event from human history. Christological concentration means not only that we have no right to speak of God apart from the history of Jesus Christ, but also that *in* the history of Jesus Christ we see precisely how little right we indeed *do* have to speak of God at all. This is the way in which we have to understand that it is the specific Christological content of the crisis which, for Barth, becomes the basis of theology.

Nevertheless, we have to keep in mind that Niebuhr and Barth speak from different backgrounds. In the context of a crisis theology as it would develop on the basis of *American* religious history, Barth's emphases cannot but be regarded as dangerously displaced. In American theology, "crisis" is something which affects man's faith in its diverse expressions, and as such also the total life of society. To concentrate all this in the Christ-event would be dishonest, it would mean denying the total dimensions of the crisis; and perhaps in the end, by the social effects that such a concentration would entail, it would mean denying the crisis altogether. Viewed purely from the standpoint of Barthian theology, Niebuhr's criticism of Barth is perhaps less than adequate, but viewed in the context of the theological problems that Niebuhr faced, it was quite necessary.[44]

3. **The deity of God and the conversion of the church.** The essay which introduces us to the Niebuhr of the 1930's is "Religious Realism in the Twentieth Century" (1931). It analyzes the "turn of the centuries" in much the same spirit as Tillich's *The Religious Situation* does, and it recognizes how on all fronts of the spiritual life there is a varied revolt against the anthropocentric, rather anthropocratic,[45] tendencies of the nineteenth century. Both in science and philosophy man is removed from his dominant place, and we find a fresh concentration on reality in its independence from the observer *(realism)*. So it is—and must be—in the study of religion: we turn from a sterile subjectivism and from a subordination of religion to other human phenomena to a renewed concentration on the religious *object*.[46] Such "religious realism" stresses the independence of God from experience though it does not give up its concern with experience.[47] This point reminds us once again of the fact that neoorthodoxy in its early phases

was very close to the thought of men like D. C. Macintosh. It was first of all the *European* development of theological realism which gradually separated Niebuhr from the latter.

Niebuhr indicates this himself in an analysis of "the criticism of American religious realism which is implicit in the German movement."[48] The main thrust of this criticism is, according to Niebuhr, that the American empirical realism is insufficiently critical of itself and too readily confuses the object of experience with that which experience intends; in other words, it does not have enough Kantian hesitation with regard to the object. The lack of criticism brings American empirical realism to the point where it tends to use God for man's interest and to regard individual faith as more important than historical revelation. It is not difficult to see how these supposed criticisms are in line with Niebuhr's own conception of the needs of contemporary theology. We remember that the questions Niebuhr raised in his early writing circled mainly around two problems: the entanglement of religion and culture as a problem of human commitment (is it possible to transcend social conditioning?), and the necessity to recover a true and meaningful view of the ultimate character and purpose of historical reality in the face of the contemporary events. A year before "Religious Realism" we find the same themes of this essay, combined with these specific concerns, in the article "Can German and American Christians Understand Each Other?" In this article Niebuhr fights

> a provincialism which forgets that . . . apart from his (man's) urge to identify himself with some transcendent meaning, his being and even his ethical and social interests lose all ultimate significance. . . . Our situation is indeed desperate if we must continue to confuse our ideas and formulas with the reality we seek to express in them. Christ becomes Christology, God theology, and religion psychology.[49]

Niebuhr's guiding thesis is that the situation in which we find ourselves calls for "a resolute effort to wrest from contemporary experience its ultimate significance and revelational value,"[50] and for a restoration of "the peculiarity of Christianity as revelation, or of faith as a divine *tour de force* by which the relative is transcended."[51] Under the conditions of this guiding thesis he introduces his critique of religious experience. This implies *both* a more serious analysis of the historical and cultural situation in which faith finds itself entangled, *and* an unwavering attention to the independence of the religious object. It is here that the *crisis motif* comes in, which we have sought to describe in the preceding section; and it is on this ground that Niebuhr prepares the answers to the questions raised in his early writings. Not only, therefore, is the realism of men like Macintosh criticized on the basis of European insights, it is also *radicalized* on the basis of sober observation and experience with regard to the ultimate significance of total life. This approach differs from Barthianism for it still seeks to unite the complete independence of God with human experience:

> The independence of God from experience does not imply his remoteness from experience; the relativity of historical experience does not imply the absence of an absolute content or point of reference; the presence of evil in more subtle and pervasive forms than is usually granted by American realism does not imply the absence of the good.[52]

The crisis motif that we find in Niebuhr's theology is, therefore, basically the recovery and reinforcement of a genuine element in the American tradition which, in the course of years, had gradually been replaced by more or less secularized ideas of pervasive optimism. *Critical historical realism* means that the self-evident pattern of Providence, the unquestioned goodness of cosmos and history, is under attack. It combines the search for significance of all events with the—existential rather than metaphysical—question of God's judging and redemptive presence in history.

It is this consistent theocentrism which seeks to base all thought about history on the sovereignty and freedom of God, that also marks the difference in approach between the two Niebuhr brothers.

The occasion for the only published exchange between them was an article by Niebuhr on the hotly debated question of American intervention in the Chinese-Japanese war.[53] Niebuhr's article suggests the possibility of doing nothing, of refraining from any activity, precisely on the basis of faith.

> The inactivity of radical Christianity is not the inactivity of those who call evil good; it is the inaction of those who do not judge their neighbors because they cannot fool themselves into a sense of superior righteousness. It is not the inactivity of resigned patience, but of *a patience that is full of hope*, and is based on faith. It is not the inactivity of the noncombatant, for it knows that *there are no noncombatants*, that everyone is involved, that *China is being crucified* (though the term is very inaccurate), by our sins and those of the whole world. It is not the inactivity of the merciless, for works of mercy must be performed though they are only palliatives to ease present pain while *the process of healing depends on deeper, more actual and urgent forces*. But if there is no God, or *if God is up in heaven and not in time itself, it is a very foolish inactivity.*[54]

The cited article is of central significance for the understanding of Niebuhr: it contains the themes that later develop into the core of a consistent theological thinking. Its tendency obviously runs counter to Reinhold Niebuhr's intentions, as is clear from the latter's criticism:

> I realize quite well that my brother's position both in its ethical perfectionism and in its apocalyptic note is closer to the gospel than mine. In confessing that, I am forced to admit that I am unable to construct an adequate social ethic out of a pure love ethic. I cannot abandon the pure love ideal because anything which falls short of it is less than the ideal. But I cannot use it fully if I want to assume a responsible attitude toward the problems of society.[55]

The discussion reveals that Niebuhr stands closer to Barth than his brother, in his insistence that the reflection on the freedom of man and the relevance of the gospel for a responsible social ethics be subordinated to consistent faith in the presence of God in history. *"The same structure in things which is our enemy is our redeemer,"* writes Niebuhr in his answer,[56] and man's business is not primarily to act perfectly but to clear the road by repentance and forgiveness. Man's *hope* and his *freedom* are real, but they never become self-evident. Taking God seriously means questioning man's existence; taking seriously the limitation of man by the freedom of God means raising the possibility of doing nothing, of remaining passive—if only to signify that man's action cannot heal the brokenness of which we all suffer.

It is not surprising that in both Niebuhrs the emphasis on human *sin* occupies an important place. For Reinhold Niebuhr sin is the deplorable situation of self-contradiction in which man entangles himself; for his brother it is the permanent refusal to make that which ultimately matters in history the only guide and criterion of thought and action.[57] Sin, according to Niebuhr, is basically and ultimately *distrust in being itself*, resulting in a denial of dependence and in disloyalty. It is the ultimate source of all social ills.

Closely related to Niebuhr's theocentric concern to rescue the independence and sovereignty of the "religious object" is another line in his thought of the 1930's: a consistent effort to clear all thought about God from value considerations based on preconceived human interests. Reflection on this problem was necessary precisely because Niebuhr introduced the crisis motif without wishing to alter the basic structure of his method, which keeps looking toward human experience and keeps insisting that human faith is an affair of *valuation*.

The question of whether such a being as God *exists* is subordinated in importance to the question of whether genuine experience of *deity value* is possible. In themselves, these considerations do not deviate from, for instance, those of Macintosh; but this changes in the further elaboration of this insight. The quality of God's God-ness, according to

Niebuhr, does not allow any reference to known value posited prior to the experience of God, and used for its analysis. There is simply no way from the lower to the higher reality (the unwarranted assumption of men like Macintosh and Wieman). No analysis of known values can offer any clue to the reality of God. Only a disinterested approach can lead farther. If God is not sought and loved for his own sake only, all theology will inevitably be anthropocentric and narcissistic; it will inevitably forget the relativity and the conflict of all values. The true tendency of religion, Niebuhr says, is *away from itself*; the true *religious need* is not to value, but *to be valued.*

The term "religious need" plays a central role in the thought of Macintosh—which is probably the reason why Niebuhr gives it major significance in the essay "Value Theory and Theology" (1937). For Macintosh the whole proof of God's existence ultimately depends on the religious need:

> On the basis of sinful man's need of moral salvation, the existence of God, the moral Savior, may be postulated as humanly imperative. What this argument postulates as necessary (and it is what moral optimism would find it reasonable to believe), this the religious experience of moral salvation reveals as Truth and Reality; namely, a Power, not identifiable with ourselves, that makes for righteousness in and through us, when we persist in the right religious adjustment. As a matter of fact, the only adequate proof of the existence of the God of religion is to be found in experience—and in religious experience particularly.[58]

Over against this Niebuhr:

> The religious need is the need for that which makes life worth living, which bestows meaning on life by revealing itself as the final source of life's being and value. *The religious need is satisfied only insofar as man is able to recognize himself as valued by something beyond himself.*[59]

This is revelation: to be valued. "What is revealed in revelation is not a being as such, but rather its deity value, not that it is, but that it 'loves us,' 'judges us,' that it makes life worth living."[60] "When we find out that we are no longer thinking him, but that he first thought us, that is revelation."[61] We see, here again, how Niebuhr is concerned to combine the absolute priority of God with the structure of the analysis of religious experience[62]; we see also how he seeks to bring the insights of crisis and sovereignty to bear on the concrete questions of the human situation.

There may be some question at this point as to whether Niebuhr does indeed succeed in combining both vital interests: the realistic concern with the human situation and the emphasis on the absolute priority of God. Does not the concept of religious need, however modified, tie God to preconceived schemes? Two things can be observed here. In the first place, the use of the term religious need is an auxiliary move to uncover a fundamental relation of mutual valuation between man and God. All value finds its source and origin in being valued by God; and this "being valued" is at the same time the basis of man's valuing of God *as God.* Thus, in the divine-human relation the valuation of the deity quality and the satisfaction of the religious need are always linked to and based on God's valuing.[63] Second, Niebuhr cannot escape the consequence that analysis of the human situation and knowledge of its ultimate meaning and value are no longer connected by a relation of predictability and certainty, but only by an irrational act of faith. This is the price Niebuhr pays for refusing the Barthian road. Or perhaps we should say it is the insight that religious realism *requires* this honesty of faith which *compels* him to refuse the Barthian road.

Yet in all this, Niebuhr could not really be said to have pursued his interests of the 1920's, if these reflections had not had their specific consequences for his view of the problem of the *church.* But they do. His chapters in the volume *The Church Against the World*[64] form perhaps his clearest and most penetrating contribution in these years. Here he comes close to announcing a whole program of action: "The task of the present generation appears to lie in the liberation of the church from its bondage to corrupt civilization."[65] The earlier insight, that Christianity is basically *homeless* in ideologies like communism and capitalism, now receives full meaning and content: the object of the church's loyalty is the sovereign Lord of history who stands in "crisis" over against all anthropocentric efforts to forget relativity, to smooth over the offense of compromise, and to allow the relative to become the absolute.

We will have to see clearly that the many complexities of the human situation of conflicting and parallel loyalties should not be reduced to simple terms if we do not want to lose all chance for an effective strategy of life[66]; but this necessity of clear analysis should not keep us from the prophetic distinction between false and right faith, and from the insistence on the conversion of the church. For the issue at stake is "the world in the church," which means "the confusion of the Spirit with the letter and . . . blindness to the actual shift of attention from meaning to symbol that has taken place within the church" (anthropocentricism).[67] The proper function of the church, the directing of attention toward the sovereign source of all life, must be restored. "Its main task always remains that of understanding, proclaiming, and preparing for the divine revolution in human life."[68] Only thus is it possible to fight the evils of society: the anthropocentric ideologies that feed on the cultivation of *desire*[69]; only thus is it possible to regain something of the visible movement of human life and history toward its true goal.

Chapter 2
Development of Position

A. THE STRUCTURE OF NIEBUHR'S THEOLOGY

1. **The rediscovery of Jonathan Edwards.** We continue our interpretation of Niebuhr's theological development with a brief glance at the theology of Jonathan Edwards—a remarkable eighteenth-century American who fascinates the historians by his many faces: that of a hellfire preacher, that of a speculative philosopher, and that of a dogmatic theologian. The insertion of a section on Edwards in a description of the structure of Niebuhr's theology is, in a sense, questionable; for no direct line of influence and dependence can be established between the two, and it is wrong to assume that Niebuhr derived the cornerstones of his theological thought from Edwards. Yet there are two arguments for the insertion. In the first place, the climate in which Niebuhr's theology is developed is also the climate of a rediscovery of long-forgotten Edwardean emphases, and of a fresh attention to the profundity and surprising relevance of these emphases.[1] In the second place, several significant themes of Niebuhr's thought reveal a growing affinity and congruence with themes of Edwards. We think especially of the notion of God as the great system of being in which all being finds its value (chapter 2, part B), the emphasis on love of being as the center of ethics and as the critical principle for the Christian life (chapter 3), and the effort to regard the "sovereign pleasure of God" as the key to history (chapter 4). Without anticipating our discussion of these themes, we believe that it is fruitful to review briefly how they cohere in Edwards' thought.

Edwards' theology is a miraculous combination of different concerns though its dominant characteristic is the association with Revivalism. In a sense, his thought is a profound apology for Revivalism, and as such it comprises the crucial problem of American religious history—sovereignty and liberty, theocracy and pluralism—in a living and dynamic synthesis. God's sovereignty is the center of this synthesis; the problems of man receive their proper place only when viewed in the light of this center.

God has appeared to me a glorious and lovely being, chiefly on account of his holiness. The holiness of God has always appeared to me the most lovely of all his attributes. The doctrines of God's absolute sovereignty, and free grace, in shewing mercy to whom he would show mercy, and man's absolute dependence on the operations of God's Holy Spirit, have very often appeared to me as sweet and glorious doctrines. These doctrines have been much my delight. God's sovereignty has ever appeared to me, great part of his glory. It has often been my delight to approach God, and adore him as a sovereign God, and ask sovereign mercy of him.[2]

The various factors that led to the rise of the revivals—an increasing rationalism, the pervasive doctrine of man's inability to attain grace, the demands of the changing conditions of life—are present in Edwards' thought in the framework of the divine sovereignty. Edwards is the theologian of the senses, of the emotions and passions. His sermons are brilliant examples of the effort to convey a complete emotional vision of "divine things." From here he directs his violent attacks against rationalism and Arminianism: dangerous temptations because they are shallow, barren, and *inhuman*.

Edwards presents his reflections in the framework of an idealism that he develops at least partly in connection with John Locke. The world is an ideal one; the mind of God is the only clue to the existence of anything[3]; but the ideas are conveyed only through sense experience, as it were, indirectly. The dependence of man on impressions from the outer world is thus connected with a view of the all-encompassing divine sovereignty by virtue of which the world ultimately has its existence. It is the infinite power of God that is the only reason for the existence and preservation of bodies.[4] "How truly then" writes Edwards, "is it in him that we live, move, and have our being!"[5]

The fact that Edwards combines a view of the divine establishment of law *in things* with a (Lockean) view of the human *mind* as locus of law and concepts, might warn against an exclusively Lockean interpretation of Edwards. Perry Miller interprets the same combination as an effort to unite the influences of John Locke and Isaac Newton, visible in Edwards' early distinction between the "inherent good" (which is "excellency" and "pleasure") and the "objective good" (which signifies the order of reality, the system of coherence in things).[6] The main influence of Newton, according to Miller, is that the relation between cause and effect is reinterpreted as "part of a sequence within a system of coherence"[7]— which has its profound consequences in Edwards' thought, in that the *legal* aspects of the man-God relation are subordinated to the *ethical* and *aesthetic* aspects. In fact, Edwards breaks with the Puritan covenant theory, which in its rationalistic development has shown its paralyzing effect on religious life. God and man are no longer seen as parties that behave according to a certain established code. God is seen as the system of being enveloping man wherever he turns. Redemption then amounts to a change of view in man, an adjustment of his vision to the enveloping system. At the same time this break with the covenant theory allows a strict concentration on *man:* on his faith, his will, and his conversion.

For Edwards the universe is one great system of being, of which *beauty* and *order* are the foremost characteristics, rather than its operation on certain *laws.* It is, therefore, in the beauty and order that Edwards finds the immediate presence of God, rather than in the necessary existence of a "first cause." This results in a significant emphasis on the continuing creativity of God: the existence of any thing and the perception of any order and beauty is most directly and absolutely dependent on the active immediacy of God. It follows, therefore, that our knowledge of things "depends upon the degree of our participation in the all-comprehending mind of God."[8]

Here we have reached the heart of Edwards' thinking: the immediate relation between perception and knowledge of reality on the one hand and religious affections on the other, between the sovereign presence of God and the human inclination and behavior.

This is why it is so important for Edwards to insist that "true religion, in great part, consists in holy affections"[9]: "affections are very much the spring of men's actions"[10] and therefore an expression of the whole man. Affection and action cannot be separated from perception and knowledge, it is all part and parcel of man's encounter with reality, with God. "How great cause have we therefore to be humbled to the dust, that we are no more affected!"[11]

From here it is easily understood that Edwards' insistence on the *new sense of the heart* is a crucial theme in his thought. The "new sense" is the basis of all discernment and knowledge, of all participation in the mind of God. But it cannot be acquired. It can only be given in a special act of God's grace. Of course, there is such a thing as common grace, as "partial work of the Spirit," as a "sensible knowledge of divine things," but all this is not yet genuinely and completely spiritual. The spiritual gift of the new sense amounts to an immediate taste of the sweetness and excellency of divine things, whereby the soul becomes "a partaker of God's beauty and Christ's joy."[12] It is the new sense that enables man to rejoice in the contemplation of God's holiness, of God's moral excellency, which is infinitely lovely in itself.

It is this same movement toward "God's beauty" which becomes the rule of virtue for Edwards. The consent to being which is the principle of ethics in *The Nature of True Virtue,* is founded on the same enjoyment of the holiness of God.

The Nature of True Virtue (1755),[13] a book which Niebuhr counts among the ones that influenced him most,[14] makes an essential distinction between "lower goodness" and "consent of being to being," or "universal benevolence." Self-love, moral sense, conscience are all, according to this treatise, established for a purpose—they are not in themselves evil—but they fall short of true virtue. The distance which has to be bridged is the distance between the wrong and right sense of the heart. It involves the redemption

> from self-glorification to the glorification of God, from pettiness and smallness of mind in theology and politics to wide vistas of being beyond being, from the provincialism of town, nation and humanity to citizenship in universal society, from the love of profit to the love of God.[15]

Edwards' insistence on the new sense as a gift of grace and on the necessity of *consent to being* as principle of the moral life, leads him to the question of the freedom of the will. All the elements of his thought join together in his assertion that man is perfectly free to do as he wills, but that a "freedom of indifference" as the Arminians hold, a freedom to *will* as one wills, is an absurdity. "It is that motive, which, as it stands in the view of the mind, is the strongest, that determines the will."[16] With *motive*, Edwards means that which has a tendency to excite or move the will. Determination of the will means, therefore, a certain *agreement* between the will and that which is placed before it; it is closely connected with the *sense of the heart.* Edwards removes the question of the freedom of the will from reflection about predetermination or about what goes *before* the act of willing so that all the emphasis falls on the *now* of the act. In this framework it is possible for Edwards to combine the *moral necessity* of the act of will—and thus God's moral government —with true freedom and responsibility; for freedom and responsibility are *grounded* in this moral necessity.[17] From this angle it also appears foolish to speak about the possibility of *resisting* divine grace. Man cannot choose his choices or will his will—this leads to a *reductio ad absurdum.*[18]

But it is not the phenomenology of the human will that is ultimately the issue between Edwards and the Arminians; it is the freedom and the sovereignty of *God.* The so-called self-determinists advance principles which destroy the freedom of God himself, even eliminate the possibility that the holy God has virtue.[19] The holiness of God is jeopardized by this shortsighted rationalism; and this leads inevitably to a truncated view of man. *Edwards' anthropocentricism is built on the foundation of theocentrism.* Whether or not one decides to regard this combination of anthropocentricism and theocentrism, of divine sovereignty and human freedom, as successful, it must be recognized as the underlying motif of Edwards' thinking, especially of the treatise on the will. Rationalization, either of God's superior holiness apart from the human situation, or the other way around, is in grave danger of falling short of the delight of this great system of being in which tensions between sovereignty and freedom disappear.

The emphases in Edwards' thought on the practical moral life and on rational, natural theology, have their place in the framework of theocentrism. Both these emphases become dominant in the course of the later theological development, but then without the emphatic theocentricity characteristic of Edwards. In the later New England theology the sovereign determination of God and the free moral agency of man have become two opposing principles, and henceforth the tension between them remains an important characteristic of American theology. Niebuhr's theology can be regarded as an effort to rediscover the living synthesis of theocentric thinking. But the tensions which exist, for instance, between the theological thinking of *Reinhold* Niebuhr and that of his brother might indicate that the possibility of such a synthesis has died with Edwards.

A brief glance at the nature of Edwards' theocentrism may conclude this section. The conception of God as being—in a sense the cornerstone of Edwards' synthesis—brings him close to pantheism (although his definitely Calvinistic theology keeps him at a safe enough distance) and inspires the use of the word *emanation* when he speaks about God's aim in creating the world. The great system of being is caught in a movement of emanation and reemanation of God's internal glory and fullness—a movement which serves only one end: *the glory of God.* To this end, God communicates knowledge, love, and joy to the creatures; to this end God calls his creatures to "give their consent," to partake in the movement from self-love to universal benevolence.

As we have seen, it is the new sense of the heart that enables man to give his consent, to regard the divine works as perfect and suitable, to discover the loveliness of God's majesty.

> It is the glory of God's wisdom, that it is a holy wisdom, and not a wicked subtility and craftiness. This makes his majesty lovely, and not merely dreadful and horrible, that it is a holy majesty. It is the glory of God's immutability that it is a holy immutability, and not an inflexible obstinacy in wickedness.[20]

This final observation gives way to a final question. How thin is the line between beauty and dreadfulness? Is it possible to shape one's thinking around the sovereignty of God without allowing for the thought that man is *caught* in this great system of being? That he will serve the glory of God, willingly in reconciliation or "in his unwillingness by his destruction?"[21] It has been said that Edwards' God is inherently *good,* that his God is a God of *love*, to enjoy and approach mystically; but this goodness and love are not the sure possessions of a liberalistic theology. They carry the majesty and mystery of being itself, and remain, therefore, terrifying. Perhaps the rediscovery of Jonathan Edwards is for Niebuhr one of the aspects of the rediscovery of *God*—God, who was caught in the chains of benevolence and immanence and whose sovereignty is now restored. But whether an honest restoration automatically entails *delight*, remains a haunting question.

2. Radical monotheism. In the last part of the preceding chapter we saw how Niebuhr formulates his specific concerns in the climate of crisis theology though in genuine continuity with—and affinity to—the heritage of Liberalism. The structure of the further development of his thought is determined by this beginning.

In our interpretation of the style and direction of this development we will have to give some attention to Niebuhr's second book, *The Kingdom of God in America* (1937). This book is an important milestone for Niebuhr, for here he restages the problem of *The Social Sources of Denominationalism* in the context of the particular emphases of the 1930's. His search for unity and integrity in the moral and cultural life allies itself with the insights developed in the meantime. Basically, the problem is the same, even if the topic of the book—the role of the idea of the kingdom of God in American Christianity—is a different one. His interest is the present situation:

> All attempts to interpret the past are indirect attempts to understand the present and its future. Men try to remember the road they have traveled in order that they may gain some knowledge of the direction in which it is leading, for their stories are begun without prevenient knowledge of the end . . . . Without retrospect no real prospect is possible.[22]

By retracing the convictions of history Niebuhr searches for a valid and effective combination of the sovereignty of God with human action and hope. Precisely because of this we started this chapter with a glance at Jonathan Edwards. In Edwards' thought the elements of dynamism, sovereignty, crisis, construction, and conversion are present in a coherence in which Niebuhr gradually recognizes his own basic concerns.

There is continuity between Niebuhr's first two books, not only in the problem, but also in the *method*. It is true that Niebuhr regards the answer of *The Social Sources* as "wholly inadequate,"[23] but this inadequacy does not lie in the use of the method of analysis and observation as such. No contrast or change can be construed between a "sociological" method of *The Social Sources* and a "theological" method of *The Kingdom of God*, though Niebuhr's own words suggest something like a Copernican turn.[24] Basically, the "change" occurs only at two points: the method of observation and analysis is *widened* so as to include living ideals, hopes, convictions, and to make room for the independence of doctrine; and all dogmatic presuppositions, like the conviction that social circumstances exclusively determine the shape of human faith, are relinquished. "There is, to say the least, no less of pure assumption in the conviction that human freedom or social condition is the determining force in life than in the dogma that the creative source of existence is the ruler of destiny"[25]; the only appropriate method is, therefore, to analyze the phenomena by entering sympathetically into them and to adopt, at least provisionally, the *faith* which comes to appearance in the phenomena.[26]

Considerations such as these probably lead Hans W. Frei to regard Niebuhr's method of writing history in *The Kingdom of God in America, The Purpose of the Church and Its Ministry: Reflections on the Aims of Theological Education,* and *Christ and Culture* as reminiscent of Wilhelm Dilthey,[27] and as different from the method developed in *The Meaning of Revelation,* where "a sharp dichotomy between scientific-external and normative, personal, or valuing viewpoints" is proposed. Frei seems to understand *The Meaning of Revelation* exclusively in terms of the problem of history in nineteenth-century German theology, and this prohibits him from regarding this work, too, as an elaboration of the concern formulated on the first pages of the Introduction to *The Kingdom of God.*

In *The Kingdom of God* Niebuhr does indeed not manifest a sharp dichotomy between internal and external history; but it may be questioned whether a consistent application of the method of *The Meaning of Revelation* would really lead to such a dichotomy. Furthermore, the "provisional adoption" of the faith in the analyzed phenomena *practically* means that Niebuhr writes history from the standpoint of the Christian community. This enables him to recognize the historical figures he describes—as in *Christ and Culture*—as true companions of faith, and to regard his work as a preamble to *a history of God's work* in modern civilization.[28] The pivotal interest remains the rediscovery of the presence of God in contemporary historical events. This, too, is the problem behind *The Meaning of Revelation,* and to this end Niebuhr occupies himself with the great convictions of the past.

The uneasiness that we observed in the solution of *The Social Sources* has, in this new approach, disappeared. No longer does Niebuhr see the social conditioning of church and religion as a given and, as such, deplorable situation (the disjunction between ideal and situation); no longer are "the Christian values" assumed to be capable of limiting the unfortunate consequences of cultural entanglement; *social conditioning is seen as something that happens, that takes place as a movement in which faith is expressed.* The forms in which we encounter church and religion are not in the first place incarnations of ideals, but rather expressions of a movement. By maintaining the dynamism of this movement and by relating the various expressions of church and religion to each other on this basis, we express faith in the *invisible catholic church.*[29]

The expressions of church and religion point beyond themselves, not to some essence which needs to be expressed again and again, but to other expressions of the same movement. "Institutionalized Christianity ... is only a halting place between Christian movements."[30] In other words, the only thing we have is a particular historical and relative expression: "Christianity," or "the invisible church," is an inference faith makes by discerning the dialectical character of all expressions, and the continuity in movement. We have here a special "Niebuhrian" adoption of Tillich's notion of "beliefful realism."

In addition to the theologians we discussed in our section on European crisis theology, Niebuhr is also attracted to the thought of Henri Bergson.[31] It is mainly through Bergson that Niebuhr learns to regard the approach of *The Social Sources* as one-sided: faith is not only defensive (a way to live with the "conditions"), but also dynamic, aggressive, creative—and it is this latter aspect which Niebuhr intends to emphasize in his second book. The dialectic between *movement* and *institution*—a basic theme in *The Kingdom of God*—is at least partly Bergsonian: it reminds us of the dialectic between the *élan vital* and the—necessary, but obstructing and distorting—*spatializations*. In this dialectic the crisis motif reappears: again and again the movement breaks through the institution; again and again the former must take the life of the latter in order to secure the ongoing life of the movement. No wonder that Niebuhr associates this emphasis with the thought of Barth.[32]

The typical Protestant dilemma, which we found emphasized by Tillich, is a central motif in *The Kingdom of God:* the possibility of constructive Protestantism must lie between absolutism and skepticism. Niebuhr shows how the whole American religious history illustrates this. The American Founding Fathers were forced to see that "the positive part of church reformation was not a structure but a life, a movement, which could never come to rest again in secure habitations, but needed to go on and on from camp to camp to its meeting with the ever-coming kingdom."[33] The original Puritan concern, underneath and aside from the rigid institutionalization of orthodoxy, was to give expression to a movement, to place the whole of life under the claim of the divine sovereignty, so that independence of the church and seminal presence in the world were held closely together. And Liberalism, though it presented a dynamic revolt against institutionalized orthodoxy, mainfest-ed its typical shortcomings in the loss of the *crisis* elements and thus in the loss of true dynamic movement: revolution was replaced by evolution, "a God without wrath brought men without sin into a kingdom without judgment through the ministrations of a Christ without a cross."[34]

Precisely these notions: wrath, sin, judgment, cross, are necessary to guard against petrifaction, against absolutizing of the relative, against substitution of the finite for the infinite. This is *the sin of American Christianity:* the loss of the movement which warrants the vision of the "One beyond the many."

The Kingdom of God presents the moral problem forcibly: How is it possible to give concrete expression to faith in the one sovereign God? How can we avoid petrifaction and subsequent pettiness and defensiveness? How can we learn to respond faithfully to contemporary events? It was this last question which became acute during the years of World War II. One might say that the war ultimately "made" Niebuhr's theology. Not only his historical realism (the effort to combine human reality and consistent monotheism), but also his insistence on personal moral responsibility in the content of the presence of the one God, was severely put to the test in these years. This is strongly reflected in Niebuhr's three articles on the action of God in the war[35]; here the problem is "not that of looking with God on the world but of finding God in the world, or rather that of understanding how to stand in the presence of God as I stand in the presence of every individual event, good or evil."[36] The senselessness of the events and the impossibility of finding an intelligible pattern in them, seems either to destroy the notion of divine sovereignty or to magnify it into arbitrariness beyond proportion. The effort to think "monotheistically" seems to be defeated by what actually takes place.

The articles on the war remind us of the discussion between the Niebuhr brothers in 1932 (chapter 1, part B3) on the question of *pacifism.* Both brothers ultimately reject the possibility of a pacifist position, but they do so for different reasons. Reinhold Niebuhr regards pacifism partly as impossible (the law of love cannot be applied *directly* in historical reality), and partly as immoral (pacifism means ignoring the concrete responsibility to maintain and promote justice). His brother, on the other hand, judges human action or nonaction solely on the basis of the action and presence of *God in history:* neither the action nor the nonaction of man can alter the fact that in the presence of this God all men are wrong, that all men share in the causes and effects of evil and suffering, and that only *through the shedding of blood* can the promise of new life be fulfilled. What is important, therefore, in the question of pacifism for Niebuhr is *not* what one does or does not do, but in what *context* decisions are taken: whether this context is faith in the one God who is present in all events, or some less than universal faith. If it is the latter, finite judgments on good and evil will inevitably replace the "monotheistic response," and then the exercise of and trust in retributive justice will inevitably obscure the necessity of *reconciliation through vicarious suffering.*

Niebuhr sees the historical events of the war as the action of a judging God, who judges through the vicarious suffering of the innocent. This means that our last word cannot be pessimism or bitterness, but must be repentance and hope, based on faith in the ultimate *goodness* of God: "To recognize God at work in war is to live and act with faith in resurrection."[37] Niebuhr describes this faith in the goodness of God, or in "resurrection," as *Christ-faith;* rather, his language in these articles is borrowed from Christology. Thus he intends to point out, not that Christ is a cosmic principle, but that trust in the sovereign ruler of history is a gift, connected with the apprehension of the historical event of Jesus Christ. The problems raised here are dealt with in *The Meaning of Revelation* (1941). In a sense, this book is a formalized presentation of the question as to how faith in God's work in history and the subsequent *transformation* of all thought and action, is possible, and in what sense this faith is related to the suffering of Jesus Christ—the event with which the Christian community seeks to connect all events. It was probably the impact of the war that led Niebuhr to emphasize almost exclusively the passion of Christ as the appropriate analogy for the interpretation of contemporary events. We remember that in his earliest writings this analogy was Jesus' attitude toward the Father. The Christology of *Christ and Culture* (1951) is, to a certain extent, a restoration of the balance.

Between *The Kingdom of God in America* and *Christ and Culture* Niebuhr develops the theme of *transformation* as a necessary implication of radical and consistent faith in the one God. In this period the problem of Christ and culture, of faith and social conditioning, and thus of church and society, is treated with an increasingly exclusive concentration on the phenomenon of *faith* in its diverse expressions, distortions, and conversions. This approach leads Niebuhr to phrase and rephrase many questions. Where does man's ultimate loyalty lie? Is it in the social and cultural phenomena themselves (the relative), or in the One to whom man can only remain loyal in a process of constant redirection and conversion? Is this not man's original sin: the defense of his particular situation in the name of the One beyond the many? Once Niebuhr begins to raise these questions in the context of his interest in the proper relations between Christ and culture, he is driven to the insight that the *defense of Christianity* is a basic mistake. A defense of Christianity will inevitably defeat itself, for it loses both the vision of the One beyond the many and the possibility of fruitful relations between faith in the One and response to historical events.

Under the impact of this insight, Niebuhr's concentration on the *church* gradually changes its emphasis. The church is no longer called above all to stress its distinctness from the world, but rather to exemplify the movement of redirection which must take place in the whole of culture. The churches are themselves under the constant necessity of conversion. No longer are certain ideals or values to be set apart as Christian. All is caught in the movement of monotheistic faith.

Niebuhr's book *Radical Monotheism and Western Culture, with Supplementary Essays,*[38] develops the implications of this concentration on monotheistic faith. The focus of attention here is the problem of conflicting faiths, in which our whole culture is involved, and as such *also* church and religion. The great enemy of monotheism is the "closed society with its *social* confidence and *social* loyalty,"[39] in which limited ideals of a limited group claim the faith which ought to be directed toward the principle of being itself. This fundamental distortion occurs in the *Christian* faith, too, as soon as other persons or objects of devotion are tacitly substituted for God himself, or as soon as God is implicitly conceived as the "God of Christianity," which is a limited social conception. Idolatry can present itself in an even more dangerous disguise in Christianity than elsewhere. Therefore, the principle of radical monotheism must be used as a critical principle for *any* faith. Christians cannot claim the right to associate God with their own group-faith any more than other people can. "There is religion in every man," Niebuhr said once; "much of it is idolatry, but . . . so is ours."

The striking characteristic of Niebuhr's thought to which we must draw attention at this point, is not so much that he gives full weight to the critical principle inherent to the Christian faith—this critical principle is given with Trinitarian thinking—but rather that he associates it with the position and function of the Christian faith as a relative phenomenon in the world of faiths. In other words, "Trinitarian" criticism comes not only from *within* Christian faith and thinking, it also comes from without—from the situations in which we become aware of the incompatibility between the many social faiths and the *one* God.

This is a motif which partly determines Niebuhr's attitude to Barth. In the development which we have described so far, there are apparent signs of Niebuhr's remaining appreciation for Barth. Yet the early objections to Barth remain. It cannot be surprising that an increasing emphasis on radical monotheism tends to sharpen rather than to diminish these objections. In the 1950's we see how Niebuhr explicitly turns his back on all *Barthian Christocentrism* as one of the most dangerous forms of idolatry that threaten the church.[40] In Christ-centered faith

> theology is turned into Christology .... To be a Christian now means not so much that through the mediation and the pioneering faith of Jesus Christ a man has become wholly human, has been called into membership in the society of universal being, and has accepted the fact that amid the totality of existence he is not exempt from the human lot; it means rather that he has become a member of a special group, with a special God, a special destiny, and a separate existence.[41]

In the Christocentric emphases of the documents around the Evanston Assembly of the World Council of Churches (1954), Niebuhr encountered this danger in all its aggressiveness. An unpublished paper, "The Church Defines Itself in the World" (1957), is the clearest reflection of this. The church, Niebuhr holds, cannot possibly define itself exclusively in terms of Jesus Christ, even though Jesus Christ is of crucial significance. The lapse into Christocentrism is evidence of a shortsightedness that ignores the basic questions of human society and history in the light of the presence of the sovereign God.

Again it may be argued that Niebuhr's resistance to the so-called Barthian Christocentrism is only a further development of his early position which neglected several important factors in Barth's thought. But, in addition to what we remarked before on Niebuhr's relation with the "early" Barth, we can at least raise the question of whether Niebuhr was not fundamentally correct in perceiving an important problem in Barthianism. Can it, in view of its preoccupation with the unique character of revelation and its stubbornly christological starting point, ever take the human predicament with genuine seriousness? Of course, Barth would say that those who would take the human predicament seriously too soon—that is, without placing it in the context of what is happening in the Christ-event—do not really take it seriously at all. But does not this consistency in fact lead to a practical problem? In other words, *is it possible to erect a consistently independent Christocentric theology without practically building a "closed society" and thus necessarily ignoring several basic questions of faith and culture*?

At this point, it seems to us, Niebuhr's criticism stands. For him, the basic problem of man lies in his self- and society-centeredness, in his "anthropocentrism." No theology of revelation can itself be a guarantee against this perennial temptation unless it speaks in terms of this temptation. As we suggested before, the questions Niebuhr directs to Barth are not primarily theological criticisms; they originate in a religious problem which, it seems to Niebuhr, is not seriously met by Barth.

There is little reason to view Niebuhr's increasing attack on Christocentric theology as a turning point in the development of his thought. Niebuhr himself once described his development as from Troeltsch to Barth, and then, later, back from Barth to (a reformed) Troeltsch. Characterizations like this tend to oversimplify what takes place; in this case it might obscure the fact that the so-called turn away from Barth is really a consistent development of an already existing position.

3. The major themes in retrospect. In our sketch of the main lines in the development of Niebuhr's theology, we saw how two intimately connected themes gradually come to the fore and become pivotal principles. We mean the themes of *monotheism* and *transformation*. Monotheism—a consistent concentration on the *one* God—*implies* transformation: all human thought and social expression must engage itself in a constant process of redirection toward the one God.

In the present section we intend to take a second look at the structure of Niebuhr's theology, to see whether we can confirm this provisional interpretation, and whether we can indeed regard monotheism and transformation as the centers of coherence in his thought.

Monotheistic faith comprises several elements. It means, as we have seen, that God is one, and that the one God is the only God; but it cannot exist unless it is convinced that the one God is good, that he is a father rather than an enemy. Monotheistic faith, *in concreto*, is "love of being; rejoicing in existence, in its source, totality, and particularity . . . the conviction that there is faithfulness at the heart of things."[42] It is a response to the challenge of God's cause, and a recognition of the trustworthiness of being. In Niebuhr's thought this faith gradually takes on the role of a permanent corrective of all faiths and all loyalties in human existence, including those which we are used to cherishing as "Christian." With a bow to Tillich, we might speak of a "faith above faith," or of a center of correction that never exhausts itself in any actual correction.

After *The Kingdom of God in America*, in which the Christian faith in the kingdom is a more or less self-evident starting point, however invisible in its true form, Niebuhr's critical hesitation on this point increases. In *Radical Monotheism and Western Culture* and *The Responsible Self: An Essay in Christian Moral Philosophy*, only one question is left: To what extent can man respond to the goodness of being itself in whatever he does? Human *faith* is the focus of attention. It is hardly surprising, therefore, that the phenomenon of *religion* is only of partial interest. Where God is "the One beyond the many in whom the many are one,"[43] it is no longer religion that primarily matters, but the question of "the incarnation of monotheistic faith in *total life.*"[44]

The early insight that "every civilization is conditioned in all its forms by its faith, be it idolatrous or divine,"[45] leads Niebuhr to see that it is not fruitful to isolate religion from the rest of culture as an object of analysis. Faith is exhibited *not only* in religious beliefs and practices. When we inquire how a leading idea has taken hold of men's lives in the past we learn that religion is only one of the areas of life in which it finds expression.[46] It is the conflict of faiths in which our *whole* culture is involved that is the proper object of attention; and when we wish to deal with "that great syndrome we call religion,"[47] even then we should analyze the many phenomena of faith present in it. Concentration on faith is one of the ways to keep religion from becoming more important than it is, from becoming more than only *one* particular area of response[48]—and as such it can prohibit the substitution of religion for the center and fountain of being itself.

A further danger Niebuhr sees in the isolation of religion—and here we recognize Barthian overtones—is that religion can turn into a *false response* to being itself: it can develop into the activity of *appeasement* of the source of being experienced as enemy[49]—and there can be no doubt that such an activity implies a serious stagnation on the road toward faith in and response to the One who in all action upon us acts as reconciler of the whole human life.

Niebuhr's treatment of the *church* is from the start conditioned by this treatment of religion. At points he can say that "the human response to divine action is *not so much religion as church,*"[50] and that church "is not primarily characterized by the fact that it is a religious community whose religion centers in Jesus Christ, but simply by the fact that as a community it centers in him."[51]

"Faith in total life": that is the center around which all Niebuhr's concerns and analyses have their place. More and more Niebuhr finds that the phenomenon of faith is too complex to be approached solely in terms of value or valuation or through its reflections in social and cultural conditions. Existentialist modes of thinking become increasingly important for him: *selves* become the object of attention rather than *culture;* and community is no longer primarily a cultural entity but an existential category—the counterpart of selfhood. At the same time his use of theological categories increases in frequency. This underscores, as it were, the impossibility of catching the complexities of human life only in sociological or value-theoretical terms.[52] It does not mean, however, that Niebuhr gradually "retreats" into theology; especially his reflections in *The Responsible Self* are so many-sided that even designations like

"Christian moral philosophy" and "critical reflection on the moral life from a Christian point of view,"[5 3] are hardly sufficient.

It is not difficult to see how the growing complexity and many-sidedness of Niebuhr's concentration on faith and its expressions strengthen his concept of relativism, as much as it is inspired by it. But it is not only this which counts. Niebuhr's relativism is not simply or primarily the accidental philosophical equipment or the frame of mind with which he approaches his problems; *it is itself a direct consequence of his monotheism.* It is the government of the one and only absolute God, and the conviction of the goodness of the sovereign source of being, that drives Niebuhr toward a concentration on the relativity and complexity of the relative. In the American religious tradition we noted a similar dynamic connection between the "many" and the "one"; and we will forever misunderstand Niebuhr's emphasis on relativism if we do not see that this same connection, sharpened and radicalized, is the very pivot of his thought. There are, of course, many other influences: the philosophies of Mead and Royce, Tillich's realistic admiration of the manifoldness of being, the thought of Frederick Denison Maurice, and, above all, the problem of Troeltsch, which leads Niebuhr toward his reflection on the combination of relativity, morality, and faith. The mainspring of his relativism, however, lies in the conviction of the goodness of being, revealed in the goodness of the sovereign God.

The monotheistic argument is the strongest one that can be brought against the defensiveness of the "closed society"; and as such it is also the strongest means to defeat the vain absoluteness of the relative and to open up "wide vistas of being beyond being." This amounts to a faithful enlargement of relativism. "Isaiah 10, 1 Corinthians 12, and Augustine's *City of God* indicate the context in which the relativities of history make sense."[5 4] They "make sense"—that is, they deserve full and unlimited attention—as relativities of *history* in which the goodness of being comes to appearance. For *only* in the relativities does the goodness of being appear; the most universal is found in the most limited, the largest in the smallest. But the relativities of history make sense *only* when they remain *relativities;* for the absolute remains the absolute, the one God remains the only God.

Therefore, "it is religious or theocentric relativism that is primary. Other relativisms are to be understood in the light of their conversion to and interpretation by it."[5 5] And let us not forget that, in Niebuhr's thought, the relation between the absolute and the relative is primarily an *ethical* problem. His monotheism ultimately makes sense only as the framework of reflection on human responsibility. Human sin, the absolutizing of the relative, originates in falling short of theocentric relativism. This sin may be inevitable, insofar as it is inevitable to confuse trust in the finite with trust in the infinite; but it is obviously *judged*, and therefore must be called *sin*. Self-defensiveness is not only bothersome; it is *evil*. Its contrast is theocentric relativism, formulated theologically: the necessity to recognize the Spirit that proceeds from the Father. Only with these connotations in mind can we understand Niebuhr's relativism; only from this point can we understand his correction of Troeltsch, and his position "between Troeltsch and Barth."

Troeltsch's effort to overcome relativism by faith in a movement of the divine Spirit expressing itself in historical individualities, was not influential. Why not? In his dissertation on Troeltsch, Niebuhr draws attention to a basic antithesis in Troeltsch's thought between pluralism and monism, between the nonrational totality of life and rational schemes and concepts. This tension is overcome *practically*, and ultimately, as we have seen, metaphysically. But it amounts to something like a "fencing in" of relativism: we are kept from drowning in the irrational sea of being, not by thinking through relativism to the end, but by the appeal to certain "obvious and self-evident" rational patterns. In Troeltsch's thought, the cultural synthesis is *not only* relative and accidental; it has an objective ground in the way history clearly develops. Lonnie D. Kliever rightly supposes that Niebuhr would regard this as an identification of the Absolute with the cultural synthesis and thus a relativizing of the Absolute[56]; the abstraction of faith from history—in Troeltsch faith is ultimately mystical experience—is in this connection understandable and inevitable.

Troeltsch's concept of history and historical science is probably still determined by and associated with Positivism, so that Troeltsch can only regard a consistent relativism as a dead-end road. As we have seen, Niebuhr's correction of Troeltsch consists of a sharp and consistent analysis of the entanglement of faith and history (undoubtedly Mead plays a role here) which is determined and strengthened by his emphasis on monotheism. The correction is partly made possible by the fact that Niebuhr never completely identified himself with Troeltsch but instead followed basic interests and convictions of American history.[57] Yet he is enough of a Troeltschean to refuse to abandon the Troeltschean problem.

This rather complicated state of affairs is perhaps one of the reasons behind Paul Ramsey's insistence that Niebuhr's use of the word relativism is a superfluous remnant of his attraction to Troeltsch.[58] Ramsey suggests that it is better to speak of *relational* or *perspectival objectivism*,[59] not only because the notion of relativism, if used consistently, defeats itself, but also because it is "not a necessary part of his (Niebuhr's) theology of conversion."[60] According to Ramsey,

Niebuhr is afraid to lose the possibility of a dynamic conversion of values, but, he asks, does this possibility not remain, even when we start with several absolutes or "objective norms"? "Monotheistic faith," says Ramsey, "is incompatible only with idolatry, not with all ordering and rank among the—now subordinate—centers of value in various value systems."[61] "Can there be no absolute or unchanging truths if man and his morals are subject to transformation in the light of the absoluteness of God-in-Christ?"[62]

The difference between Niebuhr and Ramsey seems to be that for the former the encounter of "objective reality" and "objective values" is always accompanied and conditioned by *some* response to the Absolute. Not even the existence of values can be separated from transformation (or resistance to transformation); there is no objectivity apart from and prior to this connection. Ramsey, on the other hand, seems to work with "orders of creation" rather than with "creative and ordering activity of God." Philosophically speaking, his thought is based on a static model of reality, to which the knowledge of God-in-Christ, and the transformation given with this knowledge, is added. This is the reason that Ramsey finds it impossible to do full justice to Niebuhr's relation with Troeltsch, and that he regards Troeltsch's influence on Niebuhr's relativism almost as an obstacle to a clear understanding of the issues involved. Yet the alliance in Niebuhr's thinking between a consistent monotheism and a Troeltschean thought pattern is one of its indispensable and unique features.

Monotheistic thinking leads to a consistent relativism that is not fenced in by objective rational patterns or systems of values. This is the correction of Troeltsch. But it only serves to bring out the full implications and consequences of the Troeltschean *problem*—the absolute value of the individual event, the presence of the universal in the particular, the danger of defensiveness, and the urgent moral problem of responsible activity—and to clear the road toward an effective and consistent answer.

Niebuhr experienced the Troeltschean problem as a permanent assignment. But before it could be dealt with effectively and sufficiently, something else had to happen. The church had to rediscover its *raison d'être*, its radical distinctness from the world; faith in the sovereign God who judges and transcends all human efforts had to be restored. This is Niebuhr's turn toward Barth. However, not for one moment does this turn lead to the abandonment of the "Troeltschean assignment"; it serves, rather, as a strengthening of the emphasis on relativity.

Niebuhr's break with Barth or "return to Troeltsch" is, therefore, by no means a second conversion, but only a consistent development. Niebuhr agrees with Barth that the nineteenth-century approach has to be corrected; but he turns away when the correction takes place with such radical force that reflection on the Christian faith is severed from reflection on the general human situation of faith(s) and culture.[63] It is precisely the content of monotheistic faith which enables Niebuhr to stay on Troeltsch's road. But a radical correction of Troeltsch is in order: there is only one stable center in the restlessness of relativity, and this one center is *beyond the many.* The most important issue between faith and culture, therefore, is no longer compromise, but permanent transformation. This does not lead to Barthianism. On the contrary, toward the end of Niebuhr's development the presence of Edwards in his thought is much more significant than that of Barth. For it was Edwards who attained a genuine combination of the reflection on human faith with the notion of the omnipresent sovereignty of God.

There is a final point to which we must call attention in this retrospective view of Niebuhr's theological development: the special consequences of his emphases for the way he speaks about the *church.* We will observe that there is a certain ambivalence at this point which necessarily follows from his stress on monotheism and transformation.

On the one hand, the Christian community is clearly the channel through which the one God is apprehended as *good* and, consequently, the consistent emphasis on relativity is made possible. The Christian faith is not merely one faith among the many; it is the specific faith that enables us to speak about a one and only God, because it speaks of *reconciliation.* The Christian faith is the faith that enables us to speak genuinely of faiths in the plural, to speak of the totality of being as a sensible totality; it *secularizes and sanctifies all things.*[64] "All knowledge becomes reverent and all being is open to inquiry . . . when man's faith is attached to the One, all relative beings may be received at his hands for nurture and for understanding . . . a new sacredness attaches to the relative goods."[65] Precisely because of this, it is the duty of the church *not* to draw men into Christianity, but to lead them to ultimate decisions in particular situations.

On the other hand, the Christian community, the church, with its necessarily institutionalized conservation of this faith, is itself radically relativized, even by itself. This state of affairs leads to a permanent tension in Niebuhr's thought at the point of the position of the church in the world. Sometimes the tension tends to be resolved in the direction of a general monotheistic principle, to which *everything* is subjected in transformation—as in *Radical Monotheism and Western Culture*—and then even the crucial significance of Jesus Christ, which Niebuhr usually underscores, becomes doubtful. At other points the confessional responsibility of the church is stressed. It is significant that a definite systematic solution of this tension is not reached. It is precisely the absence of such a solution that points to the cornerstone of Niebuhr's thought: God prohibits any other focus of attention besides himself (that is his greatness)—but the faith of the community is there to draw attention to this greatness, which includes a relativization of itself. Truth cannot become the possession of any community. If there is such a thing as truth, it can be grasped only in a permanent restless movement of *metanoia*, of conversion and transformation.

B. THE TEMPER OF NIEBUHR'S THEOLOGY

1. **The nature of God.** Niebuhr's theology calls for closer examination. What is needed at this point is not so much the addition of detail and illustration, but the search for implication, and the disclosure of underlying convictions about God, man, and world—in short, the answer to the question, "How does Niebuhr do theology?" This question leads us not to a systematic inventory of Niebuhr's dogmatic statements, but rather to an investigation of the meaning of such key words in his thought as *being* and *faith*. For it seems that crucial matters in Niebuhr's theology are not decided on the level of systematic discussion, but on the level of attitude and temper.

Our approach is called for by the fact that Niebuhr's corrections of Liberalism—the tradition to which he basically remains affiliated—mainly concern the *way of speaking:* God is no longer within the range of man except in sovereign inscrutability, he can no longer be counted upon as good except on the basis of his revelation, and he can no longer be assimilated into human value-systems though he demands absolute loyalty and permanent incarnation of monotheistic faith in total life.

How does Niebuhr speak about God? The first thing we must say is that the assertion that *there is a God* is to him second in importance to the assertion that *being is God*, which means that the source of all things is good.[1] In other words, Niebuhr stands in line with those thinkers for whom speaking about God is the same thing as speaking about *being itself*. For them this choice of words is simply mandatory if God is to be God at all; the term "being itself" takes our mind off any individual being, however high or almighty, and focuses on the being itself of that which is, on the power of being in and beyond the beings.

Niebuhr's use of the term being itself is mainly inspired by Jonathan Edwards.[2] This means that Niebuhr has no dominant interest in defining God as the perfect cause and ground of all that is, or as the ground beyond essence and existence. Niebuhr thinks primarily in terms of the system of universality in which we find ourselves and to which we are called to give consent. His use of the term being itself is more mystical than intellectual, though—in distinction from Tillich—the *encounter* between self and other remains untranscendable and basic in the understanding of being.

In Tillich's use of the term, two things are of main importance: it is the only nonsymbolic statement we can make about God, and it expresses *ultimate concern.* "God," therefore, is a quality rather than a particular being: we express *concern* by using the name; and by attaching it to that which is beyond thought and experience, essence and existence, we indicate that the concern is *ultimate.* Ultimate concern has to do with the threat of nonbeing over against being, "the concept of being . . . is the expression of the experience of being over against nonbeing."[3] At this point Niebuhr and Tillich part company. For it is impossible for Niebuhr to speak of the polarity between being and nonbeing instead of the polarity between *the self and the power of being that the self encounters and experiences*; it is impossible for him to transcend the duality of subject and object in all thought about man and God. A second important point, to which we will return presently, is that Niebuhr cannot separate language of being from language about *value:*

> The problem of ultimate concern to many men does not seem statable simply in terms of being but only of being and value; *they know of the ground of being, but what they do not know is the goodness of that ground.* The revelation with which they therefore begin is not the revelation of God as infinite being in the finite, but of his goodness in evil.[4]

For Niebuhr, being presents itself in the struggle of faith which goes on between man and the reality he encounters. This reality includes more than personal relations; Niebuhr thinks of the "circumambient world" as a totality of things, persons, and events which the self experiences, and on which the self imposes its schemes of interpretation. The dominant question in the encounter of reality is not, How shall I speak about it? but rather, What is the quality and intention of that which meets me? In other words, speaking about being cannot be isolated from a fundamental anxiety about the *character* of what goes on. To phrase it technically, ontology and faith are inseparably connected; speaking about God as the principle of *being* is bound up with speaking about him as the principle of *value.*[5] *I am up against being* always means that I value it; *I depend on the power of being* always means that I depend on its goodness. Until I consistently face my absolute dependence on the power of being and entrust myself to it, I have a confused and ambiguous view of what it *is.*

We noticed before how the Niebuhr of the 1930's is intent upon keeping together the being and goodness of God and upon eliminating all possibility of an assimilation of God into prior definitions of goodness. This is precisely the point at which he seeks to overcome Liberalism; and from here we must understand his insistence that being is not good *as such* but only by virtue of a relation to the principle of being which *reveals itself as good.*° The intimate connection between the experience of being and the attitude of faith is expressed metaphysically in the intimate connection between the goodness of being and faith in the Creator, in *the One beyond the many.* Such a relation implies the necessity of constant conversion, of constant learning and relearning what goodness is.

Speaking about God as being itself thus always includes the valuing self: "There is no such thing as disinterestedness in theology."[7] Therefore faith "always refers primarily to character and power rather than to existence."[8] Being itself is the powerful, awe-inspiring, frightening, or encouraging totality of that which is, rather than the ground behind and beyond life, experience, thought, knowledge, and revelation. A certain *nominalistic* tendency cannot be ignored in Niebuhr. Both the positing of character and power as primary and the inclination to attribute reality to the particular rather than to the universal—the term "being itself" being a means of communication about particular situations—point in this direction. We are led to ask whether, in view of all the elements discussed so far, there is any certain basis for speaking about being as good. Can we count on the goodness of God and entrust ourselves to it? Or is this basically an absurdity and a risk? Is reconciliation to being itself a possibility? We may be convinced that a final overcoming of defensiveness and exclusiveness, of the absolutizing of the relative, depends on reconciliation to being itself—but can such reconciliation take place? It is true that "without activity that is the counterpart of our desire for the good and of our fidelity, the 'ground of being' is just that and not God"[9]—but can we really speak of such activity?

It seems that our first encounter with ultimate reality is of quite a different sort. It is more like a sudden awareness of "the void of meaninglessness," for "all our causes, all our ideas, all the beings on which we relied to save us from worthlessness are doomed to pass"—and what is left but "the last shadowy and vague reality, the secret of existence by virtue of which things come into being, are what they are, and pass away?"[10] Indeed, this is the only thing we have left to *hope* for.

> All the relative judgments of worth are equalized in the presence of this One who loves all and hates all, but whose love like whose hatred is without emotion, without favoritism. To have hope of this One is to have hope that is eternal. This being cannot pass away. And to hope for the manifestation of his love is to hope to eternity.[11]

We see how any effort to absorb God in finitude, to assimilate him into systems of thought and valuation, is defeated by being itself as it gives itself to experience. Our hopes and faiths are transformed *whether we like it or not*, by being itself as our enemy and judge. What is free response to divine activity, which issues in permanent transformation, other than acquiescence to this state of affairs?

It would be possible to describe the presence of these questions between the lines of Niebuhr's thought as an inescapable consequence of his method "between Liberalism and Barthianism." But it would be more appropriate to put it the other way around: his method is a consequence of his insistence that the priority of God can be asserted only in the context of man's struggle for faith and reconciliation, and of his similarly strong conviction that good theology at least includes the question of the relation between God and fate. Two things must always be kept together: human sin and responsibility on the one hand, and fate, the judgment of being itself, on the other. To what extent Niebuhr's convictions at this point are inspired by personal experience, we do not know. But a fact is that they are an important element in his reservations with regard to both Barth and Tillich, and that they drive him closer to Calvin and Edwards, if not to Spinoza.

We are reminded of Baruch Spinoza when Niebuhr writes things like: "This One who loves all and hates all, but whose love like whose hatred is without emotion, without favoritism"; *God loves or hates no one.* For Spinoza this is only a mathematical consequence of his assertion of the infinite greatness of God, who is the one universal substance in which everything is.[12] Even the human *will* cannot be truly free, or truly in accord with this greatness, unless and until it sees itself as *not free.* Yet, though reason has the capacity to have a clear image of God and to conceive of things under the viewpoint of eternity, man usually thinks wrongly of God as *a being.* The basic cause of this tendency, according to Spinoza, is the human inclination to think in terms of *ends* rather than of *causes*, and to interpret everything that happens as somehow happening for the sake of man—which is a foolish and dangerous imagination.

True response to the active presence of the divine is possible only on the basis of *insight* into the ground and coherence of all that is. That is *living according to reason*, the "intellectual love of God," which is a delightful attainment of the highest possible knowledge. This knowledge is immensely useful for daily life. For it teaches us not only that all our action stems from God, but also how we are to behave in view of the things which we cannot control; these things, too, happen with divine necessity—the same necessity according to which the three angles of a triangle equal two right angles. The extent to which man *suffers* things is clearly dependent on the extent to which his ideas are inadequate; the more he "understands," the more active power he has to live, which means, the more power he has to resign to things that are *true* and *necessary.*

These sketchy lines suffice to show that there are undoubtedly many points at which Niebuhr and Spinoza touch. The most conspicuous one is the combination of the need for the self to move beyond the limits of its selfish view of things toward the sphere of divine necessity, and the notion of the omnipresent inscrutable greatness of being itself. But more than points where they touch we cannot establish. For the central focus for Niebuhr remains the struggle of faith, its possibilities and impossibilities. His "glance" toward Spinoza only indicates the presence of a *temper* which is caught between the assertion of God's greatness and the inescapability of his judgment.

The adoration of the awe-inspiring greatness of being enters into Niebuhr's thought as an ingredient in his correction of the smallness of Liberalism. The liberals thought they had a good God—just like that; that was their basic mistake, much more than a possible confusion of theology with other disciplines (Barth's diagnosis of European Liberalism).

> Our God is someone we try to keep alive by religious elevations, to use for solving our personal problems, for assuring us that we are beloved. He is without wrath, because we have made this image wrathless; his love is not holy love because we have painted the icon without holiness.[13]

These words were spoken in a lecture commemorating Edwards—a lecture which is pervaded by a strenuous effort to rediscover for our day what Edwards saw. Can we see what Edwards saw? "Our sense of wickedness is without repentance, our sorrow over it is not a godly sorrow leading to life, but cynical and accepting, leading to death. Our knowledge of our determinism is without struggle, because we know of no power that can set us free to be free indeed." The only way to rediscover this power is to view everything which happens in the context of being itself, for God cannot be less. This means that both the idea of a kind heavenly Father and the idea of arbitrary chance must be abandoned. Only so can we learn to renew our vision of God's sovereignty.

We noticed that even for Edwards divine sovereignty is not without fatefulness. But Edwards does not seem to be bothered by it, because all that is to be known about God has been "sufficiently published" in an established order of revelation. But is not the "sufficient publication" of revelation challenged by the renewed contemporary insistence on the *crisis* in the relation between God and the world? Can the established order, in our time, be more than a *guess*, a structure hoped for against all

evidence? Niebuhr's rediscovery of Edwards is inspired by this reinforcement of the *crisis motif*; and yet it seems that precisely the same motif
surrounds the rediscovery of Edwards' *God* with anxiety, the anxiety
over the relation of *God* and *fate*. "We will concede, perhaps, that man is
as wicked as Edwards said. What we do not know—or do not yet know—
is that God is as holy as Edwards knew him to be."

It is not difficult to see how the influences of European crisis
theology in the context of the problems to which Niebuhr speaks,
strengthen the element of uncertainty with regard to God's revelation.
Tillich's emphasis on the judgment element in revelation which
"overtakes" us, meets with Barth's well-known emphasis on the
impossibility for man to do what only God's free will can do. Niebuhr's
problem originates in *the assimilation of this crisis motif into a
restoration of the notion of divine sovereignty* in the context of a naive
liberalistic faith in Providence, or, to speak more broadly, in the context
of the struggle for the combination of sovereignty and pluralism in the
American tradition. Of course, there were other sources as well which
inspired Niebuhr to rediscover the divine sovereignty. We think especially
of his Meadian and Roycean learning, which remains an important
element in the consistent and sustained emphasis on relativism and even
provides some reason for his attraction to Spinoza. That Niebuhr's notion
of relativism seems generally untouched by his anxiety over the nature of
God, can well be ascribed to the presence of this more or less
independent tradition. Or perhaps we should say, this tradition keeps
contributing to the insight that the greatness of the source of being to
which we are called to respond, can in no way be compromised.

> When people tell us that they have the key to all theology in
> their pockets, or in their hearts, that they know who made the
> world or why, or know that everything is matter, or that everything
> is mind—then Spinoza's notion of the Absolutely Infinite, which
> includes *all* possibility, may profitably arise before us. It will come
> to us to say to those little gnostics, to those circumnavigators of
> being: I do not believe you; God is great.[14]

2. The possibility of faith. What, then, is *faith?* We can of course
analyze the phenomenon of faith, and discover that it consists of trust
and loyalty, of confidence and fidelity. We can even analyze how faith is
received, shared, and passed on in human communities. Yet these things
are not at stake here. The basic question is, What does it mean when we
say that we have faith in God—that we trust the source of being itself?
What happens when our faith is attached to that great power? Is it at all
possible? It seems that we have been driven to the edge where there are
only two possibilities. Either we are given faith in the power of being

itself or we are left to nothingness. All other possibilities have been eliminated: "Unless being itself, the constitution of things, the One beyond all the many, the ground of my being and of all being, the ground of its 'that-ness' and its 'so-ness,' (is) trustworthy—(can) be counted on by what (has) proceeded from it,"[15] *there is no God at all.*

The answer which Niebuhr gives is clear in its "confessional modesty." It does happen and it has happened. Faith has been given, and when it was given it was somehow connected with Jesus Christ.

> What is the absurd thing that comes into our moral history as existential selves, but the conviction, mediated by a life, a death, and a miracle beyond understanding, that the source and ground and government and end of all things—the power we (in our distrust and disloyalty) call fate and chance—is faithful, utterly trustworthy, utterly loyal to all that issues from it?[16]

Jesus convinces us that God is dependable:

> The word of God as God's oath of fidelity became flesh in him in this sense that he was a man who single-mindedly accepted the assurance that the Lord of heaven and earth was wholly faithful to him and to all creatures, and who in response gave wholehearted loyalty to the realm of being.[17]

When Christian theology speaks about God and faith it places Jesus Christ in the center, for the community in which its work is carried on cannot think or speak of God and man without remembering that it is to the life and death of Jesus Christ that the miracle of its faith was connected, that this is the place where the possibility of trust in the source of being was given. The community practically identifies faith in God with faith in Christ—it speaks of reconciliation "in Christ" and of God as God-in-Christ—but this identification remains a *confessional* act; it does by no means imply that Jesus Christ is the *only* place where it happens. To say this would be a distortion even of what happens in the Christian community. For what is given is not Jesus Christ, but—through Jesus Christ—*trust in being.* This is what counts; and this is a universal quest of mankind, just as the ever-dynamic movement between trust and distrust is visible in thousands of different forms.

What the event of Jesus Christ, so crucial for the Christian community, reveals, is precisely that faith is possible; that, for instance, the movement in so many human lives from distrust to trust, from unfaith to faith, even if it passes through the stage of "sober despair," is not without promise, that sober despair can be the foundation and preparation for faith. It reveals that there is justification by grace; in other words, that man is not left alone with the consequences of his lostness and failures, that his life borders not on an abyss of nothingness but on grace. It reveals that there is eternal life, that man does not simply disappear but is kept and sustained by the source of all life.

When faith is given, profound consequences follow. A continuous revolution of life and thought is begun; life is made possible on the basis of simple joy in the infinite varieties and possibilities of being. Faith is present *in total life;* it is more than an intellectual conviction—it is a personal relation to the reality we have learned to call God: *"It is the reliance of a person on a person."*[18] In other words, God has become personal—he is a *thou.* This is the core of revelation, that it is no third-person proposition, but a "direct confession of the heart: 'Thou art my God.' "[19]

This is Niebuhr's first answer to the question of whether faith in God is possible. The answer refers to *what happens when faith is given.* When man receives the gift of the personal relation of trust in which he can say, "Thou art my God," God has become a thou, and faith has become possible.

Yet the question of the possibility of faith must be pressed a little farther. For the problems of the sovereignty of God which Niebuhr seeks to face are such that they remain, even after the possibility of faith has been asserted. Is the Thou that man learns to address in Jesus Christ really the source of being, the ultimate power man is up against in his existence? Or is man, in the end, alone with himself and his idols? Is it not precisely in Jesus Christ that we "confront the slayer"?

We must remember that questions such as these follow necessarily from Niebuhr's theological method, from his honesty with regard to both the human predicament and the sovereignty of God. This is why the answer that he does give about the possibility of faith never becomes a haven in which his theology comes to rest or from which it takes its departure. This is clear from two further considerations. In the first place, Niebuhr never wishes to abstract from the actual situation in which faith is born and in which it lives, the permanent dialectic with unfaith and distrust that can only call God "it." And second, radical monotheism implies a challenge to incarnate faith in *total* life, which means that God is always simultaneously other than the Thou which man addresses; he is the total system of being which from place to place, from situation to situation, challenges man in his "circumambient world"—in other words, the I-Thou relation keeps referring to and spending itself in a total life which becomes ever wider and ever more "total."

The intimate connection in Niebuhr's thought between anxiety and faith is, therefore, no accident. It illustrates once again his distance from Barth, who insists on divorcing all thought about God from thought about fate and who is able to do so because he speaks from the standpoint of the "triumph of grace" which is hidden in the divine sovereignty as its very essence.[20] To Niebuhr this amounts to taking a shortcut to faith which damages both the divine sovereignty and the human predicament; in other words, from the standpoint of the American tradition it is comparable to the basic mistake of Liberalism.

The problem under discussion can perhaps be clarified somewhat further if we consider the possibility of a silent conflict between different thought patterns that are present in Niebuhr's theology and that can be traced with the aid of the difference between the concepts "historical faith" and "trust in being." The first points to a "Roycean pattern" which concentrates on the human communal activity of interpretation. The character of *being* is present to man in this activity of interpretation, and it is indicated by *images* or *symbols*. Jesus Christ is such an interpretative image[21]: with its aid we find meaning and coherence in what is going on.

The second points to an "Edwardean pattern," according to which the system of being appears as something that is governed by a sovereign, inaccessible, and almost unpredictable power. The *crisis motif* tends to increase the tension between the two patterns. The interpretation of being is a necessary and possible activity of men, yet being *itself* constantly eludes such interpretation. This is inevitable because of the timefulness and historicity of the self. Historical relativity *inevitably entails distortion* of interpretation, and then, as Niebuhr wrote in 1932, God, the "structure in things," becomes the cause of our suffering "when we seek to impose our wishes on him"; God becomes "the rock on which we beat in vain."[22] If our center of interpretation is something *less* than being itself, being itself becomes manifest in retaliation; if our acts of loyalty fall short of the universal order of being—and again, how inevitable this is—being itself becomes manifest as an enslaving system, encompassing history.

If we are forced, then, to speak further on the possibility of faith, there are two ways we can follow, and both are present in Niebuhr's thought.

First of all, it can be emphasized that what is given in Jesus Christ is the possibility of active, joyful response to the realm of being and hopeful loyalty to all creatures. It is the conviction that the "new sense of the heart" has been given, can be given, and will be given again; the hope that God will indeed prove himself to be loyal to his creatures, that there is indeed justification and eternal life. The total reliance on the Thou which is given in Jesus Christ is miraculously given by the source of being itself in a revelation of its trustworthiness; and its meaning is precisely that man is inspired to move on to other acts of faith, to the never-ending activity of incarnating his trust in being itself in his total life. In other words, in Jesus Christ there appears *hope* in the struggle between faith and unfaith; it is hope that connects our relative answers of faith to the ultimate reality itself. As the road "between absolutism and skepticism," it is the marrow of the permanent movement of *metanoia* in all human thought and action. For man can only partially overcome his "natural attitude" toward God; to make *being itself* the object of human faith and loyalty is only a possibility in the permanent restlessness of continuing conversion.

Second, however, there remains the strong suggestion of acceptance, of resignation to what is and is to be. To see every act of faith as a further step in the never-ending process of incarnating faith in total life, is very close to seeing faith as the end of human resistance, as the final yielding to the inscrutable system of being which encompasses history and negates all relative efforts to interpret it creatively and actively in daily life. Here, too, we can speak of hope, but it is hope in the framework of divine government, determination, and predestination. Niebuhr cannot escape these notions; that would mean belittling the divine sovereignty, whereas "to hope for eternity" is precisely man's only chance for life.

The two lines of thought remain intertwined in Niebuhr's theology. They keep his concept of faith in line with his major theological concerns. They unite his concern for genuine newness in the life of faith with his insistence that only God himself can bring this newness into being. Faith "involves us in a permanent revolution of the mind and of the heart, a continuous life which opens out infinitely into ever-new possibilities. It does not, therefore, afford grounds for boasting but only for simple thankfulness. It is a gift of God."[23]

3. The interpretation of moral existence. Our treatment of Niebuhr's theology may have suggested that the major part of his work deals with the problems of being and faith described in the two preceding sections. This is not altogether true. The problems which we considered are permanently in the background, but Niebuhr's central work as a theologian lies in the field of *ethics*, in the critical reflection on the moral life. If his lectures on Christian ethics, which he reworked year after year, had ever been published, his written work would give a more adequate image of the theologian Niebuhr than it does now. *The Responsible Self* is the book that comes nearest to indicating the concerns with which he daily occupied himself in the classroom.

However, it is the purpose of this section to show that the critical reflection on the moral life is not a separate compartment in Niebuhr's thought, but is linked to the same basic concerns which we indicated in the preceding sections. At times this seems to be different, especially when he insists that "a major part of ethics is a phenomenological analysis of man's moral existence."[24] Niebuhr maintains that it is impossible to treat ethics as a branch of theology, to ground statements on the moral life exclusively in theological assertions.

> Ethics helps us to understand ourselves as responsible beings, our world as the place in which the responsible existence of the human community is exercised. Its practical utility is in its clarification, its interpretation, its provision of a pattern of meaning and understanding in the light of which human action can be more responsible.[25]

But although Niebuhr never grows weary of underscoring the general *human* character of ethical reflection, his reflections are from the start determined by his convictions about God, man, and faith—both in character and in content.

Roughly speaking, Niebuhr uses two separate schemes for the interpretation of moral existence. One is the "center of value" scheme, in which he describes the moral life as taking place around many centers of value and reflects on the quest for one ultimate regulative center.[26] The other is the "responsibility" scheme, which is especially dominant in the last ten years of his work.[27] In it he begins with the *observation* that *all life* has the character of responsiveness,[28] and goes on to suggest that even Christ might receive new relevance through the "broader-based symbol" of *the responsible man.*[29]

Searching for the connection between these schemes of interpretation and Niebuhr's fundamental theological convictions, we are first of all reminded of his continuous and consistent use of the method of observation and analysis. This method is present from the time when, in *The Social Sources of Denominationalism*, Niebuhr studied the complex social forces which determined particular expressions of faith; and it gradually grows more differentiated and detailed. In his ethics lectures Niebuhr's close affinity to the thought of George Herbert Mead is most explicit: the moral act is carefully dissected, and everything that enters into it becomes the object of scrutiny. The moral self is seen as "a system of relations,"[30] functioning in a field of complex forces that determine and respond to each other. Niebuhr's preference for such more or less detached observation is undergirded, as we have seen, by the development of radical monotheism. The "animal faith" in the sensibility of encountered reality, the basic confidence that observation and analysis will lead to insight, receives theological foundation.

In an essay on the nature of faith, Niebuhr lists several possible approaches to the phenomenon of faith and develops a complete program for a detailed inquiry, then ends as follows:

> I have thus elucidated the "nature of faith" but have shown myself to be subject to the "faith" of our times: namely, the

confidence that analysis will lead to clarification, and that clarification will not end in chaotic pluralism but lead on-ward to the understanding of how all things hang together in a trustworthy universe, which is the cause of the faithful God.[31]

This is an evident connection between Niebuhr's method and his conviction that there is *indeed* a ground for belief in "a trustworthy universe"; namely, through the faith that knows of reconciliation to the Creator. The same connection is made in Niebuhr's reflections on the duality of internal and external history; his confidence that external observation *leads somewhere* is balanced and undergirded by a particular internal view of the way in which "all things hang together in a trustworthy universe"—a view that can be realized and "embodied" only externally.[32]

The second point we must call attention to is Niebuhr's affinity to that theological tradition which manifests obvious influence from the views of Kant, and which finds embodiment in men like A. Ritschl and W. Hermann. Here the "moral situation" of the individual—his obligations, shortcomings, anxieties, and personal fulfillments—is the starting point for all theology, and the basis for dogmatic statements. The particular heritage of this tradition is the emphasis on the "hermeneutical function" of ethical reflection. The nature and existence of God remains materially prior, but it cannot be made relevant apart from the context of the moral situation; in other words, dogmatics can never stand over against ethics. Theology can make itself heard only when man is addressed in his particular situation.

In his criticism of Ritschl,[33] Niebuhr deplores the fact that the value of "man over against nature" is made dominant in the reflection of the Christian community. But this does not imply that he chooses to abandon reflection on the moral situation as the proper context for theology. Ritschl's mistake was not his starting point but rather the introduction of "the value scale of civilized man" into Christian reflection about faith in God. He thus made God into an *instrument.* Ritschl was led to "relinquish the standpoint of faith in God and to accept the point of view of pagan confidence in man."[34] At this point, Niebuhr insists, the correction of all moral reflection must be permanent.

Over against Barth, Niebuhr maintains that the substance of self-knowledge *is not derived out of* our knowledge of God.[35] Does this mean that "knowledge of God" and "knowledge of man" become two separate compartments? If this were so, Niebuhr would not be able to meet Barth's criticism. But it is not the case. Rather, for Niebuhr "knowledge of God" is never *primarily* propositional knowledge; propositions about God always arise from an already present faith involvement. The priority of God can therefore not be safeguarded propositionally, but remains a requirement of permanent correction. It is not Niebuhr's intention—or that of the tradition under discussion—to separate action from belief and to make dogmatics the slave of ethics. Rather, in moral reflection a permanent effort must be made not to lose sight of the proper object. *Religion and ethics cannot be separated;* the moral situation remains the proper context for reflection, but the reflection cannot and must not be dominated by the false center of "man's spiritual personality."

The two points noted above are combined in Niebuhr's thought and enable him to carry on Christian ethics as a critical and consistent reflection on the moral life. From here we must understand the coherence of his themes, the relation in his thought between dogmatics and ethics, between theology and philosophy, and between Christian thought and human rational reflection. Niebuhr maintains that he never leaves the particular Christian viewpoint in his undertakings. He tries to develop instruments for *the believer's self-understanding*[36]; and because he cannot possibly abstract from the Christian relation to God, his moral philosophy must be called *Christian* rather than *theistic*.[37] Were it called "theistic," it would still be mere philosophy; and such a thing does not exist, since philosophy is always, consciously or not, conducted from the standpoint of a particular community with a particular faith.

Thus reflections on the moral situation are never "generally human," though we can conceive of such a thing from our particular standpoint. One can only speak about man's natural situation in the act of "looking back." Hence there is no such thing as a natural religion, but there *is* such a thing as *Christian natural theology*.[38] The permanent dialogue of moral existence between natural situation and particular faith can take place only *in the context* of this particular faith. How much more true is this of the *Christian* faith, which is radical monotheism and as such keeps referring us back to the human predicament and to the perennial conflict of faiths! We might say that radical monotheism constantly leads to "Christian natural theology," because it stands in contrast to all special, *social* faith that isolates particular groups of men or compartmentalizes their lives into a "religious" and a "secular" domain.

The Christian faith allows for the freedom to start freely in human moral existence, not because this *is* a common ground we share with all men to begin with, but because we can *treat it as such*, inspired by our particular standpoint. This means that we always meet moral existence in the process of constant transformation.[39] Our observation and interpretation itself is bound by the demand for transformation; the permanent transition and dialectic between faith and unfaith, trust and distrust, remains the center of gravity.

If this interpretation is correct, we cannot completely agree with Kenneth Cauthen, who interprets Niebuhr to say that the problem of the believer is to relate "his existence as a Christian to his existence as a citizen of some kingdom of this world."[40] For although Niebuhr speaks from a Christian viewpoint he does not see the ultimate issue as lying between *Christian faith and other faiths*, but between trust and distrust in being; and although he does not abstract from the Christian relation to God, he does not primarily speak about this relation but about what is given in it: *trust in being*. Though Christ is the only way for him, he can say no more than that Christ is only one way. Neither can we completely agree with Cauthen when he says that

> from the existential point of view the problem of faith and of the gods who are objects of faith *is a universal one* which arises out of the individual's existential situation in the world as a self in community with other selves in quest of meaning and fulfillment.[41]

Niebuhr would never make such an assertion; for the universality of the problem of faiths is revealed radically and consistently only in monotheistic faith, and therefore the statement that it *is* universal can never be propositional but only confessional; as such it is part and parcel of the Christian viewpoint.

It follows from these considerations that Niebuhr looks on "Christian faith" in a double way. On the one hand it is, like other "faiths," only one particular way of looking at the problems of moral existence. "To a large extent . . . Christianity represents a qualification of human practical existence, or at least of Western moral life, rather than a new and wholly different way of living; it may represent a species rather than a genus of human moral existence."[42] On the other hand, there is *an implicit Christocentrism* in Niebuhr. This means that the Christ-faith, though it may be a species rather than a genus, constantly determines his reflections.

Niebuhr cannot abstract from the Christian viewpoint. But it has to remain implicit; it cannot take the form of particular propositions which then become the standard for other propositions about man and moral existence. *Christology* cannot become the basis of our investigations. For the significance of Christ for the moral life can become clear only in terms of the patterns of moral life that are actually there and that can be interpreted by images like responsibility. The Christian moral life is not something received and begun completely new: it is a permanent transformation of the "natural" attitudes toward being in which we daily find ourselves. This is precisely why, and how, we can conduct our "interpretation of moral existence," in the widest possible sense, from the standpoint of the faith of the Christian community.

Chapter 3
The Scope of Responsibility

A. THE TRIAD OF FAITH

1. **Self, community, and cause.** An analysis of the human self usually begins by seeking a guiding principle for the understanding and interpretation of all its actions, thoughts, and feelings. It is characteristic of Niebuhr's thought that it manifests a certain hesitancy at this point. According to Niebuhr, there is no part of the self—reason, moral obligation, emotion, the unconscious, or the biological mechanism —which as such can serve as a starting point for the approach to the self's existence and unity. Even the principle of the existential givenness and freedom *as such* (as in Existentialism) cannot perform that function. This conviction allows him a wide range for ethical reflection, but it precludes any a priori statements about the being of man in and for himself. Niebuhr's thought does revolve around the self, but always around *"the self and . . ."* or *"the self in . . ."* His analysis is aimed at the situations, the patterns in which the self can be observed in action, feeling, and thought (the theoretical observation of the *phenomenon)*, and at the conditions under which selfhood is experienced and accepted (the practical reflections on existence).

There are no a priori assumptions about the self as a rational or moral being. In other words, Niebuhr accepts the Kantian distinction between pure and practical reason but without the implication of universal principles. This has two significant consequences. In the first place, his analysis of the self directly points to *the irreducible action by which the self is*, although this action does not itself become the object of inquiry. This is not a modern restatement of the moral argument for the existence of God, but an indication of man's "threshold existence." The indication is confirmed and corroborated by monotheistic faith, but it does not itself become an apologetic tool. In the second place, the self is understood, analyzed, and interpreted as *a relational self*—a self whose existence is thoroughly social, a self which cannot be posited apart from other selves. Of course, the self can and does assume purely individual attitudes in which its irreducible selfhood is realized—notably in the response to *the radical action by which it is*. But even so, the being of man can be approached only through its relational existence. Starting point is "the recognition that the self is fundamentally social, in this sense that it is a being which not only knows itself in relation to other selves but exists as self only in that relation."[1]

A distinct motive behind this approach to the analysis of man is Niebuhr's desire to rescue the "complete" phenomenon of the self from an exclusively scientific method which reserves *truth* for that which can be *known* and assigns all else to the domain of the irrational. Selves are epiphenomena in our dominant world view,[2] because our world view prefers to treat the self as if it were impersonal and at worst mechanical. That this situation needs correction is indicated by the fact "that no man in the situation of a participant in life *actually succeeds* in interpreting and dealing with other human beings on this level," and "that the impersonal account leaves large areas of our experience unrationalized and uncontrolled."[3] Just as true *knowledge* is only a limited cause which together with justice, beauty, and religion has its place in a community "that has a center and a cause beyond all these vocational ends,"[4] so also the selfhood of the self lies beyond the many approaches to it. Only a consistent and many-sided analysis of relational existence can throw light on the way in which the self as complete and unified self is present in all its behavior.

Closely connected with the concentration on relational existence is the insight that knowledge of selves is possible only through a *revelation*. The *Thou* can be known only in actual encounter.[5] Even the *I* has no knowledge of itself except through its encounters and relations: it is in social existence that the self is revealed to itself. Man is social before he is "rational" or "obedient"; to be is to be with others. Neither "I" nor "it" come to consciousness without the presence of a Thou. All decisions in which the I posits itself are in some way affected by companions and in turn affect them. Niebuhr calls this way of thought *social existentialism*.[6] When we try to trace its sources we are first of all led to observe a Kierkegaardian element, according to which the self can realize its selfhood, or make itself known even to itself, only by an irreducible act of decision to *be* a self. This Kierkegaardian element, however, is modified, if not corrected, by an emphasis on the *outward-directedness* of all decision. The irreducible realization of selfhood is not inward and individualistic, but takes place in particular situations and influences them. In addition to Kierkegaard, Niebuhr evidently follows Friedrich Schleiermacher, for whom *feeling* (the basic expression of selfhood) is present only as an accompanying element in the pattern of self-world relations.

More important, however, for the point under discussion—social existentialism—are the influences of George Herbert Mead and Martin Buber. The latter is for Niebuhr the eminent representative of a way of thought which emphasizes the basic significance of the I-Thou relation. For Buber, the encounter with the *Thou* is the key to the understanding of reality. Niebuhr acknowledges his indebtedness to Buber when he emphasizes the significance of the presence of *thous* for the self—*thous* who reveal themselves in personal encounters, and who differ qualitatively from mere phenomena in the world view of an I.[7] Yet on the whole, Niebuhr stands somewhat closer to Mead than to Buber. We must keep in mind that the gift of the I-Thou encounter *itself* never becomes the cornerstone of Niebuhr's thinking; his interest lies in *the conditioning of selfhood by the presence of other selves.* Personal encounter with another self is not an original event which qualifies the knowledge of what is encountered, but it takes place in and through a pattern of relations which can itself be observed and analyzed. For this approach Niebuhr remains indebted to G. H. Mead.[8]

The intimate connection Niebuhr makes between knowledge and communication must be understood in the context of this general approach. Only thus can his argument for *critical* realism receive its proper connotations. Critical realism is required, as it were, by the modesty of an approach that cannot begin with clear-cut conceptions of self or community but "meets" self and community in the complex process of the encounter with reality. Communication with natural objects and with persons is "a continuing movement in which correction is forever taking place and in which interpretation never ceases."[9] For although the activity of communal interpretation is always present in the encounter of the world, the reality of the world is not dependent on it. The relation to the world cannot be separated from the relation to the companion in interpretation, but nevertheless they are distinct.[10] This accounts for the complexity of the continuing pattern of dialogue in which the self and its companions are forever involved. There is no objective reality without communication, but communication always refers to objective reality.

With all this, we have only begun to indicate the elements which enter into Niebuhr's use of the terms *response* and *responsibility*—the symbols with which he generally speaks about the self and its relational existence. Their adequacy seems to lie mostly in the fact that they do not describe the essence of the self, but the structure of the pattern in which the self always exists. In the terms response and responsibility

Niebuhr comprises nearly everything that needs to be said about this pattern. Responsibility

> may summarily and abstractly be defined as the idea of an agent's action as response to an action upon him in accordance with his interpretation of the latter action and with his expectation of response to his response, and all of this is in a continuing community of agents.[11]

Two things are worth noting in this definition. In the first place, we observe that the self organizes its responses on the basis of its expectation of certain responses of others—in Mead's language, its ability to make an adequate response depends on its ability to assume the role of others.[12] The self responds following its interpretation of the action of others. This interpretation is modified by the actions which the self undergoes. Hence there is a highly complex process of action and interaction "in which correction is forever taking place and in which interpretation never ceases."

Yet this complexity is somewhat reduced by the tendency on the part of selves to *generalize* the actions of others. This is the second point we must observe in Niebuhr's definition of response. The self responds to the *constancies* in the actions upon him, rather than to all actions separately. These constancies—present for instance in "the constant meanings of a common language"[13]—form something like silent agreements on the basis of which a particular community *is* a community. Mead calls this phenomenon the "generalized other." It is of course clear that the self in its actual existence has several, if not many, of these "generalized others," for it is a member of several communities of agents. Sometimes these are like concentric circles—each one wider and more inclusive than another—but mostly the self simply lives among many *uncoordinated* or *uneasily coordinated* communities. This point clarifies what Niebuhr calls the *accountability* of the self: the self is accountable, not only to the extent that it conforms to the patterns in which it is involved, but also to the extent that it is *independent* from its immediate companions because it simultaneously belongs to another or a wider pattern, and ultimately to the community of *being itself.*[14]

There is a further element in Niebuhr's analysis of self and community to which we must pay attention, the *timefulness* of the self and of everything to which it stands in relation. The element of *time* is not merely a self-evident addition to all that has been said; it is crucial for the understanding of self, community, and responsibility. There are two aspects which must be considered, roughly speaking: the objective and the subjective. Niebuhr himself expresses it succinctly: *man is in time,* and *time is in man.*[15]

Man is in time. That is to say, all reality which man encounters is temporal and historical: caught in the flux of passing and conditioned by its particular situation. No thoughts, ideas, or systems are exempt from this "historical relativism." But "man is in time" implies more; namely, that man is the *timer*—that he is the active agent in connecting what he encounters into a pattern of past, present, and future. In all perception or interpretation there is a line of extension, of duration, which centers in the present of the self. The present of the self contains a past and a future, not a past and a future of *facts* but of deeds and sufferings, hopes and expectations.

Niebuhr seems here to be close to Heidegger, who explains factual "vulgar" time as an *abstraction* from the primary temporality of existential care (*Sorge*). But here, too, we should not forget the important role of the thought of Mead. For Mead, the perception of temporal and passing reality implies the introduction of a certain instantaneousness. From the point of view of the passing universe, this instantaneousness is wholly fictitious but necessary if conscious perception, interpretation, *and action* are to follow. "We abstract time from this space for the purposes of our conduct."[16] In reality, the seemingly timeless object of perception "is the existent future of the act"[17]; in other words, the response that I am *going to* make is present to me and thus causes some sense of timelessness. Likewise the *pastness* of the self, of its previous responses and perceptions, is carried along in the present. Thus there is a continuous duration of action and re-action in which the self is involved.

Decisions are made in the duration of time; that is, in the extension of the present to past and future. This means that decisions are modified, if not determined, by the larger temporal contexts in which they are placed.[18] In these "larger contexts" a movement toward a *universal* context is discernible—a movement which seems to have the character of hope: hope for a goal beyond time. In the extended patterns of past-present-future, man-in-time seeks to grasp wholeness and meaning; as Niebuhr wrote in 1930, he seeks to "wrest from contemporary experience its ultimate significance and revelational value." This is the problem of *The Meaning of Revelation*. The hope of man-in-time is the hope for a creator, for the trustworthiness of the One by whose action everything *is*.

But there is more. Man is not only in time, but *time is in man.* The self *itself* is not unhistorical or timeless. "The self that knows itself in encounter with others, finds itself to be absolutely dependent in its existence, completely contingent, inexplicably present in its hereness and nowness."[19] And this here and now in which the self experiences its radical timefulness, its being *thrown* into existence, is not an abstract category or principle but rather "the time of a definite society with distinct language, economic and political relations, religious faith and social organization."[20] Time-in-man points to the riddle of his inexplicable thereness, his finitude, conditionedness, restrictedness, and dependence. It points, above all, to his dependence on the radical action by which he *is*. From both aspects of the relation of self, community, and time we have thus come to the same point. Both aspects lead to the problem of history, meaning, and revelation. But this is not the chapter to pursue that problem. Rather, we must hasten to bring out the *final* and *most important* point in Niebuhr's analysis of self and community—a point we have artificially suppressed so far for the sake of clarity of argument, but which in reality pervades Niebuhr's reflections from the beginning. We mean *the triadic structure of communication* and *the basic role of faith as trust and loyalty in all interpersonal relations*.

That communication and knowledge are always triadic rather than merely dual, is a central motif in Niebuhr. In the dialogue in which the self is forever engaged, there are at least three partners: the self, the social companion, and natural events.[21] Basic for this triad—and here we reach a crucial point in Niebuhr's thought—is the a priori element of *covenant* or *commitment* between selves, which involves *trust*. Some measure of interpersonal trust is always present in knowledge and communication; and there is no interpersonal trust without the presence of a third, an "it."

There is a second triadic situation in which the self finds itself. Next to the triad I-Thou-nature we live in the triad I-Thou-*cause*. For the relation "self-other" refers to more than self and other, it refers to a third reality which binds self and other together and to which they bind themselves and each other. The *cause* sustains and feeds the relation; and a community—a more or less stable pattern of constant response and interpretation—can *be* a community only by virtue of such a common and binding cause. It makes interpersonal trust possible.

In this triadic form of interpersonal trust we find, then, a "structure of faith that is not peculiarly religious, but that is human."[22] It points to the fact that all men have faith in the sense that all men live in relations which exist by virtue of *causes*.

> It is a curious and inescapable fact about our lives, of which I think we all become aware at some time or another, that we cannot live without a cause, without some object of devotion, some center of worth, something on which we rely for meaning. In this sense all men have faith because they are men and cannot help themselves, just as they must and do have some knowledge of their world, though their knowledge be erroneous.[23]

A cause, then, is truly an object of devotion, a *god*: *"To be a self is to have a god."*[24] And *faith* is the relation of selves to each other and to their common cause. It comprises two elements: *trust* and *loyalty. Trust,* the "passive side," is the confidence that its object is good, that it gives value to the self; loyalty, the "active side," is the commitment, the devotion, the active fidelity of the self to that which it values.[25] Faith as trust and loyalty is directed to other selves who are united with the self in the devotion to the same cause; and together with these selves, it is directed to the cause. It is, in short, triadic in structure.

We have already found the motif of the triadic structure in Royce's philosophy; and Niebuhr's frequent use of words like "cause" and "loyalty" indicates his indebtedness to this way of thinking. We should not forget, however, that Royce's main interest is the realization of moral selfhood in the act of loyalty; it is the harmonious and proper functioning of the human communities, rather than the struggle for meaning among the many communities. Royce sees the "significant unity" of the self with "world-consciousness" realized in loyalty *as such.* For Niebuhr, such significant unity can never be a self-evident starting point; the confusing world of human loyalties is an indication of this impossibility.

The triad of faith is present in all relations in which the self is involved, though trust and loyalty are always mixed with some measure of *dis*trust and *dis*loyalty. Faith is the major ingredient in the relation between I and Thou: the relation in which selves are revealed, given, to each other; it determines the relation of the self to *the radical action by which it is.* Faith pervades all knowledge and communication, it colors all the responses of the self to its immediate and wider environments, and it qualifies the ways in which the self deals with its own timefulness.

Of course, the presence of faith is not merely an inexplicable miracle, though when it is given it is a miraculous gift. It is itself brought forth by specific actions which call for response. It is evoked by a demonstration of loyalty or by the disclosure of a cause.[26] I learn to trust in response to evidence of loyalty; I learn to be a loyal in response to revelation of trustworthiness. At the end of the analysis of self, community, and cause, therefore, the question appears as to the possibility of a faithful, trustful attitude toward *the most inclusive environment.* For the question of whether the movement toward the universal pattern in which the self finds itself leads to life or to death, cannot be escaped.

2. **Social selfhood and absolute dependence.** In our analysis of Niebuhr's reflections on self, community, and cause we have noticed the permanent presence of references to the principle on which the self is absolutely dependent and to which its relational and responsive existence points. This is, as it were, the only way left to speak of the self as a

unified and integrated whole. We find such reference, first of all, in the impossibility to posit a complete self as an object of analysis. The "I" is always posited in the premise: "Only if I posit the self can I refer this thinking, living, feeling, to myself."[27] We also find it in the structure of response-patterns which keep pointing beyond themselves to wider patterns, as well as in the significance of time. Finally, we notice it in the way Niebuhr speaks about faith and causes.

> To the monotheistic believer for whom all responses to his companions are interrelated with his responses to God as the ultimate person, the ultimate cause, the center of universal community, there seem to be indications in the whole of the responsive, accountable life of men of a movement of self-judgment and self-guidance which cannot come to rest until it makes its reference to a universal other and a universal community, which that other both represents and makes his cause .... The societies that judge or in which we judge ourselves are self-transcending societies. And the process of self-transcendence or of reference to the third beyond each third does not come to rest until the total community of being has been involved.[28]

Therefore, *faith—*

> the attitude of the self in its existence toward all the existences that surround it, as beings to be relied upon or to be suspected—*is fundamentally trust or distrust in being itself*... it is the chief ingredient in our interpretation of the radical act or agency by which we are selves, here and now.[29]

In this section we will take a closer look at what Niebuhr means by *absolute dependence,* and how he uses the term. On the basis of his analysis of self, community, and cause, it seems that all we can say about "the radical action by which the self is," is that it is itself unconditioned; that it is no part of any finite pattern of actions in which the self exists; that it cannot as such become the point of departure for an analysis of the self, but rather manifests itself in and through the many actions of the self. And all we can say about the ultimate reference of relational and responsive existence is that we have an unconquerable conviction of *a oneness behind everything*[30]: a oneness behind the actions *upon* the self and the actions *of* the self, a oneness which can be ignored only at the expense of integrated selfhood. But in what is said here, there is some indication already as to the direction in which Niebuhr's thought moves. We can notice two tendencies. The first is a clear affinity to the way in which Schleiermacher uses the triad self-God-world in his exposition of the Christian faith: absolute dependence of the self is always posited *together with* relative dependence on the world, so that statements about one of the three always imply statements about the other two. In Schleiermacher's triad Niebuhr finds "a certain existentialism," a pattern which expresses that self-awareness is simultaneously "Thou-awareness, now-awareness, and here-awareness."

The second tendency is visible in the heavy emphasis on the *oneness behind everything.* A Spinozistic scheme manifests itself here according to which the self and its existence can be truly affirmed only if they are included in the largest possible whole, the *one substance.* Yet in both tendencies the dominant question remains: Is this oneness, this power or action which manifests itself dimly or clearly wherever one turns, *beneficent?* Can one count on it and entrust oneself to it?

The temper of Niebuhr's theology which we have analyzed in the second half of chapter 2, is determined by these two elements: I depend on the ultimate power for existence and value, I cannot ignore it or fight it, *and yet* I travel in darkness with regard to its ultimate nature and intention. Typical for Niebuhr's thought, as we have noticed, is that he moves almost imperceptibly from statements about the self and its absolute dependence to statements about God and his actions. As we have said before, Niebuhr does not intend to restate the moral argument for God's existence; rather, his analysis consists of a back-and-forth movement between a *given* knowledge of God-in-Christ and an acquired knowledge of the human situation, analyzed *from the standpoint of Christian faith.* Faith, after all, can begin both in the givenness of personal existence, making inferences about the "larger world," and in a vision of the larger world, moving from here to inferences about personal existence.[31]

Thus, speaking about the question of how the self arrives at the acknowledgment of its absolute dependence, Niebuhr confesses three things[32]: he has learned to understand his life as a movement from knowledge of an ordering power to knowledge of a saving power, he has learned to see that distrust and enmity toward the source of being is man's "natural condition," and (*third!*) *he has learned to listen to the word of God spoken in Jesus Christ.* For Niebuhr, knowledge of God-in-Christ and awareness of absolute dependence cannot be separated; rather, they condition each other. And yet, precisely *because* of this, he can discern movements of trust and distrust toward the source of being in all men, and say that acknowledging absolute dependence is the only way to affirm and accept selfhood.

Only if the ultimate power is beneficent does life have meaning. Faith in the ultimate power, therefore, is the trust that *life has meaning.* This is *radical faith.* When asked for its possibility, we can only say that the Christ-event elicits it. In and around Jesus Christ we see how the structure of faith which we can analyze in *all* our relationships, arrives at its ultimate fulfillment; in and around Jesus Christ we see how the triad of faith appears "in a kind of cosmic form."[33] This *cosmic triad* can be seen as God, the self, and the neighbor (the theological and anthropological triad); God, man, and Christ (the christological triad); or God, the self, and *being* (the ethical triad).

In the section on the interpretation of moral existence we indicated that Niebuhr uses two schemes for this interpretation: the center of value scheme and the responsibility scheme. We will try to trace the relation between social selfhood and absolute dependence in both schemes.

After all that has been said in the preceding section, it cannot surprise us that Niebuhr's value theory is thoroughly *relational.* Already in his early essay "Value Theory and Theology" (1937) Niebuhr states that value cannot be conceived apart from the activity of valuing and the correspondence to a certain need. In his essay "The Center of Value" (1952) he gives a further theoretical elaboration of this point. Value cannot be possessed by a being in and for itself. It exists only in relations between beings: "If anything existed simply in itself and by itself, value would not be present."[34] Niebuhr tries to find a *via media* between the theory that value is an objective kind of reality and the theory that value is dependent on the feelings and desires of a subject. Value arises in the relation of one existent to another, in the relation of one existent to its own essence, or in the relation between these two relations. In all three cases it has no reality save in the presence of others for whom the existent is or becomes valuable.

In human life there is, therefore, an endless variety of possible value relations. If the word value is to have any meaning at all, this variety must in some way be organized. This actually happens: value relations find their constancy in their relation to a *center of value* by which they are coordinated and judged. Niebuhr calls such a center of value a dogmatic starting point. Every value theory necessarily has such a point and is insofar *religious in character.*[35] Yet it is likewise evident that most value theories employ more than one center; they "are caught up in a polytheism which posits two or more centers of values."[36] Over against such a polytheism, monotheistic faith makes its starting point, its dogmatic beginning, *"with the transcendent One for whom alone there is an ultimate good and for whom, as the source and end of all things, whatever is, is good."*[37] Only such a "dogmatic beginning" can at the same time be *un*dogmatic in the sense that it allows for many relative value systems.

This is a concise statement of several motifs to which we have already drawn attention in the second chapter: the relation between monotheism and relativism, the connection between the affirmation of the goodness of being and the relation with the Creator, and the dubious right of man to start with the assertion that being is good, though he depends on it for existence. In the context of this section our attention is drawn to the fact that Niebuhr's value theory contains the reference of many relative dependencies to one ultimate dependence, and that it shows how the many relative dependencies have sense and meaning only when this ultimate dependence is acknowledged.

The triad self-God-being is a triad of *valuation.* Again, Niebuhr does not state an argument for God's existence. He does not say that the evident necessity of an ultimate all-inclusive center of value points to the existence of God. He says, rather, in view of the total scheme of being which we cannot comprehend but which nevertheless comprises and determines all that is, we cannot have *any* center of value which is final. We depend, therefore, completely on the principle of being itself. Unless this is also the principle of value *there is no God,* and we are left to nothingness.

Niebuhr's value theory is thus not merely a defense of relationalism but, more significantly, of an essential connection between social selfhood and absolute dependence. It is this connection which ultimately is at stake in the critical exchange between Niebuhr and George Schrader on the former's value theory.[38] Schrader argues that the relational meaning of value is derivative, that it must be grounded in the relativity of *being.* Value cannot be constituted by relations; it must be intrinsic before it can be instrumental: "To *be* is ontologically prior to *to-be-for.*" According to Schrader, it is Niebuhr's intention to prevent at all costs that an individual being is granted unconditioned value; but Schrader says that this intention can still be honored if we begin with the priority of intrinsic value, for *being in itself is mediated.* That Niebuhr does not recognize this, leads, according to Schrader, to a juxtaposition in his theory of value-absolutism (value in self-relatedness) and value-relativism (value in other-relatedness). Especially the relation between God and the world in this theory becomes a curious thing to Schrader: "Like a line stretched in the air but without being anchored at either end . . . . Is not the act of valuing essentially that of *acknowledging* something which exists and is relatively independent both of our own existence and of our evaluative act?"[39] Schrader says that God must have primordial being and goodness in himself; being and value of man and the world are reflections of this, to be *acknowledged* in man's relation to God.

In his answer Niebuhr underscores the relational character of his value theory: even in self-relatedness, value does not exist apart from other-relatedness.[40] The heart of the controversy, it seems to us, lies at the point where Schrader speaks of the *mediatedness of being.* Niebuhr consistently avoids this term and speaks *only* of the *relational character of existence.* In other words, no assertions about being can be made apart from a (faith) *relation.* To Schrader, "Value theory is ultimately dependent upon metaphysics...it is impossible to deal with the question as to the ground of value apart from the inquiry into the nature of being and existence."[41] To Niebuhr the only thing that can be said metaphysically is that there is a oneness in which all being coheres. Further assertions about being itself are dependent upon the *relation of valuation* between creature and Creator. In Niebuhr's thought, therefore, social selfhood and absolute dependence are inseparable. At this point he refers the reader to Jonathan Edwards.[42]

We have indicated that in Niebuhr's thought the "center of value" scheme is gradually replaced by a greater concentration on existentialist ways of thinking and on the scheme of response and responsibility. In this latter scheme, too, we can observe a close connection between social existence and absolute dependence. The statement "To be a self is to have a god" is met by the statement "To have faith in the *one God* is to be a complete and unified *self.*"

> The self as one self among all the systematized reactions in which it engages seems to be the counterpart of a unity that lies beyond, yet expresses itself in, all the manifold systems of actions upon it.... I am one within myself as I encounter the One in all that acts upon me ... by that action whereby I am I in all the roles I play, in reaction to all the systems of action that impinge upon me, I am in the presence of the One beyond all the many.[43]

The growth toward oneness of self is an indication of the One in the many in whose presence I become a self. Growth toward integral personhood is, therefore, simultaneously and necessarily a movement from distrust to trust. Integral personhood is accompanied by the acknowledgment of personlike integrity of the One beyond the many. Unity of self is impossible without an I-Thou relation with God, in which the whole realm of being is accepted as the "third in the triad"; and likewise, the human I-Thou relation receives its final meaning and possibility in the acknowledgment of the One beyond the many as the common cause. In the triad of faith, then, *God can become both a Thou and a cause.* As *Thou* he gives the possibility to face the oneness of being and to respond to it; as *cause* he is that to which all self-transcending causes refer, the center of the universal community.[44] "When I respond to the one creative power, I place my companions... in the one universal society which has its center... in the transcendent one... In distrust of the radical action by which I am ... I must find my center of valuation in myself."[45] I cannot respond in the context of universal being without facing the radical action by which I am, and by which everything is—*faith in God and reconciliation with being is the same thing.*

Only on the basis of the connection between social selfhood and absolute dependence can we properly assess the relation in Niebuhr's thought between the individual self and the community to which it belongs. The dialectic between self and community is warranted precisely by the absolute dependence of the self. Of course, the temptation *par excellence* in this dialectic between self and community is the lapse into the *social faith* of the group—then I substitute the many for the One and become one of the many. Until I have achieved a relative emancipation from the group by responding to the radical action by which I am, I am no more than a reflection of the patterns in which I exist; then my particular community stands between me and being itself. To this temptation the self succumbs time and again, for

> it is painful to think of the absolute dependence in which I have been established . . . to accept the familiar pattern of self-ignoring existence to which the existentialists in modern times but many sociologists in their way also have called our attention . . . . For the word I, we substitute now the word one; the I now becomes one among many, yet not one self among many selves . . . . We might call it the situation of response to all others except that otherness by which the self is self, and of response therefore by forces in the body and the mind, but not by the self as self . . . the state of our unresponsiveness as *selves.* "[46]

In the movement toward faith in God and reconciliation with being, a self becomes a true self, a community a true community. The *accountability* of the self is fulfilled when the self faces and trusts the source of being. But though this is an individual attitude, it does not happen apart from the presence of a community or without its mediation. For revelatory moments which elicit the faith of the individual do not occur in a peculiarly religious sphere, but in the fullness of communal life, "in the midst of political struggles, of national and cultural crises."[47] And a community is only a true community when it makes constant reference in its existence to the cause beyond its immediate cause, when it keeps pointing to the universal context of which it is a relative part.

3. *Speaking of God.* The central function which the triad of faith performs in Niebuhr's thought implies that all speaking about God, if it is to be meaningful, must be part of this triad and reflect it. In other words, statements about God make sense only when they immediately involve statements about the self, the neighbor, and the world, and about their interrelationships. As we have indicated, there is a close affinity between Niebuhr and Schleiermacher on this point.

Schleiermacher's "feeling of absolute dependence" has often been interpreted to mean that God is in some sense immediate to the self. It may be more correct to say that *feeling* is the way in which *the irreducible totality of the self in its dependence* enters into consciousness. On this point Niebuhr and Schleiermacher strike the same note. They agree that we can think and speak about God only *after* acknowledging that our relation to him is not one of partial dependence and partial freedom, and that absolute dependence refers to *total* selfhood which can only be present to us in feeling. (Instead of "feeling" Niebuhr uses "sense," "awareness," or "consciousness.") Niebuhr's Spinozistic tendency contributes to this agreement with Schleiermacher. For if God cannot be apprehended in terms of quantity and difference but only as total substance which encloses and limits our selfhood, statements about him can be made only in the context of our sense of absolute dependence. Since absolute dependence is never present to us in its pure form but always as *accompanying moment* of our relative freedom and dependencies, God as object of reflection cannot be isolated from the other partners in the triad, the self and the world.[48] "The interrelations of self, companion, and God are so intricate that no member of this triad exists in his true nature without the others, nor can he be known or loved without the others."[49]

The insistence on the indestructible nature of the triad leads to the problem of the language about God. Since language is interpersonal, and a reflection and articulation of the complex processes of relational existence and communal encounter with reality, the self is driven to use thought patterns which include more than only the self—thought patterns which reflect and express participation. Furthermore, the absolute dependence of the self is, for Niebuhr, not a separate dimension of existence in the sense that it requires a separate language. The self cannot get hold of its "threshold existence" in a denotative term. Therefore, speaking about God cannot be isolated from speaking about the personal and interpersonal processes in which faith *always* manifests itself. This is not to say that the relation to ultimate reality is *translated* into interpersonal relations. It emphasizes, rather, that the only access language has to ultimate reality is through the activity of imagination; that is, through the development of symbols and symbolic patterns by which we apprehend and interpret reality in our communities.[50]

It is against this background that we have to understand Niebuhr's negative attitude toward *metaphysical language*. In summarizing his reasons for this attitude we simply give another illustration of the basic elements in his theological method which we analyzed before.

First of all, we remind ourselves once more of the insistence on religious relativism, which implies that it is possible to speak about God only from the point of view of *faith* in God.[51] For Niebuhr such religious relativism is always combined with historical relativism; that God and faith are always together is further qualified by the insight that faith is always a particular historic faith. Thus the impossibility of metaphysical language is given with the fact that the believing self remains bound not only to his faith, but also to his particular, relative, finite situation.[52]

Second—and this is even more important for his attitude toward metaphysics—Niebuhr consistently seeks to rescue the objectivity of God; that is, his radical over-againstness, his independence from all human reflection. Partly siding with Barth, Niebuhr criticizes Schleiermacher for not avoiding the temptation to direct the attention of faith toward itself rather than toward God.[53] For, though we cannot abstract from the point of view of faith, *we must begin with revelation:* that is, the religious object must be sought in its independent givenness, for its own sake, because its trustworthiness is not based on our trust; rather, we solely and completely depend on it.

The question of whether these two interests can ultimately be combined in an effective way is one of the fundamental problems of Niebuhr's thought, as he himself acknowledges.[54] In any case, the effort to combine them already draws Niebuhr away from interest in metaphysics.

What separates Niebuhr from Barth at this particular point is the problem of *analogy*.[55] Though Niebuhr would quite probably agree with Barth that the only relation between the "dissimilar entities" God and man exists by virtue of revelation in hiddenness, and that all speech about God finds its possibility here, he hesitates to draw such consequences from this insight as might lead to conceptual, "metaphysical" thinking about God and man. There are two reasons for this. In the first place, Barth's increasing concentration on the epistemological issues of faith and theology lead, in Niebuhr's view, to an overemphasis on the noetic side of faith and, correspondingly, on the importance of "right doctrine." The concept of analogy is an important factor here; it tends toward an isolation of the activity of knowledge in the self from the living context of selfhood in which it has its place. Niebuhr himself is conscious of this point when he suggests that it is his preoccupation with faith as trust and loyalty "which has led me farther away from the road that many other post-liberals—particularly Karl Barth—have taken."[56]

In the second place, Barth's concept of analogy is inseparably bound to his insistence that God's "Yes" to man is not merely "there" as a possibility but that *it has been spoken* in a decisive historical event and that consequently all our speech has to begin from there; in other words, it is based on an interpretation of the Christ-event which, in Niebuhr's view, abstracts from the predicament of historical believing men. To Niebuhr, the Christ-event indeed reveals that there is a "Yes" from God; but this is not to say that all our speech about God has to be curtailed and measured according to this event. Rather, the God who reveals himself in Christ is the One who calls us to ongoing responses to the source of being in our total life, to the never-ending road of conversion and transformation. To connect all our reflection on God—and consequently on "total life"!—exclusively to the Christ-event is to abstract from the central relation between revelation and faith.

Analogy, for Niebuhr, would be analogy of *concrete response.* Only such a concept would be capable of safeguarding the priority of revelation. For even Barth's theology of revelation cannot *as such* be said to be immune to the dangers against which it fights: "Faith in the God of Jesus Christ is' a rare thing, and faith in idols tends forever to disguise itself as Christian trust."[57] Immunity to idolatry is never a possession; it can be approached only in a constant movement of redirection of human faith toward its proper object. The basic error of men like Schleiermacher was that they desired to defend religion or faith itself, or to defend Christianity as the best religion.[58] They succumbed to the temptation of turning toward the faith of a particular group instead of sticking to the source of that faith. To begin with revelation, then, is to return again and again to the point of departure: faith in the One beyond the many—the One by whose action I am I, who calls me to be a truly accountable self in the many relations with my fellowmen. This is not a possibility we can define or localize in a particular group or in particular actions or doctrines; it has to be reenacted in every situation. It *can* be reenacted if the self allows itself to be inspired by signs of hope—hope for the goodness of God, for reconciliation.

Here lies, we believe, the third and most fundamental reason for Niebuhr's rejection of metaphysics. The center of gravity in this theology, the end of the human road, is not God or Christ or the good, but a transformation of things and relations. The question of whether there is faith in God is more significant than the question of whether God exists, not because faith directs its attention toward itself rather than to God, but because the rediscovery of the sovereign God and the redirection of faith toward the source of being is the road toward the healing of the ills of our world.

B. THE MORAL LIFE

1. The sovereign God and the moral life. After our description of the central concerns of Niebuhr and the lines of his theological development, and especially after our analysis of his triad of faith, it seems almost superfluous to point out the ethical implications of his thought. His whole theology is a "moral theology"; all his theological concerns are centered around this one *moral* concern: how it is possible to respond to the One beyond the many in my responses to the many

actions upon me. This concern is the guiding motif and determines the style of Niebuhr's ethics.

We have seen that *radical monotheism* for Niebuhr is essentially a *moral venture*; it is "the confidence that whatever is, is good, because it exists as one thing among the many which all have their origin and their being in the One—the principle of being which is also the principle of value." We can see that

> monotheism is less than radical if it makes a distinction between the principle of being and the principle of value, so that while all being is acknowledged as absolutely dependent for existence on the One, only some beings are valued as having worth for it, or if, speaking in religious language, the Creator and the God of grace are not identified.[1]

With these considerations the moral problem is set before us in a succinct way. Radical monotheism is reverence for being and universal loyalty is a moral venture: it simply does not *exist* when it is not incarnate in the total human life, when it is not expressed by the self in all its roles and relations. This in turn implies that the moral problem practically comprises all theology; the question "Who is my God?" for instance, is a question with which ethics deals, as long as it sets out to inquire how man can be so particularly loyal that he is true to the universal. Therefore, ethics of radical monotheism must immediately relate itself to Jesus Christ, for the possibility of making the new interpretation of all action upon us on the basis of the goodness of the One beyond the many is for us Christians related to this particular event.

The first indication of the significance of the Christ-event for this "new interpretation of all action upon us" is the way in which Jesus himself responds to what happens to and around him.

> What is the large pattern, what the inclusive action, to which Jesus responds with his evaluations and other actions when he encounters a natural event? He sees as others do that the sun shines on criminals, delinquents, hypocrites, honest men, good Samaritans, and VIPs without discrimination, that rains come down in equal proportions on the fields of the diligent and of the lazy. These phenomena have been for unbelief, from the beginning of time, signs of the operation of a universal order that is without justice, unconcerned with right and wrong conduct among men. But Jesus interprets the common phenomena in another way: here are the signs of cosmic generosity. The response to the weather so interpreted leads then also to a response to criminals and outcasts, who have not been cast out by the infinite Lord.[2]

In the last section of the second chapter we pointed out how reflection on moral existence from the Christian point of view is of central importance in Niebuhr's theology, though he himself conceives of this enterprise as *"prolegomena* to Christian ethics." For Niebuhr, there is such a thing as "Christian ethics proper": the analysis of the life of the Christian, who responds to being with the aid of the symbol of Jesus Christ. It seems that in this section, by observing the connection between radical monotheism as a moral venture and the event of Jesus Christ, we have entered the field of "Christian ethics proper." Yet a curious thing in Niebuhr's ethics is not only that most of it is taken up by *prolegomena*, but also that reflection on the life of the Christian leads back into the *prolegomena*. This is what consistent monotheism does; it cannot help but speak about the Christian as a man among men, rather than as a member of a special group. This leads us to observe that Christian ethics is not a discipline which derives its principles *only* and *exclusively* from the sources of Christianity, like scripture and tradition, though it uses these sources on the grounds that it orients itself to Jesus Christ.[3] The character and content of the Christ-symbol itself, and the situation of the Christian faith as one faith among the many, force Christian ethics into a permanent movement from the reflection on the Christian life back to reflection about moral life in general.

The Christian community connects the possibility of the "new interpretation" with Jesus Christ, but this does by no means imply that it has now become simple and accessible. On the contrary, in view of the fact that man is full of suspicion and afraid of the ultimate power of being, it seems almost impossible. In his response analysis Niebuhr points out that all reconciliation happens through reinterpretation of the actions upon us, and that reconciliation to *being itself* requires a revision of "our sense of the ultimate context." Our natural mind is suspicious and distrustful of God: all the broken structures of our common life can be traced back to that basic fact. Over against the faith that God is *one*, we posit our many gods, which are at strife with one another, so that we have not one self but many selves; over against the faith that God is *good*, we stick to our suspicion that he is a hostile and fateful power. Our natural attitude makes our ethics into *defense ethics* or *ethics of survival*, in which the ultimate reference is not being itself but our physical, spiritual, or social existence. It is defense ethics because it is based, consciously or unconsciously, on "an inescapable conviction about the death-dealing character of that total environment."[4] Defense ethics, though it often seems to operate with plausible value centers, actually takes place in a context of nothingness, of meaninglessness, when the center of value is something *less* than being itself.

How do we arrive at this insight in the human situation? First of all, through an increasing awareness of *"the twilight of the gods"* which pervades our culture. There are times when we simply cannot avoid seeing that "our gods are unable to save us from the ultimate frustration of meaningless existence."[5] But most of all we are given this insight when we speak and think *from the point of view of reconciliation.*[6] Man's "fundamental atheism" is revealed to us when we look at his situation with the aid of the symbol of Jesus Christ. From the same point of view we are enabled to see that a radical conversion, a radical change of heart, is necessary if man is to love being itself, to rejoice in the existence of whatever is. Such a conversion is more than a transition from distrust to acceptance, it is more than a substitution of universal principle for limited principle, though it is that too; most of all, it is the gift of *love* toward the Creator, and *love* toward whatever is.[7]

Such a radical conversion can happen in many ways, but it can never become a human possibility, so that the spirit of ethics which results from it can exist only in the relations of men to God and of God to men. All human attitudes, decisions, and actions which fall short of this relation, in which alone love to being is a possibility, are in some way or another *evil*. For *sin* means not taking God seriously as God, but replacing him by the lesser gods of our personal and social existence, and introducing value scales in which something less than being itself is the center. *Sin* is all that falls short of radical monotheism, that denies the oneness and goodness of God, the "law of being" (Maurice), and that ends, therefore, in distrust, rebellion, and defensiveness.

Only the point of view of reconciliation, the largest possible context, enables us to see the proportion of man's depravity and self-love, his lostness in the "many," his polytheism and pluralism of selfhood, his misinterpretation of the nature of god and the subsequent battle of the many "closed societies," the widespread "absolutizing of the relative" and the substitution of worship of images for worship of that which they image. For the revelation of the Absolute reveals the sin that lies in absolutized relativity, in our irresponsibleness in the larger world which includes us all though we are "responsive and responsible to each other in our closed societies."[8] This enumeration of possible illustrations of sin shows how all the themes of Niebuhr's thought enter into the picture when he speaks about the moral life. There is no adequate response in human life to anything at all until man has learned to follow the self-transcendence of all his causes and value centers.

> Patriotism is not enough; neither is the love of persons enough; reverence for life is not enough; love of humanity is not enough. For all such love is self-love though the self be made very large. And the love of self is bad, not because the self is bad, but because under the sovereignty of God or in the nature of things it is destructive of other selves and at the same time self-defeating.[9]

In Niebuhr's concept of sin two lines can be discerned though hardly distinguished. The first we shall call, for want of a better designation, the religious line. It discloses sin as essentially disloyalty to the One on whom man is absolutely dependent—a disloyalty which manifests itself in the choice of lower goods. Niebuhr uses the Augustinian pattern: sin is corruption of our love for the highest good, and our turning away to what is lower. In its emphasis on the corruption of the relation between God and the individual person, this line is mainly introspective and as such close to the views of men like Kant, Schleiermacher, and Kierkegaard. Next to this there is a second line, which draws attention to the *social* and *communal* character of sin. This is the nonintrospective view and it reminds us above all of the Social Gospel theologians. It is, in Niebuhr's thought, not merely secondary to or illustrative of the "religious line," but coextensive and equally essential. "The fundamental perversion of the movement of the self toward the transcendent One has issued and issues in the misdirection, the twisting, the mark-missing, of its manifold movements toward the finite."[1][9] A self that is not accountable and responsive in the community of being itself cannot avoid the corruption of responsive relations in any community in which it is involved.

It is in the "communal character of sin" that we find the major Social Gospel emphasis which continued to live in neoorthodoxy, although it is also in the doctrine of sin that the deepest disagreement becomes visible. The affinity between both Niebuhrs and men like Walter Rauschenbusch lies in the insight that sin can become incarnated in group structures (compare Reinhold Niebuhr's *Moral Man and Immoral Society)* and that the innocent suffer from what they have not brought about (compare Niebuhr's articles on the war). The disagreement lies in the question of the *source* of sin, which for both Niebuhrs is the corruption of human nature itself rather than certain institutions of the common life—a corruption which could not be counteracted by the "indirect means" of social betterment but only by the direct means of the confrontation of man with the radical implications of the judgment and grace of God.[1][1] At the same time, we should not overlook an important difference between the Niebuhr brothers themselves. Reinhold Niebuhr's reflections on sin begin with man's freedom, his brother's with man's dependence.

Both lines in Niebuhr's idea of sin join to underscore that it is a universal and inevitable phenomenon in human life; and that its scope, its pervasiveness, its dangerous disguises and its destructive effects can only come into view in the largest possible context, the universal community of being. Unless man is reconciled to God, and learns to respond to all actions upon him in this context, he will forever be involved in infinite evil.

2. Shaping the response. The use of the image of *responsibility* as a principle of moral philosophy has its distinct merits. It enables the moral philosopher to give a more complete description of the self-in-action and to place the response to *God* in the midst of the field of forces which constitutes the self's daily involvement. In *The Responsible Self,* as well as in his classroom lectures on Christian ethics, Niebuhr proposes this particular method of ethical reflection in connection with a discussion of the two major alternatives: *teleological* and *deontological* ethics. All three methods reveal a particular view of man as moral being. Teleological ethics is based on the image of the *homo faber:* "man the maker." It thinks chiefly in terms of ends. The question of what is right is subordinated to and made dependent upon the question of what is good for man, good for the achievement of his goals. Deontological ethics revolves around the *homo politicus:* "man the citizen." It subordinates the good to the right, and *laws* rather than ends constitute the center of its reflection.

As a third possibility Niebuhr proposes the *homo dialogicus:* "man the answerer." According to this pattern of thought—we have described it briefly in the analysis of the triad of faith—man's decisions are shaped by his responses to action upon him; and these responses in turn are shaped by his interpretation of what is happening. The question of response-ethics is not primarily "What end shall I seek to accomplish?" or "What law should I obey?" but rather "*What is going on?*" and "What is the fitting response in view of what is going on?"

This method allows for a unique combination of attention for the particular situation and recognition of the larger patterns to which the situation belongs. It does not abstract ethical reflection from daily involvement by using specific principles like "aim" or "requirement," and yet it does not forfeit the possibility of speaking about the human predicament in more general or generalized terms. Moreover, it avoids the one-sidedness of a purely formal concentration on the "moral vacuum" between God and the self, as well as of a search for concrete directives: both are varieties of "deontological ethics" (which is either entirely concrete or entirely abstract). In a sense, however, teleological and deontological thinking are always involved; even response ethics uses, at least presupposes, some awareness of "end" or "law." But it makes room for reflection on *nuances* and *dynamics* which are always present when the self seeks the realization of ends or obeys laws.

It is perhaps no exaggeration to say that one of the special attractions of response ethics for Niebuhr is that it provides a way to avoid the emphasis on *law,* with which the whole post-Kantian tradition in theology has had to cope, and which tends to obscure the relevance of those aspects of the Christian faith with which it is in tension. Especially those thinkers who are close to Romanticism and Idealism tend to consider legal thinking as an improper context for theology. Niebuhr's interest in minimizing the emphasis on law may be related to these tendencies, but in the last analysis it has a different source. By focusing on response ethics, Niebuhr diminishes the possibility of placing a moral principle *over against* the self in its existence, of positing something exterior to actuality which the self is called to follow or realize.

As we have said, there are enough teleological and deontological dynamics left in Niebuhr's ethics; we only have to remind ourselves of the self-transcending movement of causes and value centers, and of the evident necessity of making a conscious response to the One on whom all being depends. But it is significant that Niebuhr shifts the attention from formal principles to concrete values, from *prescriptive* to *descriptive* ethics, from end- or future-directedness to concentration on the situation in which the self exists; and that he connects this with a shift of attention to the action *upon* the self, to the interpretation of what the self *undergoes* and by which it is *limited* and *threatened*. We have seen how this "passivity" of the self is closely connected to and conditioned by an Edwardean emphasis on God's sovereignty.

For the ethical problem, for Niebuhr, is not so much how the self shall become *agent* of the will of God as how the self shall become *patient* of the will of God.[12] *The will of God is what he does, not what he requires,* though the latter is implied in the former. And the actions of the self are right when they are responses to what God does, to God's action in all action. The task is to discern that action, to articulate it, to interpret with it all that happens, and to act accordingly.

The process of learning to become the patient of the will of God, "the central work of revising our mythology of death into a history of life,"[13] is never completed in a lifetime; *metanoia* is not an assignment of which the self can ever be discharged. For to be a self is to be involved in self-defense. Perhaps we can only speak of the appearance of evangelical freedom in terms of "lightning flashes." In general "faith is never so complete that it is not accompanied by self-defensiveness."[14] Therefore, if the sovereignty of God is to be taken seriously, and if we are allowed to see the self-defending self as ultimately included in a universe of faithfulness, we cannot conceive of the self's process of *metanoia* without justification by grace. The relation of the self to God, as Schleiermacher taught, must be considered under the viewpoint of the contrast between sin and grace. Under this viewpoint, radical faith and its incarnation in total life point to *hope* more than to *achievement*.[15]

In previous chapters we have had several occasions to indicate and illustrate the fact that Niebuhr's theology is *a theology of hope. Hope* is the ultimate issue in the debate between the Niebuhr brothers in 1932. Here, over against Reinhold Niebuhr's assertion that there can be no absolute in history, Niebuhr insists that "history is not a perennial tragedy but a road to fulfillment and that fulfillment requires the tragic outcome of every self-assertion, for it is a fulfillment which can only be designated as 'love.' "[16] We also saw how Niebuhr's development toward *radical monotheism*, toward the emphasis on the One beyond the many *in* the many, could only be accompanied by an equally radical emphasis on hope, which remains the only answer to the question of the possibility of faith. In the analysis of the triad of faith in Niebuhr's thought we drew attention to the self-transcendence, the self-widening, of the patterns in which the self exists, and especially to the enlargement of the temporal contexts of recollection and expectation—a movement which can be completed only in *hope*. Now we can see the significance of all this for the moral life.

Hope necessarily exists in a temporal pattern; but man does not hope for the future revelation of something new or unknown. The point of eschatology is that the divine rule in the *present* will become manifest.[17] It is the goodness of God in and beyond that which happens *now* that is a matter of hope. Without hope there can be no genuine movement of the self toward the universal. Hope is the only way in which faith and love can be present. "In a sense, hope is the form which the love of God takes on the part of man in time who loves the God who is not yet manifest, the God who is the Father of Jesus Christ, God who is love."[18] Hope is the anticipated attainment of faith and love, "as when the hopeful heir of immeasurable wealth is lavishly generous on a meager allowance." *As such it affects the present,* the decisions and actions of the self here and now.

When we undertake to reflect on the one action which encounters us in all action upon us, we must begin with the assertion that it is indeed *one* action which encounters us. When we learn to speak of God as Creator, Governor, and Redeemer, we do not mean three different actions of one God, but three ways in which we experience and interpret the one divine action. More precisely we mean three different categories or qualities of events and actions, and we endeavor to find consistent action and presence of the one God in all three. Consistent monotheism implies that the One we have learned to address as the first person on certain occasions, is the first person on *all* occasions. This does not mean that our understanding of God's action is complete after one or several events, but rather that each new event contributes to and particularizes this understanding if we begin with the monotheistic assertion that God *is* active in all things and that the one divine action is ultimately trustworthy. Only on this basis can we distinguish between *creative, ordering*, and *redeeming* action of God, and treat the possibilities of response accordingly.

To respond to God the *Creator* is to recognize and accept the goodness of all being. Reconciliation with the Creator is manifested, acted out as it were, in the self's attitude to whatever is. This response goes farther than acceptance; it includes affirmation, understanding, and cultivation. As we have made clear, the divine creative action in the being that surrounds us, never becomes institutionalized in the sense that it coincides with patterns and orders which we encounter in being. The position of the self in the midst of all action upon him is so unstable, so much dependent on permanent *metanoia*, that localization of divine action in certain orders would inevitably lead to the absolutizing of the relative. Such localization would tend to ignore that a dynamic relation of faith between the self and God is fundamental to the response to being, and that only this can provide and renew the possibility of overcoming tendencies to seek the principle of value in something less than being itself.

Response to the *ordering* or *governing* action of God is trustful response to actions and events in which the self experiences limitation, ordering, and judgment. Beings meet their limits in relation with other beings. In this limitation the self is threatened with "the loss of its place in the order of being," for in it *God* ultimately asserts his sovereignty and power. Our response must be based on the faith that this limiting action is still the action of the one God—that in the end "we are not up against animosity but grace." In this faith the self knows itself to be included in the divine government. Its response has two aspects: self-denial (the acceptance of self in the context of the divine government) and the ordering and restraining action toward others (the acceptance of others in the same context).

Self-denial is not the hatred or the contempt of self, though this may be included. Jonathan Edwards, in his *Religious Affections*, distinguishes between legal and evangelical humiliation: the latter is not primarily the effort to see oneself as little and meaningless in view of God's greatness and majesty, but rather the *voluntary* and *willful* denouncing of oneself on the basis of a discovery of *God's holy beauty* and a consequent change of inclination.[19] This typically Edwardean distinction is somewhat present in Niebuhr when he emphasizes that self-denial means the placing of the self in the context of an ordered community of which the ordering God is the center, and in which the self's place is determined by its *love for this God*.

Niebuhr takes great pains to underscore that the restraining and ordering of *others* should take place in the same context. When we restrain others (in war, or in the carrying out of social justice) we do not do this on the basis of the goodness of ourselves and the badness of the others, but on the basis of acceptance of others in the community of created and ordered being. This means, concretely, that we use our power on behalf of the restrained neighbor, that we accept restraint upon ourselves, that we interpret our laws as inclusively as possible, and that we continue our responsibility toward the restrained other, as long as all of us are included in the same community of universal ordering. Though we may not be able to attain the actual realization of this community, our hope drives us to act on the basis of its reality.

The serious attention Niebuhr gives to this particular part of ethics reflects how his thought has been shaped by the experience of war and by the question of participation or nonparticipation. We believe that his answers, though less concrete than his brother's, are theologically more profound. Consistent monotheism drives him to accept the possibility of restraining *and* of being restrained, because it drives him to relativize and transcend all systems of judgment which have a finite center, on the basis of the faith that history is the road to fulfillment rather than the scene of perennial tragedy.

Response to the *redeeming* action of God, finally, is included in the other responses. For redemption "means the substitution of the assurance of eternal life for the certainty of death,"[20] and thus "appears as the *liberty* to interpret in trust all which happens as contained within an intention and a total activity that includes death within the domain of life, that destroys only to reestablish and renew."[21] Response to the redeeming action is the liberty to act *at all*, as creative and ordering selves. For it is a liberty which knows of reconciliation of the irreconciled world; it knows of a history in which there is atonement, the suffering of the innocent for the guilty. Of course, for the Christian this knowledge is connected with a particular history and a particular community; but as such it contains a reference to all men and all being. It contains the assurance that we can speak of God as *one* and *good*, and that our efforts to respond to the action of this sovereign God in our lives will be crowned with grace and fulfillment.

3. The dethronement of the gods. The response to the one divine action does not take the form of certain specific attitudes which have their place *among* other attitudes. It does that *too*, in the "primarily religious response," but generally the response to God will be found in the whole of life, and thus "as a qualifying element in all interpretations and reactions to the movements of that finite world of particular beings in which the I is involved."[22] Therefore, consistent monotheistic response means that "all my relative evaluations will be subjected to *the continuing and great correction.*"[23] For time and again the interpretation of the self of "what is going on" will be influenced and disturbed by smaller schemes of value; time and again the One *beyond* the many will be confused with one *of* the many; time and again the smaller gods will have to be dethroned, the world of the self will have to be broken open toward universal being.

Christian ethics is ethics of *universal responsibility*. As such it is not unique, though it strikes the theme of strife between universal society and closed societies in a unique way. Ultimately, it is the theme that counts, not the way in which it is struck; therefore, Christian ethics is allied with the ethics of Judaism and Stoicism in the battle against all ego- and group-centered styles of life. As such it also fights these styles in Christianity itself, though they may be disguised as genuinely Christian. For it knows that universalist protests against closed societies, thought patterns, and styles of life are justified even if they are not raised in the name of Christ or Christianity. Thus Christianity itself is under constant criticism on the basis of radically monotheistic faith, even though the Christian cannot separate this faith from his faith in Christ.

Against this background we must understand Niebuhr's book *Christ and Culture*, his famous typology of Christian attitudes toward culture. In this book "Christ" and "culture" are poles between which all concrete responses, made to the environing world on the basis of Christian faith, move and have their place: *"Christianity*, whether defined as church, creed, ethics, or movement of thought, *itself moves between the poles of Christ and culture."*[24] The types which Niebuhr discusses are certain abstractions from the many diverse ways in which the Christian sees and experiences the relation between his faith and his culture and how he approaches his daily involvements on the basis of his faith. It is true that the book operates with a rather comprehensive and impersonal concept of culture which in Niebuhr's later works, is considerably altered in the direction of complex personal relation and involvement. Nevertheless, it clearly shows his intentions.

Niebuhr distinguishes five types, in which the combination of "Christ" and "culture" is respectively antithetical, coextensive, complementary, paradoxical, and transforming. The last three are the more complex types, and as such they clearly have Niebuhr's preference. His preference increases as the treatment of the last three types progresses. Niebuhr's own view is reflected, it seems, in both the paradox type and the transformation type, but especially in the latter. This cannot surprise us after we have had occasion to discover his concern for goals and fulfillment *in history*, his awareness of the sinfulness of man, and his emphasis on the radical sovereignty of the one God who creates, governs, and redeems. Yet the "transformationist position" is not as such the thesis of the book; it is not the answer Niebuhr offers to the question of

Christ and Culture. This answer—if we can speak at all of an answer—is given in his final chapter, where the transformationist stand is taken so consistently that hardly any specific "position" is left. It is stated plainly that there is no solution except the solution which is expressed and reexpressed in particular decisions. No theoretical abstraction from daily involvement can give the final answer: transformation is permanent redirection in our relative situations.

Thus, if we try to answer the question of how the incarnation of radical monotheism as principle of universalist ethics takes place, we can say no more than this: it can become incarnated only as transforming, correcting, and redirecting power. About the responses to divine action we can speak positively; about the way in which these affect the daily involvement of the self we can apparently only speak negatively. Radical monotheism is in constant conflict with those forms in which human life is usually organized. Niebuhr calls these forms *polytheism* and *henotheism.*[25]

Polytheism is the pluralism of the objects of devotion, the coexistence of many gods to which the self pays loyal tribute in "a kind of successive polygamy." In polytheism, human life revolves around a kind of pantheon that is sometimes full of inner strife—the pluralism of self and society—sometimes in uneasy harmony. Uneasy it will be, for "each god in turn requires a certain absolute devotion and the denial of the claims of the other gods."[26]

Henotheism is the more dangerous of the two. For this type of faith chooses one of the many objects of devotion and turns it into the *only* one. This is social faith, the center of the *closed society.* It is dangerous, especially because it so easily disguises itself as monotheism. Many forms of faith which are practically built around reverence for *life* or for *mankind* are really forms of henotheism because they stop short of being itself.

In this sense *humanism* "remains a kind of henotheism"[27] insofar as it is the religion of humanity. However, its legitimacy is obvious when we see it as a movement of protest against forms of henotheistic faith—especially in religion—that stop short of humanity.[28] Furthermore, humanism very often is much *more* than "the religion of humanity": it "rarely exists in separation from a reverence for life and a reverence for being that point to the presence in it of more than loyalty to mankind."[29]

It should be sufficiently clear by now that Niebuhr's most vigorous attack on henotheism is directed toward the most widely present disguises of it: the forms of henotheism in Christianity itself. In this attack Niebuhr merely points to the necessity of the self-transforming movement of monotheism, to the "faith above faith" which is present as continuous corrector. With the aid of this principle we are able to see how the deification of *Christ* or the *scriptures* can develop into forms of henotheism and social faith, which prevent the correction to which they themselves testify.[30] For these unique temptations of church and Christianity we should be on our guard, not because we ought to relativize our particular faith on the grounds of a brotherhood of all men, but because our particular faith directs us to the source of being in whose sight all being has value. No closed society can be an effective witness of a faith which speaks of reconciliation to the Creator.

Chapter 4
The Revelation of God in Christ

A. THE POSSIBILITY OF HISTORICAL REVELATION

1. **The problem of history.** That history is a problem is a commonplace observation in twentieth-century theology. The problem itself is, of course, as old as man's consciousness of himself as a historical being, entangled in a time process with some hidden meaning or goal. But it became more puzzling as the conception of *universal* history made its entrance and the fixed schemes of divine planning—the original frame of this conception—were secularized. Since the rise of the *science* of history, and the impact of Lessing's famous dictum about accidental facts and universal truth, the problem claims at least a chapter in all philosophy and in all *prolegomena* to theology.

Nevertheless, the problem of history in our days is a more explicit theme in theology and philosophy than ever before. Two factors contribute to this state of affairs: in the first place, the insight that man's being and thinking are completely determined by the historicity of all things; and second, the special nature we have learned to attribute to *historical reason.* This second point calls our attention to the gradual overcoming of the "naturalizing of history," the treatment of historical facts as analogous to facts of nature. The lines from Dilthey to Heidegger and Collingwood and from Kant to Rudolf Bultmann illustrate this development.

Both factors, taken together, force us to see that human nature can no longer be regarded as standing over against history as it stands over against nature, that it is not something that—to speak with Collingwood —"stays put" in its activity of knowing.[1] History begins with our own historicity; historical knowledge is primarily self-realization of the knower, who in his own history encounters and reenacts the history of his "objects." "Facts" are abstractions from this process.

Niebuhr's approach to the problem of history is from the start determined by the development indicated. It begins with a recognition of the thorough historicity of the self, the determination of all that the self is by the conditions in which it arises.

For men like Bultmann such a view of the historical self would be related to the abandonment of the question of *meaning* in history.[2] In Niebuhr's position, however, it is only a starting point. It serves to bring out the question of *meaning* with more earnestness. The historicity of the self threatens to dissolve all its strongholds of meaning; the efforts to recapture these, the searches of faith for a genuinely trustworthy object, are themselves caught in a process of passing. But this does not lead to abandonment of the question of meaning. Niebuhr's relativism is not so consistent as to erase all traces of the (idealist) search for sensibility in totality.

The realization of selfhood in the midst of determination and conditioning is not merely a matter of deciding to *be* a self; it is a problem of *faith*. A self is a self when it has learned to entrust itself to the total system in and beyond the seemingly irrational powers it encounters. The meaning of history is grasped in the historical process of faithful interpretation and response. Niebuhr thus combines an emphasis on complete external conditioning with an emphasis on the significance and necessity of internal faith attitudes, without abandoning one for the other. In other words, he modifies Kant by pointing out that reason is historically conditioned in all its activity, but he keeps insisting that there are two ways of looking at history.[3] Insight in this combination of emphases is indispensable for the understanding of Niebuhr's distinction between internal and external history.

The problem of history arises for Niebuhr in the context of his major theological concerns. There are two recurring points at which we specifically encounter it. The first is the relation of the particular insights of the *Christian community* to other points of view and to a general human understanding of meaning in history. The second is the problem of the self over against the total historical reality and of its search for wholeness and direction in it. Analogous to these two points we can indicate two more: the relation between the truth which I see from my standpoint, in my—historically developed and conditioned—faith, and "objective," communicable, verifiable truth; and the problem of the intelligibility of history *as such*. Niebuhr's treatment of the problems of history and Christology must be understood against the background of these concerns.

Several aspects of the problem of history in Niebuhr's theology have already been indicated in the first three chapters of our study. In chapter 1 we became acquainted with the many sources of Niebuhr's historical relativism. The insight that all knowledge is conditioned by the standpoint of the knower, that our thought is not eternal and transcendent, that the images in our mind are not universal, though we speak and think about the eternal and the universal,[4] is an axiom for Niebuhr; it is connected with influences from American sources, from Royce and from Troeltsch, but also with an attraction to Tillich's "beliefful realism" with its emphasis on the significance of the present moment. An insistence on the ever-present possibility of a relation with meaning and direction of the whole—his association of historical and religious relativism—keeps Niebuhr at a distance from the dangers of skepticism and solipsism, and enables him to regard the recognition of relativity as the prelude to *faithful critical work.*[5]

In chapter 2 we saw how faith in the greatness and sovereignty of God is, for Niebuhr, the only valid framework for historical relativism. The interpretation of being itself by relative beings is constantly subjected to the dangers of distortion and "absolutizing of the relative"; this interpretation can take place, therefore, only in the form of constant transformation and *metanoia,* of which faith as *trust* in being itself is the major ingredient. This theme is of central importance in *The Kingdom of God in America:* petrifaction of the permanent movement means loss of the possibility to "make room" for the Absolute in history.

In chapter 3 we analyzed the way in which the problem of history arises from the timefulness of the self and of the communal interpretations. Not only is man in time, but time is in man: man's search for meaning and goals is assigned to him by the fact that he is in history "as the fish in water."[6]

It should be clear that for Niebuhr the problems of history and of Christology are inseparable. For not only is Jesus Christ the decisive issue between the particular insights of the Christian community and other communities: the problem of meaning in history, grasped in faith at a particular point of history, is as such a christological problem, at least in a formal sense.

Only after the premise that Niebuhr's view of history is part and parcel of his particular theological interests can we proceed to establish that it is Ernst Troeltsch who bequeathed to Niebuhr the problems of history which haunted nineteenth-century theology in Germany. We observed that Niebuhr's permanent attraction to Troeltsch has significant consequences for the structure of his thought, but that at the same time his correction of Troeltsch is fundamental and radical. For in spite of all his indebtedness to Troeltsch, Niebuhr remains devoted to the effort to see history as a field of divine action and to resist all devaluation of the visible historical development. We saw how this effort is related to his most serious concerns. It leads him to a basically different understanding of history and man-in-history, which, nevertheless, does not fall back behind Troeltsch's achievements.

Troeltsch's thought gives evidence of particular difficulties in connection with the rise and emancipation of historical science. The object of this science, the "historical fact," gradually received such independent authority that all kinds of Hegelian interpretations of the historical development became questionable. There was only one way left to combine "accidental fact" and "eternal truth"; namely, in the individual experience of absolute validity. This experience could not receive expression save in ways mediated and conditioned through history, but it had its own independent ground in the *religious a priori*: the venture to regard a particular historical situation as a manifestation of the divine Spirit. In other words, the split between objective knowledge and subjective interpretation—which had threatened the philosophical development ever since Kant—was practically complete. It is, says Troeltsch, a *delusion* to think that the Absolute can be present at one point in history.

Central to Niebuhr's correction of Troeltsch is the combination of historical relativism and *theological* or *theocentric* relativism.[7] We can describe and summarize its effects on the understanding of history in three points.

First of all, monotheism leads to a more radical and more consistent relativism. It destroys all the strongholds that still seem to be present in Troeltsch's relativism: the "evident rational patterns" which stand between the individual and a complete skepticism. These cannot serve to illustrate and defend the presence of divine action and planning in history. The one God is active in all events alike, as judge (his apparent absence) *and* as redeemer (his transforming and renewing presence). The first thing that must be said about the relation between observation and knowledge on the one hand, and certitude of faith on the other hand—stronger and more radical than Troeltsch put it—is that it is *paradoxical.*

Troeltsch admits, of course, the contrast between certitude of faith and scientific certainty: the reason why *faith* can never be defended on the basis of historical reality. Yet the decision of faith is, for Troeltsch, a provisional actualization of a truth which will become evident but is already indicated in the patterns of historical development. The tension between pluralism and monism is solved metaphysically; it is not of a paradoxical nature, as in Niebuhr. Niebuhr insists that the only center in the restlessness of total relativism is *beyond the many.*

At this point Niebuhr's correction of Troeltsch originates partly, as we observed above, in the divergence between American nonreflective anthropocentricism—and faith in an accountable Providence—and the German academic problem of faith over against knowledge. But it also clearly springs from Niebuhr's correction of the American anthropocentric and "providentialist" tradition *itself*—a correction which is accomplished with the aid of the crisis motif, especially as it appears in the early Barth.

But, in the second place, paradox is not the last word; monotheistic correction implies more. We noticed how Niebuhr, much more than Troeltsch, occupies himself with the historicity and timefulness of the individual *self*, and how the relativities of history include for him the relativity and conditionedness of the self in all its activities, *including its faith*. The investigations of George Herbert Mead enable Niebuhr to give concrete content to his conception of the social and historical mediation of all knowledge and faith. Even the act of believing itself cannot be exempt from external investigation and explanation. This extension of analysis to all the patterns in which the self lives, does not imply the abandonment of all meaning and all absolute value. On the contrary, it is demanded by a truly monotheistic search for meaning.

The monotheistic correction implies, in the third place, that the historicity and timefulness of the self are radicalized in its *subjectivity*. The self is always and in every situation a concerned subject, dedicated to gods, trusting and distrusting. The self is such in all its actions; in all its encounters with the circumambient world *some* response to the Absolute is involved, not as a special religious act of faith, but in and through all other responses. All its relations of valuation are accompanied by an attitude to the one center of value beyond the many. All its knowledge is related to some internal pattern of faith. At this point the problem of history appears for Niebuhr as the problem of conflicting patterns and conflicting loyalties; the absolutizing of one particular pattern is the source of all evil. This leads a step beyond Troeltsch.

The three elements in Niebuhr's correction of Troeltsch come together at the point of his insistence on radical transformation—a point where Troeltsch speaks of the inevitability of compromise. Crucial elements of Troeltsch's problem—the value in the individual event and the possibility of adequate response—are thus maintained in a new dynamic framework. Consistent monotheism demands that no pattern in history is—even provisionally—identified with divine action, that all things are radically relativized, that we begin the never-ending "pilgrim's progress" of acknowledging the One beyond the many in our attitudes of faith. In other words, *history and faith are present together in an inescapable and permanent duality*, in a movement of continuous dialogue and readjustment. All our encounters with historical reality are inescapably *also* encounters of faith. But if the movement of this duality is petrified in particular institutions, in particular "syntheses of faith" (Troeltsch), we have established a closed society, we have absolutized the relative, and can no longer be called radical *mono*theists. Our faith, the faith of finite historical beings who need to be reconciled and converted to being, may always be fragmentary[8]—it indicates that the historical development is not without structure and meaning, that the sovereign God is truly *in history*.

Niebuhr's insistence on this permanent duality illustrates his refusal to abandon or smooth over consistent historical relativism, and to confine all *meaning* in history to internal acts of faith. He thus maintains Troeltsch's consistency over against Bultmann and his followers who seek refuge in the famous distinction between *Historie* and *Geschichte*. Niebuhr does not reject Bultmann's intentions; for him, too, the *meaning* of history cannot be established and verified externally but requires a decision of faith. But this nonverifiability does not itself become the principle of his historical method, as is the case with Bultmann. Niebuhr's thought is arrested, it seems, at the point where the historical self confronts the possibility of meaning in the circumambient reality. It is not enough to say that "meaning" lies in a free grasp of future possibilities, for this does not answer the question of the ultimate nature of the power that acts upon me. This nature can never be presented to us unequivocally in any particular occurrence, but we do cope with it in all particular occurrences.

The future is intended in my present responses (Mead); but the intricate threads and patterns of which this intention is part, point to a structure, a center of meaning, in history itself, which takes revenge for all my efforts to ignore or to fight it, and to which I must learn to entrust and commit myself. My historicity, and my encounter of historical reality, is always "of one piece": the two attitudes toward history may be distinct, but they cannot be separated.

2. Revelation and the duality of internal and external history. When we begin to explore and analyze Niebuhr's distinction between internal and external history, we must again remind ourselves that Niebuhr treats the problem of history as the problem of revelation, and, more particularly, that his reasoning about history begins on the basis of the given revelation in Jesus Christ. He does not begin with a general or neutral concept of history, and he does not inquire into the possibility of revelation on the basis of such a concept. He begins with the presence of a Christian community and a Christian witness, and proceeds to analyze how this witness looks at history and is present in history.

The two problems which we distinguished in the preceding section—the relation of the Christian community to other communities, and the historical self-searching for meaning and intelligibility; or the relation of particular and personal truth to objective verifiable truth, and the intelligibility of history as such—remain intertwined. This is evident when one looks at the structure of *The Meaning of Revelation*. In this book an exposition of the way in which Christians speak about their history, tell the story of their lives, precedes the distinction between "history lived" and "history seen" (chapter 2). Only the character of the Christian witness itself, *not* the distinction between internal and external history, leads us to see that scriptural records and natural events must be interpreted through our own personal history and faith if they are to have any meaning, and that Christian faith and *impersonal, unhistorical thinking* are incompatible. The distinction between internal and external history serves, as it were, to illustrate and explicate this point.

The distinction itself points to two ways of looking at history: external observation and personal participation. We speak here not of different events but of different *perspectives, aspects*, or *contexts*,[9] their difference being roughly similar to that between *things* and *selves*. It is internal history which is the realm of faith and the *locus* of revelation. For *faith* is the major constituent of selfhood, and *selves* do not appear in external history. "Inner history and inner faith belong together, as the existence of self and an object of devotion for the sake of which the self lives are inseparable."[10]

Inquiring farther into the way in which Niebuhr deals with the self's activities of knowing and believing in this duality of internal and external history, we are directed to the concept of *imagination*, a word which crossed our path in the analysis of the triad of faith. Imagination is the tool with which reality is made intelligible; it integrates successive impressions into a unified picture and it develops central images, with the aid of which new encounters receive their place in our schemes of unity and meaning. Niebuhr stresses that man is a symbol-making creature, that the development of images is essential for him. In the communal development of knowledge and language certain master images play their roles, often unacknowledged yet always influential, as for instance the images of the *machine* or of the *mathematical system*—often used and proclaimed as images of being itself.[11] Images accompany human knowledge from its earliest stages, and in their more developed form serve as foci of communication and carriers of meaning for certain communities. Only after the premise that *all* knowledge takes place in communities of selves can we proceed to distinguish between "internal" and "external."

Even in the observation of "facts" and "things" the idea of a universal community is at least "eschatologically" present, as in Josiah Royce. We can never speak of externality as the indestructible core of objectivity, and of internality as the addition of subjective interpretations. Rather, external observation implies a *detachment* from direct personal participation, for the sake of a communication which points to universality; and at the same time, internal history means much more than "subjectivity" for it speaks of *communal* verifiability. That the distinction must be made is an inescapable lesson from all critical philosophy,[12] but it is essential that we do not lose sight of the intimate connection between what is distinguished. Thus, the difference between the external observer and the internal participant does not exclude that all knowledge is basically participation. External observation represents a shift in emphasis, a detachment from participation; no one is *merely* an impartial spectator, though impartial spectatorship is recognized and postulated as necessary from the point of view of one's own historicity and one's own communal participation.

The relativity of the distinction between external and internal history which we seek to emphasize here, stems from the nature of historical reason. There is no historical knowledge save through personal reenactment—external knowledge of "facts" is an abstraction from this, for the sake of a more universal or "scientific" communication. We may have to face the *fait accompli* that there are two ways to do history; but they are both part of the dynamic processes of selfhood in community, and they find their unity in the self which knows and relives history as a historical being.

Both internally and externally there is, therefore, a permanent and necessary cooperation of reason and imagination. External images create patterns in which facts are brought together in reasonable wholes— patterns which are applied to and verified by subsequent observation. Internal images create intelligibility of meaning and direction; but here, too, the work of reason is indispensable. Niebuhr accepts, in other words, the Kantian separation of pure and practical reason (roughly similar to the external-internal distinction), but he never tires of emphasizing the unity of the self in all activities of reason: "The separation has often led us to ignore the practical or ethical elements in our knowing as well as the observing, interpreting elements in our doing."[13] In the distinction of internal and external history the unity of the self is presupposed, and its realization in the permanent duality between internal and external history is, therefore, a continuous assignment. But it is an impossible assignment without a *revelation* and a *faith* in which reconciliation to being and thus unity of self becomes visible as a possibility.

Revelation is the gift of an image with which a self, or a community of selves, makes sense out of history. It is the gift of an image which enables the reasoning heart to understand the happenings in which it is involved. In this sense the revelatory image is *revelatory because it is rational*[14] and because it posits itself as adequate over against all inadequate images with which selves keep trying to illuminate their lives. Niebuhr retains a sense of the powers of "natural reason" here, though natural reason never exists in its pure form and, furthermore, gives permanent evidence of its profound corruption. The gift of the revelatory image takes place, for the Christian community, in the event of Jesus Christ. This event opens up the possibility of trust in being itself, a trustful attitude toward *all* action upon us, and truly unified selfhood; it is therefore the one adequate image which unmasks all other imagination as *evil*. Most evil images center around the interest of selves; they magnify the glory of man and in their defensiveness lead to destruction.[15] The revelatory image enables us to see how the evil images petrify history into a particular state of affairs, how they break the movement of *metanoia* in rigid, defensive "closed societies." The heart that reasons with the image of revelation, however, keeps discovering "the possibility of the resurrection of a new and other self, of a new community, a reborn remnant."[16]

When we keep in mind that the problem of history in Niebuhr's thinking is also—perhaps mainly?—the problem of the particular Christian point of view in relation to other points of view, and that in *The Meaning of Revelation* the distinction internal-external tends to coincide with the distinction between the Christian community and other communities, we can understand how the question of meaning in history can be treated as the question of the presence and the effects of the *revelatory image*. In other words, the problem of history is linked to the problem of conversion, of accepting all events as fitting in the divine plan.

One immediately thinks of Jonathan Edwards' "new sense of the heart" at this point; and indeed, there are striking similarities between Edwards' thought and Niebuhr's reflections on the reasoning and the imagination of the heart. Edwards distinguishes between a mere theoretical understanding of things and a spiritual understanding, which is inspired by the glory and beauty of God. All discerning and knowledge of the interrelatedness, meaning, and beauty of being flows from the new sense of the heart, Edwards emphasizes in the treatise on *Religious Affections*. The world becomes comprehensible and beautiful when we are enabled to see "the divinity of Divinity." And, as Niebuhr speaks of evil imaginations, Edwards speaks of "imagination or phantasy" as "that wherein are formed all those delusions of Satan, which those are carried away with, who are under the influence of *false* religion, and *counterfeit* graces and affections."[17]

It is obvious that for Niebuhr the compatibility of reason and revelation is hardly a problem. Without the revelatory image the work of the reasoning heart ends in error and destruction; but without reason revelation illuminates only itself.[18] Only through reasoning with revelation can we bring intelligibility in history: in the sufferings (compare the articles on the war) and joys, in the sins and reconciliations present in the lives of men. Reason is illuminated by revelation. This illumination enables us not only to describe the significance of the revelatory event in conceptual terms, but especially to find guidance in what we are now doing. Therefore, the issue does not lie between reason and revelation, but rather between reasoning in faith and reasoning in unfaith or in some other faith.

The work of the reasoning heart continues; in this sense revelation may be called *progressive*. This "progressiveness" does not imply that new events will yield new revelatory images. Rather, our revelatory image clarifies subsequent events and is itself clarified by them. Its meaning is not dependent on the events; but without a continuing interpretation through each new event it remains forever hidden, or it is confined to a few events, or to a particular community *only*. Character and content of the revelation in Jesus Christ warrant its continuing critical function in this respect: "It requires of those to whom it has come that they begin the never-ending pilgrim's progress of the reasoning Christian heart."[19]

From here we can understand why the duality between internal and external history is necessary. If there is no fruitful interaction between the two, the distinction between objective and subjective truth stagnates, and with this the borderlines of the many closed societies would receive eternal sanction. Precisely because trust in *being* is the issue of Christian revelation, there is duality of internal and external history.

The relations between internal and external history are concentrated on four points.[20] There is, in the first place, the awareness of external accounts of our personal and communal history, including the revelatory event of Jesus Christ. These accounts are not to be ignored or depreciated on the basis of our own standpoint, but they must be internalized as a form of divine judgment. Second, there is such a thing as *faithful external history*, the effort to regard all events in world history and in church history as workings of the divine will. Unity in history must be sought, though we are forever confined to a double and partial knowledge of events. Revelation takes place in our history, but this does not mean that it is the presence of revelation which separates our community from others. Third, the Christian community engages in the effort to see itself "from the outside"; that is, *with the eyes of God*. This remains an attempt, but it is nevertheless required by revelation itself. It is a way in which the community keeps reaching out to a point where the duality between internal and external history is transcended. This point is never reached, but the effort keeps the duality in process. Finally, there can be no internal history save through external er odiment. Faith does not exist unless it is incarnated in particular structures which can be observed and analyzed, though its certainty is not dependent on these analyses.

The unity which is the presupposition and goal of the duality is the unity of the self, and this unity of the self is dependent on an adequate and successful relation of internal and external history. A self cannot really be one self until it faces the ground and origin of its being: "I am one in my manyness in myself and so responsible as self, as I face the one action in the actions of the many upon me."[21] Now we see that this is not only a religious necessity but that it is required by the revelation of the trustworthiness of God in internal history, by the revelatory image which makes the duality of internal and external history an inescapable and hopeful *duty*. Only through revelation can I embark on the journey toward the unity of the self.

The road of this duality leads, as we have seen, in the direction of something like universal internality, a universal community of interpretation. Yet precisely because of this, external history has its own genuine significance. External history is not less true or less important than internal history, for it points to *the way things are in the eyes of God*. Between the lines of Niebuhr's book *The Meaning of Revelation* there is a strong bias for external history. Internal images are inescapable, and a vision of the coherence of all events is given only in the struggle of permanent duality, but what is ultimately to be realized—the universal community of interpretation—is just as much intended in external history, because *God is one*. This is the (theological) reason why internal views must be checked by external accounts.[22] The eschatological tension in the duality of internal and external history—Niebuhr compares it to the paradox of Chalcedonian Christology[23]—is given with the unity of God himself. We will observe in the section on the Trinity how for Niebuhr the problems of Christology and history are dominated by and subsumed in the problem of the unity of God. It is this unity which prevents the duality of the two histories from becoming a destructive stalemate. Without a living duality our faith becomes a "unitarianism of the Son," and then we have denied the Spirit which proceeds from the Father also.

In the remainder of this section we must analyze briefly how Niebuhr's insights about historical knowledge and faith apply to the Christ-event itself. For the Christian community appeals to a particular *event* when it speaks of revelation. The revelatory image is not an arbitrary miraculous gift; it is connected with a particular man in our history. A full treatment of Niebuhr's Christology will appear in the second half of this chapter; in this context we must be content with a few indications.

We can understand Niebuhr's warning that revelation cannot be localized in external history, as is done by Fundamentalism. "For such history, abstracting from human selves, must also abstract events from the divine self; and furthermore, while it may furnish motives for belief in the occurrence of certain happenings, it does not invite trust in a living God."[24] And yet revelation is connected to the historical event of Jesus Christ. This event is *remembered* by the community as unique and indispensable. We have seen how internal and external history must be distinguished with regard to Jesus Christ. We have seen also how the duality of internal and external history is an inescapable duty—and this, too, applies to Jesus Christ. Externally, Jesus is a man among men. We cannot regard this external account as defective; we cannot even regard it as only half the truth. Jesus Christ is not *also* a man, or *first* a man; rather, he is *ultimately*, *eschatologically*, a man like us. In God's view there is no such thing as a unique event. Only because of the inescapable duality of internal and external history, communal uniqueness necessarily remains. For the community that shares this particular history, Jesus Christ is truly a Son of God.

These remarks only serve to indicate that the revelation in Christ does not point to itself, or propagate itself, as an indispensable starting point. Rather, it is present as a converter of evil images; it opens up a possibility for *man* to trust God. In doing so, we might say, the Christ-event promotes the disappearance of its own uniqueness as it promotes the coming of the kingdom, the universal community of men, and as the unique revelation which it brings to us becomes event again and again in other events.

Although the memory of Jesus Christ and that which happens through this memory cannot be separated, they are distinct.[25] The "revelatory effect" of the event, its appearance in new events in a transforming and clarifying way, cannot be possessed like the memory itself; yet both belong, strictly speaking, to the *event*. The nature of historical reason makes it clear to us that the *event in itself* is not given to historical knowledge, for it belongs to the character of an event that it becomes event *again*, in the continuing process of interpretation. The event *in itself* is the event in connection with *all other events*, and as such it is known only to God, whereas "men are confined to a double and partial knowledge which is yet not knowledge of double reality."[26] There is no metaphysical but only a practical solution for this problem.

Precisely because the revelation in Jesus Christ directs us to the God of *all* events, and as such binds men not only to a certain limited past and to a future marked by the boundaries of a particular closed society, but rather to the past and future of all mankind, the uniqueness of this revelatory event must be discussed with care. The uniqueness is *real*—the possibility of faith in God is connected with Jesus Christ—but it is *provisional*. Though *The Meaning of Revelation* is perhaps the most Barthian of Niebuhr's books because of its Christocentrism, it contains many traces of his later emphasis on the possibility of other perspectives besides Christ through which one can apprehend God's trustworthiness. This is not a change of mind in Niebuhr; rather it represents a greater concentration on the problems of the self over against the meaning and intention of the action upon it. In *The Meaning of Revelation* these problems still coincide with the problem of relating the Christian community to other points of view. This coincidence disappears later. Yet in *The Meaning of Revelation*, too, the religious problem of the self is the dominant issue, to which all reflection on revelation in historical events is subordinated.

The solution of the duality between internal and external history can only be practical and eschatological; there is no other way to speak about the event of Jesus Christ. The eschatological solution does not imply that internal history will be validated by external history, but that there will be a progressive realization of the universal community through ongoing interpretation of events. In this process each new event presents a possibility to deepen, undergird, and clarify the faith in the One who rules all.

The revelation of God in Christ is itself part of the larger problem of the relation between the self and God. Basically the distinction between internal and external history is auxiliary to a problem which is religious. It concerns the nature of the historical development of the faith of the self which partakes in the "never-ending pilgrim's progress of the reasoning Christian heart," and ultimately it concerns the nature of the God who reveals himself in history. Is he an active self or is he the structure in things, "the way things are?" Is our faith and hope a genuine movement toward something new, or does it amount to a gradual adaptation of our self-centered faiths to "the way things are?" We have observed before that both tendencies are present in Niebuhr. The same thing is true of his reflections on history and revelation.

3. The community and the interpretation of history.

If the historical limitations of all thought about God demand that theology begin consciously with and in a historical community, its limitations as an inquiry into the nature of the object of faith require it to begin in faith and therefore in a particular faith, since there is no other kind. Because God and faith belong together the standpoint of the Christian theologian must be in the faith of the Christian community, directed toward the God of Jesus Christ. Otherwise his standpoint will be that of some other community with another faith and another God. There is no neutral standpoint and no faithless situation from which approach can be made to that which is inseparable from faith. Whatever freedom the Christian and the theologian may have, there is no absolute freedom for them in the sense of complete uncommitted-ness to any supreme value.[27]

After our previous analyses it is hardly necessary to elaborate on the points succinctly expressed in the above quotation. A faith means a history of selves in community; faith in the God of Jesus Christ means the Christian community. Reasoning about God and man with the aid of the image of Jesus Christ, therefore, implies the choice of this particular community.

A community—as we saw in the analysis of the triad of faith—is made up of timeful selves who are bound together by a common cause. The element of time in this "community of faith" is essential[28]; it means that such a community is always a *community of memory* and a *community of expectation or hope.* The extended patterns of time in which a self lives—patterns of remembered responses and sufferings and of expected responses—are, and become, patterns of a *community.*

The revelation of Jesus Christ creates a particular historical community. It is qualified by the fact that Jesus Christ is present in its history, determining its past and future and its interpretation of things and events. Such "common memory" and "common expectation" are not always the same thing. The fact that we talk of *Anni Domini* and of *Christian culture,* indicates that the presence of Jesus Christ can be conceived in many different ways. Not only is he present in several larger communities of which we are part (the history of Western culture, the world church) but also in a diversity of smaller communities, which each remember him differently. Jesus Christ is always remembered, "minded," together with many other things and events; never is he the only binding element. In each case the significance of this remembered image may be different; in each community a particular aspect may be overemphasized. But in any case, where a community of selves is present, where people gather around common meanings and common outward expressions which in some way center in Jesus Christ, a process has begun in which, with the aid of the image of Jesus Christ, private memories, private inner histories, are *converted* toward each other and toward the common image.

This process of conversion cannot come to rest at the boundaries of one particular community which remembers Christ in a particular way. Nevertheless, it often happens that way: "Every part of disunited Christendom interprets its past through an image of itself and holds fast without repentance to that image."[29] Christendom often manifests itself as a conglomeration of *closed societies,* and thus the common possession of the memory of Jesus Christ is prevented from doing its converting work. And still

> we cannot have an invisible church of the Spirit unless we are *united by our memories;* unless we separated groups, divided into confessional and national churches, remember not only the common past in which we were united, but also *that past in which we opposed one another* or separated from each other.[30]

This process of conversion which must be permanent, involves us in serious study and restudy of the past, not in order to strengthen the present defenses of our closed societies (though we can always annex past facts for these purposes), but to enable ourselves and others to adopt one another's histories.

The study of the past as a conversion of memory and as a genuine movement of our disunited communities toward one another will be impossible unless we are able to attack the last ground of our defensiveness—unless we are able to revise our sense of the ultimate context in such a way that defenses are no longer necessary. This is precisely what can happen with the aid of the memory of Jesus Christ. Other communities, with other central images, are perhaps unable to proceed beyond the point of noticing the fateful necessity of mutual strife between human communities; the community which centers in Jesus Christ knows more.

For in Jesus Christ we remember more than only the founder of our particular society; through him we acquire a historical past that stretches far beyond him. He connects us with the history of Israel, and farther even—the universal history of mankind. In this history Jesus Christ is the incarnation of "the principle of redemption." He does not introduce this principle as something radically new into a history which, up until then, was a history of darkness; rather, in him the principle of redemption comes to *new power:* through him we see that it has always been there.[31] Through Jesus Christ the Christian community learns to see that nature, history, and society are related to redemption. Participation in brokenness as well as reconciliation becomes visible in his cross.

This is the way in which the memory of Jesus Christ refers us to the world, to the universal society of mankind, instead of strengthening the boundaries of the closed Christian society. Through the memory of Jesus Christ, through the inner history of the Christian community, *I learn to adopt the past of all human groups.*[32] "Through Christ we become immigrants into the empire of God which extends over all the world and learn to remember the history of that empire, which is of men in all times and places, as our history."[33] This is the universalism of the

Christian faith. It is not based on the belief that all men are brothers, or even that all men *will be* brothers, but on the belief that the principle of redemption, manifested in new power in Jesus Christ, is truly a divine principle, and therefore universal. It is based on the insight that *God is in Christ:* that the eternal is truly present in history and reveals himself in the particular history of Jesus Christ; and on the insight that *Christ is in God:* that what is revealed in Jesus Christ is truly divine.

We have seen before how Niebuhr's emphasis on relativity, monotheism, and transformation causes tension in his concept of the Christian community. On the one hand, the community is the necessary channel through which the revelation of God's trustworthiness is apprehended; on the other hand, it is relativized by the content and effect of its own inner history. In these sections on the possibility of historical revelation, we have seen how the tension reappears at practically every point. The problems of the historicity of the self, together with the way in which Christians speak about revelation in their history, show how a permanent duality between internal and external history is necessary; this duality is practically identical with the continuous self-relativization of the community, with the *metanoia* toward God and the world.

The uniqueness of the event of Jesus Christ is caught in the same process. It seems that the eschatological tension in Niebuhr's thought about particularity and universality implies a never-ending, never-completed, *self-elimination of the particular Christian community.* This does not in any way mitigate the emphasis on the necessity of external embodiment for the continuation of our inner history. But because these external embodiments serve the continuing effect of *this* inner history, the function is something more than the stabilization and institutionalization of this community, though this, too, is implied. Above all, they assist the continuous self-relativizing reference to universal history and universal society.

B. THE UNITY OF GOD AND THE WORK OF CHRIST

1. Trinity. After the prolegomena on revelation and history in the preceding half of our chapter we are now ready to investigate how Niebuhr speaks more concretely about the revelation of God in Christ: about the triune God who reveals himself, and the particular event in which this revelation is apprehended. Perhaps we will observe that all we can find is a further illustration of that which has been said already; but in that case we will at least have gained some insight into the coherence of the different elements in Niebuhr's thought, and in the persistence of his central concerns.

The theme of the *unity of God* is of crucial importance for Niebuhr. The only possibility for a faith which speaks to the predicament of man who seeks in vain to find unity, intelligibility, and hope in his history and selfhood, lies in the unity of God. It is the only possibility for unity of self; it is the only ground for the permanent duality of internal and external history. If God is truly one, then his presence in all the action upon us as the ultimate hostile power, and the goodness in which we have learned to believe with the aid of Jesus Christ, point to one and the same God. Though we may never surmount the difficulties involved in the effort to see him as one and to express this unity adequately, *radical monotheism* can be the driving force of our search for integration and direction.

For Niebuhr the unity of God is the framework in which the problems of history and Christology have their place. It is appropriate, therefore, that an inquiry into the way Niebuhr speaks about this unity—and particularly about the question of God as *three in one* —precede the analysis of his Christology.

Faith in the unity of God is expressed in the permanent *metanoia* from closedness to openness, from self-centeredness or community-centeredness to God-centeredness, from petrifaction and stabilization (compare *The Kingdom of God in America*) to dynamic correction of absolutized viewpoints and institutions. In the preceding section we noted that this movement is represented not only by the movement of Christian communities toward each other, and thus toward full and complete *doctrine*, but also by the movement of the Christian community toward all human communities. For ultimately the question of the unity of God is the question of man who confronts many confusing actions upon him and searches for wholeness and intelligibility.

From here we can understand why Niebuhr approaches the question of Trinitarianism in two ways. We can roughly distinguish these as "historical" and "existential."

In the first approach Niebuhr calls our attention to the presence of *three unitarianisms in the history of Christianity*,[1] generally represented by Deism, Unitarianism, and Spiritualism. Each of these "unitarianisms" represents a one-sided emphasis. The one-sidedness may be inevitable, the mutual correction and complement is mandatory; for the three unitarianisms are logically dependent on one another. Faith in a "first cause" never exists without some awareness of its goodness; faith in a good God consciously or unconsciously operates on the assumption that this good God is also the first cause; and Spiritualism meets its challenge in the two questions of ultimate power and ultimate goodness.[2] There is no way to unite these unitarianisms conceptually: what the unity of God is, is "dynamically exhibited in the movements of faith in history."[3] The unity is not an afterthought but rather the basis of the interdependence of the three unitarianisms.

This particular theme is obviously present in Niebuhr's book *The Kingdom of God in America.* The idea of the kingdom of God in American history is illustrated through the exhibition of three successive emphases—the sovereignty of God, the kingdom of Christ, the coming kingdom. These are not three more or less related ideas which followed each other in the course of history, but three—inevitably one-sided— manifestations of the same basic motif: the presence of God in history. The history of the idea itself shows how the emphases cannot be separated.

> An ideal of the coming kingdom, divorced from reliance on the divine initiative and separated from the experience of the Christian revolution, showed itself insufficient to rouse to new life the party of the kingdom of God. . . .
> There was no way toward the coming kingdom save the way taken by a sovereign God through the reign of Jesus Christ.[4]

We see that the unity of the three elements is an essential presupposition, but it cannot be present save in a dynamic interrelation of the overemphases. The unity of God cannot be truly confessed unless we manage to refrain from closing off the separate emphases against one another.

In connection with this first approach to the doctrine of the Trinity we might call attention to two related points. In the first place, Niebuhr's attitude to *doctrine in general* becomes manifest here. Doctrine cannot be an effort at conceptual transcendence of the entire history of faith into a comprehensive system; it is the articulation of a particular faith which has a necessarily limited standpoint. Furthermore, it cannot abstract fully from the actual relation with God. Given this situation, it is impossible for doctrine to give adequate expression to the *unity of God*, since such expression can be given only by all times and all places together. Thus Niebuhr's Trinitarianism clearly reflects and illustrates the general attitude toward metaphysical language that we analyzed in chapter 3.

The second point to which we call attention in connection with this first approach to Trinitarianism is this: the dynamic interaction of particular unitarian emphases is at the same time a moral problem. Or, better yet, the problem of *Christ and culture* is a *Trinitarian* problem. Only the transformationist position can avoid all the unitarian temptations that threaten the others. The major defect of the position of "Christ above culture" and "Christ and culture in paradox" is that they tend to present static models, in the latter case almost an ontological bifurcation of reality.[5] Only a view which keeps the different segments of moral reality in dynamic interrelation can claim to be true to the unity of God.

In this last remark we have broached the second, "existential" approach to the Trinity. It is implied in the first approach: the unity of God is basically a problem of *man's enduring crisis*. In more unitarian systems of faith the problem tends to be less perplexing; that is, as long as the complementary challenges of the particular system do not make themselves felt. As soon as this happens, the relation of Jesus Christ to the almighty Creator of heaven and earth, for instance, becomes a fundamental issue, not in the sense in which correct or complete doctrine can be an interesting assignment, but existentially. For the deity of the Creator (that is, his goodness), the deity of Jesus Christ (that is, his power), and the deity of the Spirit (that is, the possible presence of a *holy* Spirit among all spirits) are fundamental religious questions that cannot be solved independently from one another. They are manifestations of the fundamental human predicament.

> The problem of man is how to love the One on whom he is completely, absolutely dependent; who is the Mystery behind the mystery of human existence in the fatefulness of its selfhood, of being this man among these men, in this time and all time, in the thus and so-ness of the strange actual world. It is the problem of reconciliation to the One from whom death proceeds as well as life, who makes demands too hard to bear, who sets us in the world where our beloved neighbors are the objects of seeming animosity, who appears as God of wrath as well as God of love. It is the problem that arises in its acutest form when life itself becomes a problem, when the goodness of existence is questionable, as it has been for most men at most times; when the ancient and universal suspicion arises that he is happiest who was never born and the next fortunate who dies young.[6]

Viewed like this, the problem of God's unity is the problem of the unity of his wrath and his mercy. Reconciliation and hope are dependent on it; in other words, the problem of reconciliation is subsumed within that of the divine unity, of the unity of divine power and love.[7] We cannot ignore the fact that our first awareness of God's unity is an awareness of unity as *hostility*—an awareness of one ultimate power who destroys all value, negates all little gods, and rolls all things together in meaninglessness. The revelation in Jesus Christ—in him we find an eminent manifestation of this "slayer"!—does not, as if by magic, erase this awareness. It introduces, or strengthens, the faith that God is love and thus *assigns* the problem of divine unity.

God's hostility is not transformed into love—not if we take all segments of our life as historical beings with equal seriousness and avoid the traps of unitarianism—but *both* hostility *and* love are brought together in a unity which seems at first totally enigmatic and mysterious. This leads to great restlessness, to a permanent rethinking of all our concepts of God, of love, and of power. The ultimate result of such restlessness cannot be precluded, either in a resignation to fate (though this will always be present), nor in a premature identification of God with "love" (though we cannot do without *some* identification). This tension is the tension of Trinitarianism; it is the heart of Niebuhr's theocentric theology.

Because Niebuhr insists that the knowledge of the divine unity is a permanent exercise of faith and reason, it is rather difficult to analyze his position with the aid of categories borrowed from classical Trinitarianism. Niebuhr makes it quite difficult to grasp the divine unity in and through the different values. Frei speaks of "economic Trinitarianism,"[8] and adds that such a position does not allow a firm grasp of the unity of the three persons in the one deity, that it cannot observe the rule *opera ad extra indivisa*, and that it can offer no clue to the being or existence of the divine persons. In dealing with these objections, we must bear in mind that the question of God is, for Niebuhr, a question of human response.

The conception of God in himself apart from God in his revelation has no place in Niebuhr's theology. Does this imply economic Trinitarianism? It does, to the extent that Niebuhr regards God's unity as something to be sought in a situation in which a certain threeness is given. For this implies that the threeness is not immediately grounded in God himself, whereas the oneness is. But we must not lose sight of the center of gravity in Niebuhr's thought; in seeking God's unity man seeks his own unity. Hardly any more can be said than this: *God is one, whereas man is not. This* is the reason why it is difficult to "grasp the unity of the three persons in the one deity." Monotheistic transformation means the effort to grasp the One beyond the many, so that this threeness can become a threeness in a "nonliteral sense," and the "external works" of the triune God can be called *appropriationés.* The rule *opera ad extra indivisa* is thus not so much a rule as a crucial matter of faith.

On the other hand—and this is just as important—Niebuhr speaks of a unity of God which must be transformed into triunity. We are aware of God as one in his power and hostility. This awareness is not merely an error, to be corrected by revelation in Jesus Christ. It is a unity which also manifests itself in Jesus Christ and which threatens to undercut all trust we attach to revelatory images. And this is *not* the unity which is the end of the road of faith. Rather, monotheistic transformation transforms this unity into *triunity.* Thus, in another genuine sense, the oneness of God is given and his threeness—rather, his three-in-one-ness—is sought.

Considerations such as these make us hesitant to speak of Niebuhr's position as simple economic Trinitarianism. But it must be said that Niebuhr does not provide a clear alternative either, precisely because the problem of history and being is still "open." Or, phrased theologically, the work of the Holy Spirit prohibits the completion of an "immanent Trinitarianism" in which the unity of God is firmly stated.

Niebuhr's second approach to the problem of the Trinity—from the point of view of "man's enduring crisis"—also has significant ethical implications. The problem of *love versus justice* (crucial in the thought of Reinhold Niebuhr) cannot be a problem of mere paradox or of dialectical relationship. It is the problem of transformation and as such it is a *Trinitarian* problem. Neither love nor justice, as mere "human" concepts, can claim the right of ultimate priority. In responsible existence they are perennial partners on the road of transformation. If we attribute highest priority to love and thus are forced to make a distinction of stages, we are led to other divisions: ethics versus religion, man's work versus God's work, or even one God versus another God.[9] God's judgment and God's redemption are not to be separated; so neither can we, in our response, separate between actions in justice and actions in love. Restraining action is also part of our response to the *redeeming* action of God, and as such connected with trustful self-denial.

Up to this point it might seem that Niebuhr's Trinitarianism is mainly *bi*-nitarianism, because his chief problem seems to lie in the relation of the creative power and the God of grace. This, however, should not lead us to overlook the importance he attaches to the Holy Spirit, even though this aspect does not receive much explicit attention. In a sense we might say that the way in which Niebuhr conceives the Trinitarian problem tends toward heavy emphasis on pneumatology.

We receive some clue to this in Niebuhr's insistence that the Spirit proceeds from the Father as well as from the Son[10]; in other words, a corrective emphasis is placed on the words *from the Father*. We cannot think of the Spirit only in terms of Christ; this is crucial for the unity of God and, as such, for the unity of man. Thus the identity between the Spirit which proceeds from the Son, and the Spirit which proceeds from the Father needs to be rediscovered again and again in the perennial task of *metanoia*. The Spirit of God is found with the aid of the Spirit of Christ,[11] but also "there is a spirit in man to which the Spirit of Christ makes appeal."[12] Ethically this means, for instance, that self-denial (the Spirit of Christ) needs to be balanced by self-affirmation (the Spirit of the Creator); rather, ultimately they cannot and must not contradict each other.

The crucial point in Niebuhr's emphasis on the *ex patre* is that it is an effort to grasp the true meaning of the rule *opera ad extra indivisa sunt.* We do not get hold of the undividedness of the external works of the Trinity if we do not see that the Spirit does not proceed only from the Son. Of course, Niebuhr does not deny that the Spirit proceeds from the Father through the Son—such denial would seriously jeopardize the connection between the unity of God and the revelation in Christ, nor does he seek to solve the question of unity between Father and Son solely in the direction of the Father by not valuing the *filioque.* Rather, he seeks to correct the one-sidedness which interprets the unity of God only on the basis of the Spirit of Christ without seeing that it is precisely in the relation between this Spirit and the Spirit of creation that the problem of the unity of God is given. Thus, the oneness of the Holy Spirit which is the unity of God is present to us in the duality of our historicity.

All this is just another way of saying what the significance of Christ is in the history of men. Jesus Christ is not a new creation but a man like us in our created world; as such he teaches us what it is to be a man who trusts the one God. The revelation we receive in this history, which we confess to be truly of God, continually refers us to our history as created men, in which the Spirit of the one God truly moves us to respond to the world around us in the faith that it is being reconciled to the Creator. This determines the position of the Christian community.

The problem of the Holy Spirit contains and comprises the problem of the relation between God and Christ and of the relation between the church and the world. With regard to both relations Niebuhr's thought is based on the conviction that the Spirit of Christ is indispensable for monotheistic faith, that with its aid we learn to speak and think adequately about a trustworthy triune God and to respond accordingly. But the Spirit of Christ does not replace the Spirit of the Father, it is not the sole criterion for its presence. We might say the Spirit of Christ *confirms* the Spirit of the Father and leads to a recognition of its presence. For Jesus Christ, and the community in which his Spirit lives, do not refer to themselves, nor to God through themselves. They refer to God as the trustworthy Creator and Governor of the *world,* and to *man* as he is related to God in distrust and defensiveness. Likewise the Spirit of the Father *confirms* the Spirit of Jesus Christ the Son. That the principle of redemption is indeed a universal principle is not merely a bold assertion of the Christian community; it receives answer, confirmation, and illumination in history wherever the source of being is trusted even outside of Christ. That the principle of redemption is universal has its ground in the unity of God himself, in the fact that the Spirit proceeds from the Father *and* from the Son, and from the Father *through* the Son.

2. Reconciliation and Christology. The problem of the unity of

God is the problem of the reconciliation of man to the One beyond the many. The Christian community confesses that in Jesus Christ this reconciliation takes place. With the aid of the image of Christ it has learned and is learning to trust God and to rely on his unity. This is the context of Niebuhr's Christology.

Reconciliation as the restoration of the man-God relation is at the same time the answer to human sinfulness. Sin is, as we have seen, for Niebuhr basically distrust in the power behind all powers, and subsequent defensiveness, isolation, self-centeredness, and a permanent absolutizing of the relative. We saw how sin involves whole communities, how it manifests itself as a communal network of distrust and disloyalty, and thus also as a communal network of suffering. "The threads of responsibility run back and forth through space and time, from person to person in such an intricate pattern that none of us is uninvolved in any cross."[13] Serving certain limited values implies the destruction of other values served by others. This makes the brokenness of the human community seem inevitable; therefore, if there is such a thing as reconciliation, it is clear not only that it must come from a point beyond human possibilities, but also that it must have "communal effect." It must be a creative deed of loyal love[14] which restores the spirit of the broken community. For Niebuhr, such deeds can only be grounded in a revelation of the trustworthiness of being, in other words, in a manifestation of *divine loyalty.*

The "crosses" we experience in the communal sin and reconciliation in which we are forever involved, and the cross as the symbolic expression of that which happens in the Christ-event, interpret each other. Central in this mutual interpretation is the notion of the vicarious suffering of the innocent.[15] In innocent suffering we encounter the irrevocable effects of communal sin and in this irrevocability we experience the judgment of God. But through the cross of Christ we have learned to see that this vicarious suffering is a principle of hope, that through it reconciliation takes place. Through Christ we see that God

> gives his best-beloved rather than to allow the work of his creation to dissolve into the anarchy of existence which can recognize no order, to decay internally. The intense seriousness of the love of God, as revealed in Jesus Christ's death, is confirmed and recalled and illustrated and reenacted in the vicarious suffering of war.[16]

Therefore we are called to respond to events in history with *faith in resurrection;* for in facing the destruction of Jesus Christ "we have the demonstration in this very instance of a life-power that is not conquered, not destroyed."[17]

The cross of Jesus Christ reveals that all human righteousness is unrighteousness which for its justification depends only on the graciousness of God. It is through suffering, more precisely through the suffering of the *innocent,* through *crucifixion,* that we learn to see that the end of the human road is not the result of man's efforts but justification. Not that this insight comes naturally; it is miraculously given at the moment that we have every reason to believe in the finality of sin, including its irrevocable effects.

Response to divine graciousness in our communal involvements, therefore, cannot ignore or bypass the suffering. On the contrary, only through suffering and reconciliation is such response possible. Under this perspective we are called to live with and respond to our neighbors. In this sense, the neighbor becomes a *christomorphic being;* the ubiquity of Christ is seen in all suffering neighbors,[18] because this suffering is part of a pattern of reconciliation and hope.

We have noticed before how strongly Niebuhr emphasizes that Jesus Christ does not and cannot become an object of faith in itself. Our redemption is historically related to Jesus Christ but it is dependent only on the activity of God. The memory of Jesus Christ is inseparable from our faith in God, but the former is not the cause of the latter. The Christ-event is indispensable in the struggle of the self for unity and integrity; but it does not eliminate or even mitigate this struggle—rather, intensifies it because of the seeming absurdity of what it brings. Jesus Christ is the cornerstone on which we build[19]; but the unity of God, on which the unity of self and the eternal value of the Christ-event—the divinity of Christ—depend, is not unequivocally manifested in him. His presence transforms and redirects, but it does not solve or eliminate the problem of a faithful response to the One beyond the many. This emphasis is part of Niebuhr's conviction that the trustworthiness of the one God, the source of being and Lord of history, is the sole quest of man. This trustworthiness is given and not given, realized and sought ever again. All this reflects Niebuhr's resistance to a weakening of the eschatological tension in the permanent process of transformation and *metanoia* by a christological concentration.

The image of Jesus Christ which is present in our history, however, is larger and more inclusive than a mere instance of innocent suffering through which we learn to believe in justification by grace. For this innocent suffering happens in a life which survives as a clear paradigm of a trustful and loyal relation to the principle of being. It is the image of a man in whose total life the radically monotheistic faith is expressed in such a way that it becomes mediating. Jesus' mediatorship is reflected in the double direction we see in his life: in him we see man directed toward God and God directed toward man; more precisely, "He is a single person wholly directed as man toward God and wholly directed in his unity with the Father toward men."[20] As such he is a focusing point of the continuous alternation of God-man and man-God relations. His relation to God is one of perfect trust; because of this he is trustworthy in his faithfulness toward men and thus manifests *God's* trustworthiness and faithfulness.

Niebuhr finds an adequate designation of Jesus' relation to God in the term sonship. "His confidence and his fidelity are those of a Son of God—the most descriptive term which Christians apply to him as they contemplate the faith of their Lord."[21] It is Jesus' moral *sonship* which makes him the moral mediator of the Father's will toward men.[22] This implies that God is revealed in the way in which Jesus is a man; his manhood is the context and the bearer of his revelatory significance. We noticed before how Niebuhr speaks of incarnation as the presence of radical faith in the complete structure of a moral existence. In this sense we should understand Jesus' *total life* as the incarnation of his sonship. *In this incarnation God is revealed.* For God is present where unified selfhood is present.

We arrive at the same conclusion when we consider how Niebuhr regards Jesus' *virtues* as the point at which his mediatorship becomes apparent. Before we accuse Niebuhr of identifying perfect humanity as such with divinity, or of connecting the revelatory significance of the Christ-event with the virtuosity of the man Jesus, we should remember that a *virtue*, for Niebuhr, is never a human quality which can be known or analyzed apart from a relation to God. In a (unfortunately unpublished) paper "Reflections on Faith, Hope, and Love," Niebuhr makes clear that the word virtue designates a particular relation, or pattern of relations, to beings, and thus also to being itself.[23] A virtue, then, is not so much a habit or a constitution of character of a particular human being, but a relation which either perverts or reveals the true quality of being itself. Virtues are gifts of God which have no power or existence apart from the relation of giving.[24] In this sense, too, Jesus' moral perfection reveals the "beauty" of being itself.[25] "Thus any one of the virtues of Jesus may be taken as the key to the understanding of his character and teaching, but each is intelligible in its apparent radicalism only as a relation to God."[26]

In a sense, then, it is adequate to say that in all human response patterns the "divine" and the "human" are *in some way* together. From here Jesus' mediatorship would appear to exist by virtue of the fact that *his* responses are *more* trustful and loyal than those of anyone else we know, and that *his* moral existence therefore has *more* power to elicit our trust and loyalty than those of another man. That alone would not be sufficient for an adequate Christology, especially because it would ignore the basic classical distinction between the way in which the Spirit is present in Jesus and the way in which it is present in us. This is not a distinction in degree but in kind. But Niebuhr's christological departure enables him to say more. The Christ-event becomes an *original* image for us insofar as it reveals how God *is* present in being and history. It brings this revelation into a situation in which the sense of God's presence was lost and is lost again and again. It elicits trust and loyalty in moral situations warped and obscured by distrust and disloyalty. True, in and through Christ we see that "faithfulness at the heart of things" has *always* been there; but "without the historical incarnation of that faith in Jesus Christ we should be lost in faithlessness."[27]

This approach to Christology enables Niebuhr to avoid several difficulties which make themselves felt in contemporary thought about Christ. The first—we associate it roughly with the name of Barth—lies in the tendency to overemphasize Christ's deity at the expense of his humanity, and consequently to shift the attention from "reconciliation in historical actuality" to "revelation of a state of affairs"; in short, to separate Christology from the historical Jesus. Frei calls this "epistemological monophysitism."[28] Niebuhr's major objection to this type of thinking, it seems to us, lies in the fact that the acknowledgment of God's revelation in Christ is no longer seen as a process of actual orientation to Jesus but becomes, rather, an axiomatic starting point for the consideration of his historicity and humanity. In other words, this point of view does know of an appreciation of the humanity of Christ and as such of the humanity of man, but this appreciation is not itself part of the process of discovering God's presence in Christ. Rather, the acknowledgment of God's presence in Christ becomes the epistemological condition for understanding his humanity. Though Niebuhr would agree that only as Son of God does Jesus Christ have historical existence, he does not, as we have already indicated, draw the epistemological consequences from this insight; rather, he becomes increasingly aware of the dangers of such a step.

The second difficulty that Niebuhr is able to avoid finds its origin in a careful and consistent separation of faith and historical knowledge, characteristic of much German Liberalism. The necessity to find a particular link between Christology and historical knowledge of Jesus —for instance in a "messianic self-consciousness"—already presupposes such a separation and clearly involves a depreciation of the direct christological significance of Jesus' full historicity. The consequences of this position are manifest in Bultmann, who regards all historical facts of Jesus as irrelevant for faith. The major difficulty here lies in the identification of Jesus' concrete historicity with his humanity, and the subsequent disappearance of both in favor of a nonobjectifiable existential decision which grasps the eschatological significance of the Christ-event.

In avoiding the two tendencies mentioned, Niebuhr is able to retain a concrete historical Jesus who is not as such identical with God's revelatory act but in whose full historical and moral existence the revelation of God takes place. This enables Niebuhr to place significant stress on the revelation of Jesus Christ *of what it means to be a man.* His disclosure of what it means that God is, and is good, *could not,* says Niebuhr, *take place without the illumination of what it means to be a man.*[29]

The structure of Niebuhr's Christology illustrates the way in which he deals with the problems of history and revelation in *The Meaning of Revelation.* There the "two natures" of Christ have become "two histories," "two ways of understanding one event." More concretely, it is *in* the total human life of Jesus Christ that the word of God is spoken; it is this concrete historical person we—internally—remember as mediator. There are two histories here: the history of God with men *and* the history of men. Yet this is not to say that we can resign ourselves to an eternal dichotomy, even though the duality between internal and external history and the process of transformation and *metanoia* may never come to rest; the insistence that God is truly in history compels us to say that ultimately the two are one, even as God is one. Or, more precisely: ultimately, eschatologically, it is the history of men that counts—the history of men who respond faithfully to one another and to God. The communal uniqueness of Jesus Christ lasts as long as we need to be referred to this possibility.

In all this, however, it remains true that our ability to see and describe Jesus as the moral mediator between God and man is not dependent on any analyzable state of affairs. It springs from a miracle by which *resurrection-faith* was and is introduced into the history of the Christian community. Without this, Jesus Christ would have survived, if at all, as an eminent example of the malevolence of the ultimate power of being. But now, irrational though it may be,

> it is our conviction that God is faithful, that he kept faith with Jesus Christ who was loyal to him and to his brothers; that Christ is risen from the dead; that as the Power is faithful so Christ's faithfulness is powerful; that we can say "our Father" to that which has elected us to live, to die, and to inherit life beyond life.[30]

Resurrection-faith is the only clue to Christology. Yet it does not banish all relevance of Jesus' concrete historicity: it is a definite historical man of whom we say that he rose from the dead. Therefore, the statement that only a primordial miraculous faith in the trustworthiness of God can enable us to see Jesus Christ as mediator, must be *complemented* by the statement that this particular Jesus Christ elicits faith in God.

3. History, God, and Christ. We have thus reached the point where we speak of two complementary statements: The resurrection-faith enables us to speak of Jesus Christ as mediator, and Jesus' moral existence elicits faith in God. The question with which we have to deal now is how this complementariness must be understood. It is the question of where we must locate God's self-revealing presence: in the miracle of resurrection-faith or in Jesus' total life; in the existence of the Christ-image or in Jesus' moral sonship. If we emphasize resurrection-faith and Christ-image, we place the "irrational confession" in the center, and with that we are tempted to loosen the connection between this faith and the actual history which we live and experience, and thus to increase the closedness of the Christian community. If we concentrate on total life and moral sonship, we are tempted to stress Jesus' "consubstantiality" with us (his presence in the history of men) to such an extent that there is hardly room for his uniqueness.

The christological problem formulated here is a problem of history and hermeneutics and as such typical for the twentieth century. It seeks to relate the significance of Christ to history and eschatology; in other words, it asks for the structure of the triad history-God-Christ. In trying to interpret Niebuhr's approach to this triad we simultaneously seek to establish the final link between his Christology and his Trinitarianism.

In much nineteenth-century theology the interpretation of the Christ-event and the search for the "historical Jesus" took place in a framework in which *history* and *God* were concepts that carried a generally accessible meaning. Jesus Christ exemplified or illuminated a certain structure of faith and existence of which there was a sensible pre-understanding. For Schleiermacher, Jesus Christ was the perfect embodiment of the God-consciousness; in the more Hegelian schemes, Jesus became the exemplification of the essence or the ultimate development of history, or the embodiment of an eternal truth about man.

Through the development of historical criticism and the more and more widely accepted dichotomy between fact and faith, however, it became increasingly difficult to relate the event of Jesus Christ to the more general convictions about history and God. When, especially in the early twentieth century, the awareness of the historicity of the self and its knowledge grew and many an optimistic vision of history and God collapsed, the resulting historical skepticism provided a climate in which the emphasis in the triad history-God-Christ had to be shifted toward

Christ; that is, toward the unique revelatory significance of the Christ-event. Thus Karl Barth made faith in God as the Lord of history dependent on the event itself, and Rudolf Bultmann focused on the immediate awareness of God's address to man. With that, the problem of revelation and history was phrased in a new way.

The transition between the nineteenth and twentieth century with regard to the triad history-God-Christ can be illustrated with Martin Kähler's essay on the historical Jesus and the biblical Christ.[31] In a situation where history and faith could no longer be connected in an unambiguous way, the faith of the church had to rise to defend its particular interpretation of the historical Christ over against science. Kähler contrasts the creation of historians with the apostolic witness which is based on a faithful impression of the total picture of Jesus: the former is ephemeral; the latter lasts for it has the authority of tradition and proclamation. All factuality and all further historical detail may be freely investigated as long as it is subordinated to the totality of the biblical Christ.

The difficulty of this position is that Kähler in fact isolates a particular interpretation of the historical fact of Jesus Christ as authoritative, and that his limitation of the value of pure historical investigation appears, therefore, as rather arbitrary. Kähler remains a figure of the nineteenth century, in that he does not yet share in the more radical thinking about history and faith. Two things are characteristic of this radicalization: first, the insight that *all* so-called facts are present to us as parts of patterns of interpretation and that historical knowledge means participation and reenactment; and second, the insight that faith is a unique encounter with God which speaks to the heart of our existence and is not conditioned by any external fact. These insights mark, for instance, the difference between the "quest for the historical Jesus" and the "new quest" of the post-Bultmann scholars; and they indicate part of what is at stake in the shift of emphasis in the history-God-Christ triad.

The peculiar character of Niebuhr's Christology is indicated by the fact that as a twentieth-century thinker, he fully shares the changes in the thinking about faith and history and the accompanying shift in emphasis toward "Christ," but at the same time seems to defend the nineteenth-century approach, according to which Christ "exemplifies" the larger structure of history. Though he follows Barth in the latter's insistence that revelation is a unique miracle and that we learn to understand this in the history of Jesus Christ, he cannot regard this history as such as revelation-history, nor can he give up his concern with the interrelation between the many faiths of man. And though he agrees with Bultmann that revelation means a challenge to realize authentic selfhood and that such revelation can never be *possessed* with the memory of Jesus Christ,[32] he cannot lose sight of the particular historical context in which the decision of faith is shaped and conditioned—neither of the historical context of Jesus Christ nor of the historical context of the community in which the self lives and believes.

Niebuhr's reservations about the Bultmannian attitude toward the history-God-Christ triad are perhaps somewhat less clear than his relation to Barth, in view of his indebtedness to critical philosophy for the distinction between external and internal history as compared to Bultmann's Kantian distinction between *Historie* and *Geschichte*. Yet the two distinctions are by no means similar. For Bultmann, the believing self stands in a vacuum between God and material history; it is, of course, shaped and conditioned by its history, even in its faith—but in the act of faith and decision itself it seems to transcend it. Niebuhr's indebtedness to men like Mead and Spinoza points in a different direction here.

At first sight the "return to history," more particularly to the historical Jesus, that is practiced by post-Bultmannians like Gerhard Ebeling, seems to meet the objections which can be raised against too sharp a divorce between faith and history. Ebeling focuses on the relation between the historical reality of Jesus and that which "comes to word" in him. He proceeds significantly beyond Bultmann by no longer connecting the revelatory character of the Christ-event to its pure thereness; rather, the response to what "comes to word" in Jesus is always at the same time response to a concrete historical content.[33]

Yet we remain on Bultmannian ground to the extent that there is a basic separation between investigation of what comes to word in Jesus and the existential certitude which is the key to Christ-faith. In other words, the nonverifiability of faith remains the constitutive principle of the theological method. This is not the same thing as saying that the gift or the givenness of faith is an inexplicable miracle. The latter statement can still be combined with a more complex attitude to historical reality which speaks of duality rather than of separation, and thus seeks to avoid the rather arbitrary Christocentrism which always threatens the Bultmannian way of thought. It cannot surprise us that the "new hermeneutic," because of this, has been criticized for neglecting the *cultural ingredient* in the human response of faith.[34]

In any case, Niebuhr's hesitations about some of the major twentieth-century developments make his own position with regard to the triad history-God-Christ seem somewhat ambiguous. Starting from this observation, we must seek Niebuhr's answer to the question we raised at the beginning of this section. Which side do we emphasize in speaking of God's revelation in Christ: the Christ-image and the resurrection-faith, or the moral sonship of Jesus' total life? We shall look at each possibility in turn.

It is clear that Niebuhr speaks of "the miracle of resurrection-faith" rather than of the "resurrection." This is not to be interpreted in a strictly Bultmannian sense, as though the reality of the resurrection coincides with the eschatological significance of the cross, grasped in faith; Niebuhr's way of speaking originates in his insistence that the acknowledgment of the "lordship of the living Christ" can never be separated from the life of faith in a particular community—moreover, is related again and again to the total life of little faiths, through which the historical self finds its way. The factuality of the resurrection is not seen as something that is valid in itself as a certain and visible manifestation of the new humanity which is expected and hoped for in history. Faith, of course, is directed toward the living Christ as the image of the new man, but this faith is so much involved in the complexity of the many histories and the many faiths that it must be confirmed and reaffirmed in every situation in which a choice must be made between faith and unfaith—the mutual confirmation of the Spirit of Christ and the Spirit of the Father! Such confirmation and reaffirmation includes the assertion of the factuality of the resurrection. But apart from the complexity of man's moral existence, and the duality between internal and external history, such an assertion is either superfluous or arbitrary, for we cannot take ourselves out of history to a vantage point above it.

Those who would assert the factuality of the resurrection apart from man's faith do so, of course, in order to maintain that the renewal of man and world is something which *has happened* and *is going to happen*; but nevertheless it can be asked whether this does not lead to a depreciation of actual history and thus to a weakening of the major driving force of human hope—and these would certainly be Niebuhrian questions. At the same time, however, we cannot overlook the fact that, for Niebuhr, we are *completely dependent*, for our faith and our trust in the graciousness of being, for all we are and all we have, on the truth of the resurrection; that is, on the gift of resurrection-faith or a similar image. Again it seems as if Niebuhr seeks to grasp both horns of the dilemma. However this may be, the problem of faith formulated in this way can hardly be more stringent and more baffling.

It is clear from these considerations that for Niebuhr the factuality of the resurrection is not a problem which can easily be solved. He would never say, for instance, that its existence practically coincides with the existence of the Christian community, as John Knox does, who regards the existence of the church as the essential and continuing meaning of the resurrection.[35] Nor would he find it sufficient to vindicate the character of the resurrection as historical event on the basis of its functioning as such in the Christian community.[36] For the problem of the resurrection-faith of the community is precisely its functioning in a world of many communities and many faiths. As such the resurrection is related to the ultimate meaning of history, whereas the Christian community itself does not and cannot manifest this meaning in an unambiguous way. *As such, too,* the resurrection is a problem of historical science; to disregard this, would mean to jeopardize the oneness of God in history.

The second possibility that we mentioned—the location of God's self-revealing presence in the moral sonship of Jesus' total life—clearly has Niebuhr's preference. This preference is also manifest in the tendency of his Christology to sacrifice Jesus' uniqueness, to a certain extent, to his consubstantiality with man. For the main emphasis lies on Jesus' life as a "paradigm of responsibility."[37] This is not the same thing as saying that it is an example to be followed, for the crucial point is not Jesus' virtuous example but the way in which the graciousness of the source of being is revealed in the pattern of Jesus' total life. Nevertheless, here, too, we are referred to more. For in spite of all emphasis on the role of faith in patterns of response, the question of how faith comes into existence is not thereby answered in a satisfying way.

The *source* of the "inexplicable givenness" of faith, both in the historical situation of Jesus himself and in the situation of the Christian community, is not itself part of the patterns in which it functions; it does not lie, for instance, in a certain predisposition of man that only needs to be strengthened by certain actions or examples. For the natural disposition of man, though he is forever involved in the search for centers of trustworthiness, is hostility and suspicion toward being itself. In his lostness, man completely depends on the miracle of the gift of faith. But when this miracle occurs it comes to him through history, through the complex patterns in which he lives, and it does not take him out of that history; indeed, it binds him to the history of Jesus Christ, his own history, and the history of the world. Along this way he learns what revelation is, and who it is that reveals himself.

We have reached the point where we must draw our final conclusions about Niebuhr's Christology. Our analysis so far has shown that for Niebuhr the triad history-God-Christ is determined by the problems of the basic triad history-God-*man*, and that the tensions of this situation cause a *disjunction* between Jesus Christ and God. Or, in terms of the christological analyses above: what in others' thought becomes the disjunction between *Historie* and *Geschichte*, becomes in Niebuhr's thought a disjunction between historical revelation and the unity of God. Any Christocentrism, whether it stems from Barthian thinking or from a Bultmannian distinction between faith and history, abstracts from the fundamental problem of the fragmented self over against the one God in all events. For this insistence, Niebuhr sacrifices the unambiguous character of God's presence in history at one particular point, precisely because he also refuses to return to the schemes of Liberalism. In other words, his insistence that the one God is present in history causes a certain remoteness of God, which is not identical with his remoteness from human experience but rather serves as a reminder of the unfinishedness of the road of *metanoia* and transformation of the duality of history.

Jesus Christ refers to God and this means, for Niebuhr, that he does *not* refer to himself. *Christocentrism compromises the unity of God.* For on the one hand, it leads to a closed society with a separate God; it does no longer truly seek dialogue with and entrance into the community of universal being, to which the God-faith elicited by Jesus Christ should refer. On the other hand, Christocentrism "misjudges the world that is without knowledge of Christ as without any awareness of God"[38]; therefore, the interpretation of God-in-Christ which we carry on in the church, is not *complete* without an interpretation of Christ through the Spirit that proceeds from the Father.

> The most prevalent, the most deceptive, and perhaps ultimately the most dangerous inconsistency . . . arises from the substitution of Christology for theology, the love of Jesus Christ for the love of God, and of life in the community of Jesus Christ for life in the divine commonwealth. . . . When the proposition that Jesus Christ is God is converted into the proposition that God is Jesus Christ . . . as if the Spirit proceeded only from the Son . . . as if Jesus Christ were man's only hope . . . his very character, his sonship, his relation to the One with whom he is united, are denied.[39]

All this is not to say that we cannot call Jesus truly God. Niebuhr's solution of the Trinitarian problem is not as simple as that.[40] On the contrary, precisely because it is *God* who is revealed, the point at which he is revealed must be related incessantly to all other points in history. Here lies the importance that Niebuhr attaches to the Holy Spirit and to the function of hope. As Jesus' own hopefulness was *heroic*,[41] so the function of his image in our history is to create and renew hope—heroic hopefulness with regard to a God whom we cannot possibly trust on the basis of our daily experience. Any theological or christological model which precludes the outcome of this fundamental struggle of faith and hope is defense against the threat of his struggle and thus also against its promise. Radical monotheism and radical godlessness are permanent partners; were this not so, there would be no way to transcend the defensiveness of the closed society. There is no third alternative next to entrusting oneself to being itself or constructing another defense. Hope to proceed on this road has been given and can be given again. It is related in particular to the life of Jesus Christ. In a sense, the hope created by him includes the hope that he himself will be shown authorized to create hope.

Yet a major factor in all this is Niebuhr's insistence on God's *greatness* and *sovereignty*, and this insistence tends to increase rather than to weaken the disjunction which we observed. At certain points in Niebuhr's writings[42] it seems that God has become the great X in the triad history-God-Christ, and that because of this, his pneumatology must necessarily remain silent or underdeveloped. At those points hope almost becomes resignation—resignation to the unity and the power of the mysterious system of being which can in no way be compromised by finite men.

Chapter 5
The Church

A. THE CHRISTIAN COMMUNITY

1. The confessional attitude. It may seem to the reader of the first four chapters that Niebuhr's reflections on the church represent an afterthought which is included only because it cannot be left out, but which, with regard to its content, falls prey to the general vigor of monotheism and transformation that characterizes Niebuhr's thinking as a whole. Our constant reference to the tendency of Niebuhr's thought to relativize, almost to eliminate, the Christian community, might strengthen this impression. Yet we suggest that Niebuhr's theology revolves around the church from beginning to end. In this respect he holds a special position among other neoorthodox thinkers,[1] although the way in which he speaks about the church distinguishes him from many other church theologians as well.

This last chapter serves to illustrate this point. The first half will occupy itself with the prolegomena, with certain themes in Niebuhr's thought which underlie and determine the way in which he speaks about the church. The second half will deal with his conception of the church. One thing about this conception should, however, be mentioned at the outset. For Niebuhr any exercise of theology, any occurrence of Christian faith and witness, presupposes the existence of the Christian community, the church, and takes place in its context; with the givenness of the church something else is also given: the larger contexts in which the church lives, moves, and has its being. The church presents itself as an inalienable part of a particular society and a particular culture, and is determined by it. Christian faith and the Christian church can never be analyzed only "from the inside"; there are *several* worlds in which they live, to which they refer, and in view of which they should relativize themselves. This is so not only because the larger world in which we live forces us to accept some sort of relativism, but especially because the God to whom the church points is the God of more than only the church.

This fundamental conviction is reflected, first of all, in Niebuhr's insistence on the necessity of the *confessional attitude*. This is consistent with what we have analyzed above with regard to history, faith, and community. "Theology finds itself forced to begin in historic faith because there is no other starting point for its endeavor."[2] There is no way to transcend the historical relativity of a particular faith; "Men lack standards by which to judge their standards"[3]; there can be no superior comparison and evaluation of the many faiths. To be a Christian is simply part of one's fate, and therefore we can never say that there is such a being as a *Christian God*—even though Christians cannot abstract from the *Christian relation to God*.[4] In addition to these considerations about faith, history, and community, reflections on the person and work of Christ also lead us in the direction of "confessionalism." For Christ is unique and central because and insofar as he refers us to God, the neighbor, and the world. The nature of the Christian faith demands that nothing but the object of faith be placed in the center.

> The faith of Christian revelation is directed toward a God who reveals himself as the only universal sovereign and as the One who judges all men—but particularly those directed to him in faith—to be sinners wholly unworthy of sovereignty. To substitute the sovereignty of Christian religion for the sovereignty of the God of Christian faith, though it be done by means of the revelation idea, is to fall into a new type of idolatry, to abandon the standpoint of Christian faith and revelation which are directed toward the God of Jesus Christ and to take the standpoint of a faith directed toward religion or revelation.[5]

> A faithful external history is not interested in faith but in the ways of God; and the more faithful it is, the less it may need to mention his name or refer to the revelation in which he was first apprehended—or rather, in which he first apprehended the believer.[6]

There is only one attitude, then, which the Christian community can legitimately assume: "We can proceed only by stating *in simple, confessional form* what has happened to us in our community, how we came to believe, how we reason about things, and what we see from our point of view."[7] Any other attitude necessarily leads to the defense of self or community. Needless to say, such defense is a permanent temptation and it is never wholly absent, but it remains the basic destructive element in all presentations of monotheistic faith. We can never *possess* what happens to us in revelation; acting as if we do means a denial of the fact that the transition from unbelief to faith, from distrust to trust in the One beyond the many, is never more than partial. Self-defensiveness denies the necessity of justification by faith.[8]

In his insistence on the necessity of the confessional attitude

Niebuhr turns against all *apologetic use of revelation.* Apologetic statements, which seek to defend the legitimacy or reasonableness of the Christian faith on the basis of some common ground shared by the "defender" and the "despiser," necessarily distort both the character of revelation and the status of the receiver of revelation. Defense inevitably confuses ultimate with finite ends, and ends up treating the *self* as the object to be defended. This error, "the inversion of faith whereby man puts himself into the center, constructs an anthropocentric universe and makes confidence in his own value rather than faith in God his beginning," is more prevalent and more dangerous than we usually think; "for faith in the God of Jesus Christ is a rare thing, and faith in idols tends forever to disguise itself as Christian trust."[9]

It is obvious that Niebuhr's rigid distinction between confessionalism and apologetics has its consequences for the theory of missions: reconciling men with God is in no way identical with conversion to Christianity.[10] Niebuhr has been criticized for making the Christian witness outside the community completely meaningless,[11] but such criticism is not entirely justified. Niebuhr underscores the specifically missionary character of the Christian community, which is grounded precisely in its confessional and self-relativizing attitude,[12] for only in such an attitude can the community *effectively* refer to God! The community is missionary to the extent that all proselytizing is avoided.

There is another critical question which must be more seriously considered: Does not the confessional attitude which Niebuhr prescribes for the community always involve *some apologetics?* It can hardly be denied that there are so many traces of a rational explication of the Christian faith in Niebuhr's thought, that his insistence on confessionalism seems somewhat isolated. Many critics have called attention to the fact that the confessional emphasis on Jesus Christ stands next to what looks like a rational defense of radical monotheism. John B. Cobb, Jr. speaks plainly of an "apologetic for radical monotheism."[13] Kenneth M. Hamilton attributes to Niebuhr

> the assumption that the complete and perfect faith which is radical monotheism is something entirely intelligible in and by itself, that this intelligible faith is illustrated or "incarnated" in specific instances which can be judged to embody the ideal to a greater or lesser extent.[14]

Kenneth Cauthen puts it even more sharply: "Neibuhr moves logically from an analysis of the universal problem of faith arising out of man's existential situation into the confessional framework of Christian theology."[15] Also Lonnie D. Kliever: "Niebuhr makes guarded apologetic use of this apparent inescapability of faith," and: "Niebuhr's confessional approach does not exclude theological apologetics."[16]

There seems to be some ground for these criticisms when one looks at statements such as these:

> To the monotheistic believer for whom all responses to his companions are interrelated with his responses to God as the ultimate person, the ultimate cause, the center of universal community, there seem to be indications in the whole of the responsive, accountable life of men of a movement of self-judgment and self-guidance which cannot come to rest until it makes its reference to a universal other and a universal community, which that other both represents and makes his cause.[17]

It is not clear to what extent Niebuhr wants to restrict the "indications of the movement of self-judgment and self-guidance" to the particular vision of the "monotheistic believer" who confesses himself as such. This unclarity does not wholly disappear by Niebuhr's assertion that he only occupies himself with self-understanding in the community of believing men, or by the fact that statements about human faith are made from the Christian point of view.[18]

The questions which arise here can be answered only by a closer look at the possible meanings of the word apologetics and the meaning which Niebuhr attaches to it. It seems that in the nineteenth century, generally speaking, the defense of "true religion" on a rational basis became increasingly obsolete and was replaced in three ways. The first was the interpretation of history as the development of an ideal principle, of reason, of true religion, or even of true religionlessness. Christianity was seen as a particular point in, or illustration of, this development. The second was the positing of the legitimacy of the particular Christian faith on the basis of an authority which could not itself be defended because it stood in a direct relation to the subject of revelation. The faith of the community was rationally defended on this basis, though the basis itself did not become the object of defense. The third was the postponement of *all* apologetics in favor of a purely scientific approach to all religious phenomena. In a sense, the "Barthian revolt" against the nineteenth-century developments consisted of an exclusive concentration on the second of these ways.

Many hold that this attempt is successful in avoiding a relapse into the defense of "true religion." Others, however, are not so sure; and it may be partly because of this, that "after Barth" attention to the other two possibilities of apologetics is developing. This takes the form of a reflection on fundamental principles, an encounter in communication, an effort to account for the way in which one believes; and it does not primarily reflect the need for self-justification of the Christian religion, though it is of course difficult to make final judgments here. Niebuhr, who like Barth takes his starting point in the unique authority of the revelation which itself cannot be an object of defense, is driven on as it were by his fear of a renewed and disguised form of self-defense that he sees present in the Barthian movement. Thus, in order to be a consistent confessionalist, he seeks to balance his starting point by the other possibilities of apologetics which were present in nineteenth-century thought. His attraction to Ernst Troeltsch is at least partly rooted in this concern.

Troeltsch does not abandon the possibility of defending the reasonableness of Christianity by critically studying its phenomena, recognizing a metaphysical element, and analyzing religious experience in general. Of course, as we have seen, Niebuhr rejects even this possibility; but in doing so he retains the structure of the Troeltschean question, which means that he always guards against the dangers of overemphasizing the irrational origin and existence of the Christian faith.

Niebuhr is thus able to distinguish between a defensive argument for the validity and reasonableness of the Christian faith (which he rejects), and a rational explication of the Christian faith (which characterizes much of his thought). In other words, the incarnation of radical faith in total life has a rational side, it can be approached rationally; *but that this is so, does not itself become rational.* The gift of faith itself can be witnessed to only in simple confessional statements; but what the faith is and does, can and must be made visible rationally. Because of this distinction, the latter action can and must be completely without any traces of self-defense or defense of community.

The problem of this approach is, of course, that the emphasis on the necessity of confessionalism is accompanied by a divorce between witness to the Christian faith and the particular symbols in which the community has learned to express it. That God is more than the God of the Christian community implies that witness to him is not bound to the particular language of this community. We should not forget that the emphasis on the confessional attitude is a consequence of the emphasis on monotheism and transformation: confessionalism means reference to the largest possible whole in which self and other are included, the universal community of being. Only such continuous reference can liberate men from the ever-returning necessity of self-defense, which often disguises itself as true confessionalism. It is not *necessary* to shield or defend God, for his sovereignty is always more inclusive than our efforts. We cannot even return to apologetics in order to defend a particular conception of God which we suppose to be more *true* than other conceptions.[19] *Such* apologetics is necessarily self-defense. And we are not called to defend our faith, but to serve the glory of God.

2. **The authority of scripture.** The conspicuous absence of a

satisfactory doctrine of scriptural authority in neoorthodox theology causes many benevolent conservative observers to venture the suggestion that this might turn out to be the Achilles' heel of the whole movement. Although we would not subscribe to the implication that without sufficient attention for the authority of scripture no theology can be called adequate—the major importance of Niebuhr's theology lies in his particular style of thinking rather than in reinforcement or modification of doctrines—it is clear that a fresh occupation with scriptural authority in contemporary theology would not be a luxury. The contemporary concentrations on the origin and effect of faith, on the problems of language and hermeneutics, on the sociological aspects of the Christian community, seem to leave little room for reflection on the Bible. In Niebuhr's case, the authority for the Christian faith seems to rest almost exclusively in the historical communication of faith itself, and his insistence on the confessional attitude seems to belittle the authority of particular documents. The doctrine of scriptural authority cannot be left untouched by all these emphases; it is desirable, therefore, that it become the object of fresh scrutiny.

The style of Niebuhr's thought underscores the problem, not only because his ideas about history and revelation—revelation is *embodied* but not *localized* in external history—raise questions about the Bible, but also because *authority as such* is no longer a self-evident thing when we speak about incarnation and communication of faith in a total life. In "total life" we find ourselves in a complex field of many authorities. Can there be any absolute or ultimate authority here? How does the Bible function for us in this context? These are the questions for Niebuhr.

Reflection on the Bible must, for Niebuhr, begin in the particular Christian community and therefore simultaneously in the larger historical and cultural contexts of this community. Definitions of scriptural authority which absolutize the relativity of scripture—"closed society" definitions!—are a basic error.[20] Moreover, our reflections can never reach the point where authority originates. Beyond the relation between scripture and community which actually exists and functions in a variety of ways, nothing is accessible to us. Niebuhr is "ill at ease with theologians who deal with the scriptures as a nonhistorical book and undertake to explain it as though they were nonhistorical men."[21]

Niebuhr illustrates this, first of all, with the results of the past hundred years of biblical scholarship. Instead of destroying scriptural authority, this scholarship has produced a new awareness of the close association between book and community, so that "scriptural and communal authority begin to fuse." The same conclusion is reached, second, by reflection on the authority by which the pastoral ministry is exercised. In this authority, too, there is no clear separation between the scriptures and the particular community in which the ministry functions.[22]

The Bible, then, is a truly historical book—it contains the documents of a particular society, or particular societies; it can, therefore, be approached only in a way which does full justice to this historical character. This means not only that the Bible can be *fully* subjected to historical criticism, but also that those who reckon themselves to belong to the same community of which the Bible contains documents, must read the Bible *backward through their own history* if they are to understand it as revelation.[23] This implies that there is a two-way movement, a reciprocity, between the scriptures and its readers.[24] In all this, Niebuhr opposes what we might call a *biblicism of derivation.* Present assertions of faith do not have their ground and truth in the fact that the Bible suggests them to us, or that they can be derived from the Bible; rather, the relation between the Bible and present assertions of faith is one of dialogue, comparison, and compatibility. In this relation the Bible has authority because in it we are likely to hear the *"reverberation"* of the commandment and promise in which the Christian community first found its *raison d'être.* The Bible contains the dictionary and the grammar of the language in which God speaks to us, rather than that language itself.[25]

A second point of consideration suggests itself in the observation that the scriptures are by no means the *only* source of authority for the community. It is obvious that many voices besides scripture speak to the contemporary community of believing men. What else can be expected among historical and social beings? The tradition—that "dynamic structure of modifiable habits without which men do not exist as men"[26]—contains the presence of many other men and communities besides those of the Bible, so that the dialogue with the Bible is truly a "multilogue." This point is brought home to us by the character of the Bible itself—it contains the language of other communities besides Israel and the early Christians—and by the character of our present moral existence. These things make it impossible for us to draw a simple diagram of authority or even to discern which authority ranks highest for us. Here Niebuhr opposes what we might call a *biblicism of isolation.* The Bible is never our *sole* source or *sole* authority; in the actual life of the community it shares its authority with many other things. This observation only illustrates and strengthens the conviction that the Bible is not the only word that God is speaking.[27]

If these two considerations were not accompanied in Niebuhr's thought by the conviction that we are allowed and enabled to speak this way precisely because of the truth of the revelation which does come to us through Bible and community, they would probably destroy all unique authority of the scriptures. But these considerations are not meant to destroy or even to limit scriptural authority; rather, they determine the way in which it should be approached. It would, of course, be dishonest to say merely that the Bible has authority *in spite of* its historical, communal, and relative character. Authority defined by such a statement would not have any relevance to a faith incarnated in total life. Rather, the character of faith leads us to see that genuine authority does not exist apart from a *decision* which—as it were—allows it to function. This is true not only for the authority attributed to the Bible as historical source or educational guide; but especially for its authority as the story of God's self-disclosure.

We observed before that acknowledgment of revelation in a particular event, or, in this case, in a particular document, expresses itself in a continuous *metanoia* which is Trinitarian in structure. The Bible, as the story of God's self-disclosure, has, in this respect, a function similar to that of the Christ-event of which it contains the documents. Its authority consists, so to speak, in its ability to refer men to God, neighbor, and world.[28] Precisely this underscores the limitations of scripture as a book, historically and culturally conditioned; it remains impossible to treat the uniqueness of its authority as nonhistorical and as eternally valid, precisely because of the character of this authority.

Niebuhr's designation of the Bible as the story of God's self-disclosure in Jesus Christ raises the question of his approach to the *Old Testament.* At first sight his utterances on this point seem very scarce and insignificant. A closer look, however, teaches us that the Old Testament is, for Niebuhr, a supreme illustration of particular emphases he seeks to make in connection with Jesus Christ. The Old Testament has its relevance precisely because the significance of Jesus Christ implies that he is not the *only* significant one.[29] Three points may illustrate this.

a. Jesus Christ—who is central in the memory of the community and whose image determines the authority of the Bible as a whole—is not a nonhistorical figure, but he brings with him his own particular faith and that of his people. Accepting Jesus Christ means accepting his faith and his history, which are the faith and history of Israel.[30]

b. The story of Israel contains unique examples of the incarnation of radical faith in total life, *just like* the story of Jesus Christ. In the faith of Israel all human relations were transformed into covenant relations[31]; its history is a history of revelation.[32]

c. The Old Testament can deliver us from a Christocentrism which without correction develops into a destructive henotheism. Renewed attention to the Old Testament in recent years has often brought a fresh awareness of the living monotheism with which the Israelites encountered the actions of the sovereign Lord of history in all events. The universal ethics of the Jewish people can save us from a polytheism and henotheism "into which we gentile nations are forever tempted to fall."[33]

The unique authority of the scriptures as story of God's self-disclosure, then, cannot be possessed. It is linked to the ever-returning decision of the community to see, acknowledge, and "incarnate" this self-disclosure; and as such it is linked to the power of the Spirit who enables us to recognize the action of the sovereign God in our history. Such communal decisions have been taken by the establishment of the canon and by the restitution of scriptural authority during the Reformation; they are taken today whenever other authorities are subordinated to the authority of the God to whom the Bible points.

This unique authority does not increase the value of the Bible as sourcebook or as educational guide, but it determines the way in which we use the Bible as sourcebook or as educational guide. To say that the Bible is *word of God* means that it enables us to hear the many words God is speaking. If we wish to discover and rediscover *this* scriptural authority, we must be on our guard against a mere identification of Bible and word of God; not only because such identification obstructs our view of scriptural authority, but especially because it deprives the term "word of God" of a genuine meaning. "When the two are identified so that word of God means Bible and Bible means word of God, nothing meaningful is being said anymore about the symbolized reality or about the symbol."[34] With this problem, however, we have broached the subject matter of the following section.

3. The symbols of the Christian faith. The question of what the specific characteristics of the Christian community are—its attitudes, its sources, its way of articulating faith—cannot be answered without some attention to the symbolic character of religious language and to the way in which the Christian community uses or ought to use it. Niebuhr's reflections on language are clearly not determined by the questions of the analyst who looks for logically consistent patterns and for conditions related to the meaningfulness of certain types of speech. His questions are, rather: How should we use our language, and the prelogical patterns by which it is "organized," in such a way that it truly reflects our encounter with reality and our interpretative response to it? How should we organize our speech about *God* in such a way that it not merely reflects others' ideas about him (so that our world becomes "a room plastered with bad copies of copies of copies of such original paintings")[35] but truly our own experience in the relation with the One beyond the many in the many? Language can become a creative means to

evoke encounter with reality and with God; it can also become a prison that binds us to particular traditional schemes in which living symbols have become stale copies.

A long tradition, reaching back to American Revivalism, shapes Niebuhr's thought on these points. Names that come to mind are Edwards, Bushnell, and Mead. Important is, first of all, Edwards' distinction between *sign* and *idea*. To have an idea of the things we speak and think about, means to have a *vivid experience* of those things.[36]

In actual speech and thought, however, we use signs to represent the ideas; this is necessary though it leads men to a multitude of errors. There is, therefore, a distinction between mere cognition and ideal apprehension; and knowledge of "divine things" can only be of the latter kind. In other words, as John E. Smith puts it, in Edwards there is a "fusion of the descriptive and evocative functions of language"[37]; when language about divine things is no longer evocative, its descriptive function also deteriorates. Bushnell, in his *Dissertation on Language*, in a comparable sense concerns himself with the relation between the mere use of words and "the great universal grammar of the soul and the creation."[38] Much senseless strife results from the confusion of form and truth: as in poetry, truth might well assert itself through the multiplication of forms and words, which are often contradictory among themselves. Next to this emphasis, Bushnell's *Dissertation* is a significant example of the effort to analyze language as a social and contextual phenomenon. From here we can draw a line to Mead, for whom signs and symbols function in a pattern of response, in a process of conveying and expecting attitudes. All the emphases mentioned are present in Niebuhr.

Niebuhr's attitude toward religious and theological language—there is not a very clear distinction between the two—is, next to the anti-metaphysical motifs which we discussed earlier, determined by this approach. As a result, we can make three observations. In the first place, doctrinal speech must retain its dynamic, *teaching* character rather than institutionalize itself in static authoritative formulas. "We should discover our dogmas as persons and communities of persons rather than proclaim them."[39] Second, doctrines must be seen as articulations of the actual processes of faith and response; the latter cannot be made subordinate to the former, just as dogmatics has no priority over ethics.[40] Instead (this is the third point), the Christian community is engaged in a constant effort to relate its language about reality to the pattern, the "myth," of Jesus Christ; rather, to relate the latter to its daily life, to the history which it interprets, and to the future which it expects. The symbols of the Christian faith therefore have to be seen as fruits of this ever-present interaction between faith and "total life," and they can perform their proper function only if they are permanently reconnected to this process.

Of course, this is not only a matter of individual effort. The whole church or the whole culture can be caught in an atmosphere in which the traditional symbols have lost their vitality and are no longer sources of inspiration. Then nothing less than a new reformation can rescue faith. These considerations are behind Niebuhr's concern for *resymbolization of the Christian message.*

> I do not believe that we can meet in our day the need which the church was founded to meet by becoming more orthodox or more liberal, more biblical or more liturgical. I look for a resymbolization of the message and the life of faith in the one God. Our old phrases are worn out; they have become clichés by means of which we can neither grasp nor communicate the reality of our existence before God. Retranslation is not enough; more precisely, retranslation of traditional terms—"word of God," "redemption," "incarnation," "justification," "grace," "eternal life"—is not possible unless one has direct relations in the immediacy of personal life to the actualities to which people in another time referred with the aid of such symbols. I do not know how this resymbolization in pregnant words and in symbolic deeds—like the new words of the Reformation and the Puritan movement and the Great Awakening, like the symbolic deeds of the Franciscans and the social gospelers—will come about. I do count on the Holy Spirit, and believe that the words and deeds will come to us.[41]

It is clear that Niebuhr's concept of resymbolization is intimately connected with the general observations listed above. Resymbolization is as much a rediscovery of the character of language as it is a rediscovery of the character of faith in total life. Above all, resymbolization of the *Christian* message is based on the specific character of Christian faith which prohibits the closed society, the isolation of a "sacred" religious language or a normative body of doctrine. Mere adaptation of ancient terms to modern thinking is not enough; it might even be dangerous because it can overlook what is really at stake. Resymbolization can grow only out of a living experience of the meaning of the gospel with the aid of contemporary ideas.[42] It is, therefore, not similar to demythologizing, though Niebuhr confesses kinship with Bultmann's intentions.[43] It does not seek the core within and behind the complexity of mythological language; the primary thing is communication with neighbors and God, and through this the reformation of culture. Or, as Niebuhr himself says, "Our real concern in the church is with the dialogue rather than the kerygma."[44]

B. THE CHURCH IN THE WORLD

1. Purpose and perspective.

Jonathan Edwards once said that the trouble with men was not that they had no ideas of God or that they were atheists, but that their ideas of God were too little and too small. This is doubtless the most important problem in theological education—this problem of helping men to understand the greatness of God. But in connection with it, it is important that they should understand the greatness of the church in its complexity but also in its marvelous unity, its present modern existence but also its existence in all times, its distinction from Israel but also its unity with Israel. *Let us try to give men a big idea of the church* in everything that we do in theological education.[1]

This quotation undoubtedly reveals Niebuhr's specific concern with the church, and it also indicates the context and the perspective of this concern. What is "the greatness of the church" for Niebuhr? We might indicate Niebuhr's frame of thought with regard to the church by the following key words: factuality, indispensability, relativity, and reference. Niebuhr always begins with the fact that the church is there, both in given structures and in given patterns of relation to the social and cultural environment in which it lives; in other words, Niebuhr's reflection on the church begins with its tangible thereness, rather than with an abstract theological concept. As we have observed before, the *indispensability* and the *relativity* of the church can only be asserted together, though it is in the church that we receive and retain the central image which determines our vision of being and history; and also *because* of this, no definition of the church is adequate unless it takes account of the church as part of the world—unless it uses more terms of definition than only Jesus Christ.[2] For it is the task of the church to *refer* men to the greatness of God, and with that to the permanent transformation in which the Christian community is learning to adopt the histories of all human groups as its own.

This basic scheme has been present in Niebuhr's thought from the very beginning. It has determined the changes that he went through with regard to the church-world relation, and is not merely a result of these changes or a passing stage. This becomes clear as soon as we start to formulate the changes of emphasis that actually took place in Niebuhr's thought.

In the precritical period, of which *The Social Sources of Denominationalism* is the major example, the problem of the church is clearly that of social determinism and ultimate loyalty. Its ultimate loyalty—its "reference"—can be realized only if men seek to transcend the social conditioning which makes relativity into a threat to loyalty, by adhering to the ideal of love exemplified in the gospel. The critical period—especially *The Church Against the World*—shows a major emphasis on the church's responsibility to divorce itself from all forms of idolatrous anthropocentricism and to witness to the sovereignty of God as a critical corrective. By shifting the problem from "social determinism vs. ultimate loyalty" to "anthropocentricism vs. sovereignty and judgment" it is radicalized rather than defined in completely new categories: it is brought closer to the problem of the sinful nature of man and his tendency toward self-defense and distrust of being. In the critical period (roughly the years 1935-41) this means serious attention to the specific nature of the church in distinction from the world; in the following years (the forties and the fifties), however it leads to an effort to restore the balance *in view of the remaining basic pattern of the church-world problem.*

The distinction between church and world should not allow us to lose sight of the fact that its particularity—its historical conditioning, the image of Jesus Christ—remains relative in view of the universal context to which it seeks to refer men: God, neighbor, and world. The problem of the church is precisely the balance between indispensability and reference: if we overemphasize distinctness, the danger is isolationism; if we overemphasize universal responsibility, it is worldliness.[3] The task of the church in the light of this dual temptation is to exemplify in its apostolic, pastoral, and pioneering responsibility what it means to be world-before-God.[4]

In all this, however, Niebuhr's attention is still focused on a purified concept of *the task of the church.* Gradually this interest seems to recede in importance. In *The Purpose of the Church and Its Ministry* (1956), the particular purpose of the church is compared and related to the many purposes of cultural life; in other words, the "world" is no longer seen as an undifferentiated whole used as a pole in the definition of the church. It is telling that the major dangers for the church here are no longer worldliness and isolationism but "Christian humanism" and "ecclesiastical institution."[5] In other words, the problem is now the relation between distinctness and pervasiveness of the Christian faith, or even the place of the Christian faith in the world of the many faiths.

This "second radicalizing" of the church-world problem which is implied in Niebuhr's work of the forties and fifties, becomes explicit in the significant paper *The Church Defines Itself in the World.*[6] Here Niebuhr insists more strongly than before—apparently in reaction against a Christocentrism and church-centrism which he sees present in contemporary ecumenical thinking—on a definition of the church in the context of created and inspired humanity, in view of "the worldly character of the church and the churchly character of the world." This does not weaken or even eliminate the particular character of the church but rather leads to a clear conception of its missionary position, which is grounded in the fact that "the church knows itself to be 'world' before God while the world does not know this but thinks it can be like God."

It is clear that in this whole development the basic scheme in which Niebuhr defines the church-world relation does not change in spite of the shifts in emphasis. His conception of the purpose of the church, though formulated only in *The Purpose of the Church and Its Ministry*, can be seen as a concise summary of his whole thinking on the subject: it is the increase among men of the love of God and neighbor.[7] It is not, in other words, the effort to draw men to faith in Jesus Christ, although this is necessarily involved. The main element in Niebuhr's thinking about the church remains the church's complex relation to the whole of culture, both factual and perspectival. The church must recognize itself as a relative part of the total life of a human culture and a human history, and the freedom implied in the vision of reconciliation to the Creator which it has received does not really exist if it is not radiated throughout this total life. The basic task of the church is, and remains, the exercise of the pastoral ministry of reconciliation to the unreconciled world.[8] Reviewing the development of Niebuhr's thought we might say that at first the most important thing is that the *church* must do this; later he increasingly stresses that it is *this* which must be done. Neither of these "poles" ever wholly disappears from Niebuhr's thought, even though in the later years there are hints of a pessimism with regard to the church, parallel to his resistance to Christocentric ways of thinking.

Niebuhr's conception of the work of *theology* significantly reflects his thought about the church. For the work of theology is linked inseparably to the existence of the church, and its character is determined by the character of the complex relations between church and world.

> Being in social history it cannot be a personal and private theology, nor can it live in some nonchurchly sphere of political or cultural history: its home is the church; its language is the language of the church; and with the church it is directed toward the universal from which the church knows itself to derive its being and to which it points in all its faith and works.[9]

This indication of context has its immediate consequences for the definition of the object of theology. Theology is linked to the living reality of faith; it is therefore not merely the science of God,

> for it knows that the Transcendent Universal is known or acknowledged only in acts of universal loyalty and in transcending confidence, precedent to all inquiry and action . . . it calls attention to the way in which every individual, group, and institution is

directly related to the Transcendent—whether positively in trust and loyalty or negatively in distrust and disloyalty.[10]

Yet neither is *faith as such* the object of theology. The object is the interrelated objects and subjects which are present when faith is present. Theology concerns itself with God in relation to self and neighbor, and with self and neighbor in relation to God; the proper study of mankind is God *and* man-before-God in their interrelation,[11] in the context of the church's ultimate purpose: *the spread of love of God and neighbor.*

A concise statement of the subject matter of theology is given in Niebuhr's (unpublished) lecture "The Position of Theology Today":

> Theology as theology is always concerned with God, yet only with God in relation to man or to ourselves—as our creator and the creator of our world, as our ruler and the ruler of our world, as our savior and the savior of our values. A knowledge of the divine which is concerned with its relation to nature and natural powers abstracted from man is not theology but metaphysics; a knowledge directed toward the ultimate ground of being in relation to all beings, simply considered, is ontology.
>
> Though theology can have fruitful dialogue with such metaphysics and such ontology it will always resist equation with them for its own knowledge is directed to *God-before-man*, to God in relation to men, or better, to ourselves. For theology as knowledge of the divine as it might be in itself apart from man fearing, hating, and loving God; apart from ourselves as being created, judged, and redeemed by him, is not knowledge of God at all. . . . And so it never proceeds without reference to the subjective pole—man. It is not, by the same token, primarily concerned with man in relation to natural existences—the study of that subject is natural anthropology; or with man in his relation primarily to fellowmen—that is the concern of sociology and social anthropology. The subject matter of theology is always man-before-*God*, man-related-to-God so that the knowledge—or at least acknowledgment of God—is implicit in all theological anthropology.

Theology, then, is the intellectual side of the direction toward wholeness of life and unity of self; it is the *intellectual love of God*. Its mission is "to show in practice as in theory how Christian faith in the One, the triune God, moves toward wholeness in life and thought, in person and community."[12] As such it is placed in the widest possible, *human*, context, like the church itself. It is "the search for human wisdom about the wisdom of God . . . the movement of the mind toward the hoped-for God and the hoped-for neighbor," which cannot hope to reach true understanding unless it is directed by *love of being.*[13] As it can be said about the faith of the church, that it functions both in a particular community and in "total life," it must be said about theology that it is not only the articulation of a particular faith but also the critical questioning in the midst of *all* scientific thought and activity. Theology has a genuine task at the university where it conducts a never-ending struggle with the half-gods, and endeavors to direct all life and thought to the One beyond the many.

Needless to say, in this activity theology can by no means be queen.[14] It fulfills the humble role of a handmaid. In this respect, too, it reflects the church as a whole and its task in the world. This "humble role of a handmaid" is a result of the inevitable tensions between particularity and universality which characterize the position of the church. In a sense, Niebuhr summarizes his whole conception of the church when he says about theology, that it *"must be content to spend no small part of its energies in the correction of the errors which ensue from its necessary mode of working."*[15]

2. The institutional pole. In many contemporary theological circles, notably those associated with the World Council of Churches, the *institutional* character of the church is the subject of intensive discussion. Since *institutionalism* was discovered as a major nontheological factor hindering church union, and since there is more and more communication between theologians and sociologists on the subject of church renewal, there has been increasing attention both to the self-perpetuating tendency of given church structures and to the changes in relations between the church and the "autonomous" and "secular" patterns of society. Against this background there is a widespread tendency to see basic conflict between the church's calling to mission and active participation in the problems of modern society on the one hand, and its institutional, conservative structures on the other.

We make these generalizations about the contemporary discussions on relevant missionary structures of the church only to emphasize that Niebuhr's reflections on the "church as institution" move in an entirely different climate and would be misunderstood if they were associated with these discussions. First of all, there is in Niebuhr no trace of the latent church gnosticism which conceives of the essence of the church as spiritual and noninstitutional, and regards its incarnation in human structures of social, political, and economic life as a limitation of its true being and mission. Instead, as we have observed before, Niebuhr's reflection on the church begins with reflection on the given structures— there is no other way to approach the problem. Second, there is no implication of a contrast between task and calling of the church on the one hand and its existence as an institution on the other. The fact that in modern society the church has lost much of its relevance is, to Niebuhr, only a symptom of a much deeper illness in the relation between church and culture, and the position of the church cannot be improved by any shortcut to social relevance. The present ills cannot be cured by encouraging "relevant" participation in the problems of society. Indeed, concentration only on the symptom might be dangerous as far as it obscures the basic purpose of the church, the exercise of the pastoral ministry of reconciliation, the redirection of the human spirit toward the greatness of God.

All this does not imply that the institutional character of the church does not present any problems to Niebuhr. For him the typical problem of the institution is that it organizes the human response patterns in such a way that it can block the living movement of a community or prevent a dynamic encounter between a self and its "circumambient world." This happens when the institution no longer sees anything except itself; more precisely, when it has lost sight of the other pole with which it should be held in tension, or by which it is connected, as it were, to its *raison d'être* and its purpose. This is the reason why Niebuhr prefers to speak of the church in terms of *polar relations*. There is always the pole of the institution—but it is balanced, relativized by other realities; and precisely in this polar tension the character and purpose of the church is clarified. We mention three of these polar definitions, and remind ourselves at the outset that they do not represent a chronological order, or an order of preference. They are used simultaneously and each serves to bring out aspects of the conception of the church which are permanently present in Niebuhr's thought.

The first is the polar relation between communal life and institutional organization, or, in shorthand, between "inward" and "outward" life of a given community. Though "institution" in this sense can be a more inclusive and less obligating entity than "community," it is clear that neither one can be conceived apart from the other.[16]

The second polar relation that figures in Niebuhr's thought is what we might call the "critical" one, and it is formulated in different ways. We meet it first in *The Social Sources of Denominationalism* as the polarity between ideal attitude and restrictive institutional embodiment. That this does not lead to a depreciation of the institutional *as such* is clear when we follow the development of this polarity in *The Kingdom of God in America*, where it becomes the tension between *movement* and *institution*. We must not lose sight of the fact that in this later book the major problem is not institutionalization itself, but rather the petrifaction of the movement of institutionalization, or the closing of the institutional forms against the possibilities of dynamic correction by the revolutionary character of the Christian faith itself. This point is completely overlooked in the German translation of *The Kingdom of God in America*, in which "institutionalization" is translated with an equivalent to *reification* that suggests immobility.[17] It is certainly not Niebuhr's intention to suggest that true Christianity consists of a permanently flowing movement *only*, though it must be conceded that his Bergsonian choice of words often suggests such an interpretation. At other places his intention is stated more clearly.[18]

Niebuhr's main point in this critical polarity is the tension between ultimate concerns and private interests; in other words, the danger lies in the closed society rather than in the institution as such.[19] This is also the way in which Niebuhr's use of the polarity Protestant-Catholic must be understood: the necessity of incarnation, of representation of the infinite in finite form, must be balanced by a continuing protest against confusion of meaning and symbol.[20]

The third polar relation we draw attention to is the one between the wide range of incarnations of faith in the total life of culture and the institutional conservation of church activity; for instance, the organized rites. There is some implication here of personal engagement over against impersonal participation, or of freedom and variety over against isolation. In this connection Niebuhr can speak of *two distinct ecumenical movements*, one of the institutional church and the other a movement of unity in spirit in our culture as a whole.[21]

Though we have indicated that these three polarities exist side by side throughout Niebuhr's work, we have to point to a shift in emphasis in the problem of the institutional pole, similar to the one we discovered in Niebuhr's thinking about purpose and perspective of the church. We can say that Niebuhr's attention shifts from the problem of denominationalism to the problem of the manifold incarnation of faith in culture. This is not to say that the church in its institutional form is depreciated, but rather that the institution of the church cannot be the central self-propagating model for the incarnation of faith. Consistent critical monotheism leads Niebuhr to see that the problem of the incarnation of faith is deeper and wider than the problem of the form and life of the church—rather, that the church, though it remains the bearer of the revelatory image of Jesus Christ, also in its institutional conservation is no exception to the general lot of other human communities.

In this connection two other points may be briefly mentioned. In the first place, Niebuhr's development shows that he does not see the church as a species of what might be called "the religious institution." As Niebuhr makes clear in his article "The Norm of the Church," a definition "from within" knows only Jesus Christ and does not begin with other assumptions about itself. In other words, any human association can become the church when it centers in Jesus Christ.[22] Second, the development of Niebuhr's thought implies the conviction that the *denomination* can no longer be regarded as the exclusive pattern for the presence of the church in the world. The church is where love of God and neighbor is increased, where God and neighbor are served.

Thus Niebuhr's final problem is that of cultural man and his God, not that of the ideal and the institution. Even in the critical polarity we discussed, this final problem is permanently in the background; perhaps it is Niebuhr's increasing awareness of the danger of the "henotheism of the church" which brings it out more explicitly.

3. **The vision of unity.** In *The Social Sources of Denomination- alism*, Niebuhr raises the problem of social conditioning and ultimate loyalty. With this, the whole issue of denominationalism and dividedness lies before him. In it he sees primarily "unacknowledged hypocrisy," "moral ineffectiveness," and "ethical weakness."

> The evil of denominationalism lies in the conditions which make the rise of sects desirable and necessary: in the failure of the churches to transcend the social conditions which fashion them into caste organizations, to sublimate their loyalties to standards and institutions only remotely relevant if not contrary to the Christian ideal, to resist the temptation of making their own self-preservation and extension the primary object of their endeavor.[23]

Niebuhr calls the churches to repentance and to radical commitment to the ideal of love; but soon afterward, in the Preface of *The Kingdom of God in America*, he confesses that this solution is "wholly inadequate." From this moment on, he opposes all superficial ecumenical movements which bypass the fundamental implications in the problem of denominationalism. *Unity* stands at the heart of Niebuhr's theology, but the problems here are so deep and wide—having their roots in human distrust and defensiveness, in "evil imaginations of the heart"—that a movement of church union can only lead men astray from the real issues. Like his brother, he is very critical of all solutions which do not search beneath the manifest dividedness of the church for what is true and false in the church, for what is genuine and destructive in human faith. In the paper "The Church Defines Itself in the World," Niebuhr warns against treating the famous "nontheological factors" as nonessential, for precisely these factors can lead us to see the worldly character of the church and the churchly character of the world; they can prevent us from defining the church too narrowly in terms of Jesus Christ and from seeking easy solutions. The problem of unity, too, is complicated by the fact that he who concentrates on the church can never concentrate on the church *only*.

There are no easy solutions; nothing short of a *conversion of memory* will do. "Every part of disunited Christendom interprets its past through an image of itself and holds fast without repentance to that image."[24] Unity depends on a truly common memory and a common hope; it depends on the appropriation of the "catholic vision" which is *more* than church union.

The catholic vision is, as it were, handed to us by the development of biblical studies, historical research, and the rise of science in the past century.[25] These things provide a new awareness of the unity of men in many different societies and histories, and they call our attention to the fact that no definition of Christianity except by its *total history* is adequate.

> The invisibility of the catholic church is due not only to the fact that no one society or nation of Christians can represent the universal, but also to the fact that no one time, but only all times together, can set forth the full meaning of the movement toward the eternal and its created image. One of the great needs of present-day institutionalized Christianity, perhaps particularly in America with its denominations, is recovery of faith in the invisible catholic church.[26]

The catholic vision implies more than church union, because the ultimate issue is not the unity of the church but the unity of God and the world—the unity of the many histories in which men live and in which they search for wholeness and intelligibility. Precisely *through Christ* "we become immigrants into the empire of God which extends over all the world and learn to remember the history of that empire; that is, of men in all times and places, as our history."[27] Neither Christ nor the church can, therefore, be the center of our search for unity. For apart from their reference to God and to *his* unity, both Christ and the church become principles of closedness and defense. The unity of the church is visualized in its true context only when we direct our attention to the unity of God, which we cannot grasp apart from a continuing dialogue with the world around us, with the many histories that challenge our particular history, with the many forms of faith that are present besides ours.

The church loses its particular character and mission when it seeks unity in terms of itself. For then it has not touched the basic problem of human defensiveness and distrust, elements which seek again and again to organize bulwarks of unity against the threat of a totality of being which seems unintelligible and malevolent. Therefore,

> no unity achieved or given in integration around any principle save the one God can really unify or endure. Insofar as we seek a unity in Christ otherwise than in his oneness with the Father and the Holy Spirit, or confess him Lord otherwise than to the glory of God the Father, we are in peril of worshiping the principle of our Christian unity, not the principle of the unity of being.[28]

And when we begin with the unity of God, we might find unity in our world "in a wholly different manner than we desired or imagined."[29]

Once the unity of God has become the center of our attention, the unity of *men* becomes prior in importance to the unity of believers. The latter remains important, to be sure, but it is no more important than other unities; for instance, that of families, communities, or nations. When the unity of God is the focus of orientation, church unity can be no more than one aspect or one part, even if it is the church that directs men to the unity of God and that seeks to increase among men the love of God and neighbor. The present church-centrism which is prevalent in many circles of the ecumenical movement makes it impossible, according to Niebuhr, to get a clear picture of what is at stake.

Needless to say, the emphases we find here are similar to the ones we discussed in the preceding sections on the church in the world. Niebuhr's sensitivity to church-centrism, even in the context of the church union movement, is so great that the message he leaves for the church in this respect is far from clear. The factuality and the perspective of the church's relatedness to culture, seen and reinforced in the context of radical monotheism, lead Niebuhr to insist that there can be no significant unity if it does not reflect the unity of God in the world; in other words, if it does not focus upon the major problem of man's irreconciledness to God. Any church unity which is sought apart from this theocentric approach is a dangerous thing. For "the ecumenical world of those who are unreconciled to each other is the world of those unreconciled to God. This strange human race has never been reconciled to God—but now its irreconciledness is more conspicuous than ever."[30]

Concluding Remarks

1. THE SIGNIFICANCE OF NIEBUHR'S THEOLOGY

We suggested in the introduction that the importance of Niebuhr's theology does not lie primarily in a forceful systematic thinking which regroups the problems of theology around several leading ideas and in this way inspires and influences the schools and currents of contemporary thought, but that it lies, rather, in the particular style with which he approaches the dilemmas of his theological heritage and with which he reacts to those who largely determine the direction of theology today. Throughout our study this impression has been confirmed. At crucial points in Niebuhr's thought we looked in vain for clear solutions of complicated issues; and many times, in discussing certain problems, we had only implications of his general thinking to work with. On the whole, however, his style is clear and consistent; and it is here that we must look for the significance of his theology. His way of thinking not only summarizes and indicates several basic problems of twentieth-century theology, but also suggests a direction in which theological thought must move if it wants to avoid the pitfalls and dead alleys that "critical theology" in all its varieties sets out to expose.

To a European observer, Niebuhr's theology seems to reflect the major outlines of the journey of twentieth-century theology. It begins in those movements of thought which seek the ultimate value of human life and history in the context of men's scientific, moral, and religious ideals; it moves on to the consistent recognition of the unique source of grace in God's absolute sovereignty; and from there on—without abandoning either of the two preceding "phases"—it proceeds to deal with newly arising fragmentary questions about the why and the how of theological language, of situational relations between church and society, and so on: questions which arise in a general atmosphere of dissatisfaction with the "giant theologies" that arose before, during, and after World War II. All this does not make Niebuhr's theology as such into an alternative to Barth's—it can still be maintained that his direct reactions to Barth's theology do less than justice to the latter's intention—but it does mean that Niebuhr's theological style reflects several concerns and possibilities that can and should be taken seriously in a situation in which the effects of Barthianism are more and more subject to criticism.

Determinative for this style is, of course, as we have had occasion to point out, its American background. To say that American religious thought, in its attachment to a pervasive faith in Providence, has never been hospitable to critical philosophy, is perhaps too simple and too academic a statement; yet it does indicate that church and theology in America have lived in an atmosphere of self-evidence, established in the cultural life as a whole, and that there have not been significant movements, academic or otherwise, which really formed a threat or a challenge to their existence.

Contrary to the European scene, where secularization has a popular social basis and the church has been forced time and again to take specific stands and stress its distinctness from the surrounding world, including the academic world, American theology has, therefore, developed particular interests and problems. It has, for instance, been able to speak about the church in a much less emphatic way and about human faith in a much more general way, as a phenomenon generally implicit in moral attitudes toward neighbor and society. In such a situation the effects of "crisis-thinking" simply *had* to be different, and it is here that we have to look for Niebuhr's significance. Characteristic here is that a radical view of human lostness and divine sovereignty is brought to bear on consistent "liberal questioning," with the result that the Christian faith and church are placed in the context of a *human* problem of unsuspected dimensions, and decentralized with a view to this problem.

It is not surprising that the theology of Reinhold Niebuhr offers significant parallels. We find here a concentration on the structure of the moral life with the aid of a radical-Christian questioning in such a way that the problem of theology becomes larger and more general—though not less radical or crucial—than the problem of the Christian faith only, even though the latter remains involved in it in a unique way. It seems to us that this is the specifically American, neoorthodox way of relating crisis-thinking to theology; and it is here that its influence and significance on the contemporary scene will be felt most deeply.

In general, it can be observed that the crisis motif, in whatever form it worked its way into theology in the 1920's and 1930's, has led theological thought to several obvious terminal points. The discovery that the statement "Man is on earth and God is in heaven" should become a leading *theological* principle is, in a sense, a *final* discovery. It enables theology to proceed only slightly—though significantly—beyond the stalemate Liberalism-Orthodoxy; for with it theology also seems to have revealed the limits beyond which it cannot go without dropping the crisis motif and running the risk of falling back into older positions. This generalization may prove less than adequate when tested consistently; yet at least it indicates a problem of contemporary theology. The anthropocentricism or church-centrism, for instance, which is a major object of attack in *both* Barthianism *and* American neoorthodoxy, is only kept silent by virtue of the crisis motif. If the latter is mitigated, or even lost completely, the objects of attack return in disguised form: Barthianism without crisis becomes faith-absolutism, and neoorthodoxy without crisis becomes social activism. Assuming that one values the crisis motif, then, the major question before us is whether we can proceed theologically without being forced into one of the ready-made alternative "terminal" positions. It is from the standpoint of this question that we seek to discuss the significance of Niebuhr's theology.

The major importance of Niebuhr's theology which arises from the situation sketched above is, in our 'opinion, the strong emphasis on the *missionary structure of the Christian faith.* We do not use the word missionary here in its traditional meaning, related to the effort to "carry the gospel to the ends of the earth," nor do we suggest any connection with the ecumenical study project called "The Missionary Structure of the Congregation." We use it, for want of a better and perhaps more Niebuhrian term, in order to indicate that the Christian faith with all its forms, symbols, and structures, is directed toward incarnation in total life, toward the world as human world-before-God; and that its "mission" is not so much to bring this human world about or to promote its own growth and enlargement, as it is to draw attention to the dimensions and problems implied in the effort to live toward this world. "Missionary structure" implies that the factual conditioning of the Christian church by the relative historical situation in which it exists should be turned into creative involvement, not so much to become pioneer in the improvement of social and political conditions, but to share in the general human lot, seeking to live with and to incarnate the faith it has received.

Niebuhr's theology is able to bring out this missionary structure because he combines the opposite poles of detailed observation and reference to the "universal society of being." Precisely because theology speaks about the latter, it can spend its energies on the former; only in the view of the one source of being does relativity become true relativity. A vision of the largest possible whole sets free for genuine attention to the smallest possible detail, the intricate patterns with which men relate themselves to one another and to their world. It is in this context that the Christian faith is placed, *both* as a phenomenon among the phenomena *and* as vantage point from which to keep the human problem in its true perspective. This both-and, though it leads to a theological method which remains unfinished and somewhat ambiguous, is essential for the missionary structure of the Christian faith. A theology that begins here may never become more than fragmentary. Its genuine perplexities reach for an eschatological solution; in other words, theological thinking meets one of its true limits at its very methodological starting point.

The development of Niebuhr's thought testifies to the fact that, in order to retain a clear view of the missionary structure of the Christian faith, it is of the utmost importance that we prevent ourselves from making a final methodological choice between speaking from the standpoint of the Christian faith *and* speaking from the standpoint of human faith. This, it seems to us, is the reason why Niebuhr keeps resisting all efforts to concentrate theology in Christology, or to define the church's position in the world exclusively with reference to Christ.

We illustrate our designation of the significance of Niebuhr's theology briefly by drawing attention once more, by way of example, to his remarks about language and resymbolization.

It could perhaps be argued that Niebuhr's fear of metaphysical language is, in view of the motives behind it, not really necessary, and, in view of the "indicative side" of his statements about God, man, and world, not really honest with regard to his own thought either. Yet we might be able to penetrate a little farther into Niebuhr's intentions by viewing the problem from the point of view of the missionary structure of the Christian faith, including its language. In the analysis of theological-metaphysical language the question of verification is solved in a number of ways (except of course in the strictly neopositivist position, which regards all language about God as nonverifiable): by reference to subsequent conduct, by reference to a community in which it functions, and so forth. In most of these approaches theological-metaphysical language is implicitly seen as a specific language type in which the word God functions as the key word. The question of verification of metaphysical language, then, practically concerns the direct relation between such a "theistic" language system and a verifiable context.

Though the importance of this question can hardly be over-estimated, we cannot, of course, go into it here; our only intention is to explicate against this background the possible meanings of the missionary structure of the language of the Christian faith. It seems to us that Niebuhr would not recognize the implication that the language of theology as such can, by definition, be isolated as a specific type of language which stands in need of direct verification; speech about "God in relation to man, and man in relation to God" should even resist such verification because it awaits "eschatological" verification in that situation in which "being" is revealed unambiguously as coherent, true, and universally intelligible. Any verification short of this universal verification may have its limited value but dodges the basic problems involved in the use of theological-metaphysical language. Perhaps the neopositivists, or logical empiricists, with their strict verification requirements, see this point more clearly than other analysts.

All this is not to say that eschatological verification is of a static nature, which would mean that the difference between those who use a specific type of religious language distinguish themselves from others by the fact that they "see" its meaning whereas others do not. Eschatological verification is dynamic, which means that it is foreshadowed, intended, by the reference of theological-metaphysical language to ever wider communities of verifiability. The effects of Christian God-talk must be verified in the larger world of human communities in which the Christian community lives, moves, and functions: not because a key word like "God" stands in need of verification, but because it has to become apparent how the dynamics of faith present in *all* language are affected by the language of Christian faith. In other words, to Niebuhr the problem of verification includes the problem of human faith, and the intelligibility of theological-metaphysical language is contingent upon the problem of man's relation to the principle of being which affects *all* areas of his total life. With this, of course, we have left the field and the intentions of language analysis. But we have also indicated what the basic reason behind Niebuhr's hesitations with regard to "metaphysics" is, and what is behind the "analogy of concrete response" that we mentioned in chapter 3. We summarize it in the expression "the missionary structure of the language of the Christian faith."

Niebuhr's concern for a *resymbolization* of the message has the same background. Niebuhr hopefully expects a revival of religion which is at the same time a revival of the total life of society, relating it more directly and personally to God. At first sight these concerns seem to be quite different from contemporary emphases on social relevance of the church or on existential relevance of the kerygma. Yet we have to remember that in American religious thought there has always been an intimate connection between Revivalism and social relevance. The Social Gospel exemplified this connection, though it remained bound to the "spirit of the times." Niebuhr's criticism of the Social Gospel consists basically of an effort to rediscover the right relation between religion and the life of society. There can be no shortcuts in this relation: reformation of society can occur only on the basis of a spiritual religious reformation. We have a clear indication here that Niebuhr's concern for the missionary structure of the Christian faith, for all its emphasis on involvement, relativity, and reference, is based on a search for "religious depth" in total life; in other words, its basic objective is to place clearly before men's eyes who it is that they are responding to in all their actions.

2. THE PROBLEM OF NIEBUHR'S THEOLOGY

We arrive at the problematic aspect of Niebuhr's theology as soon as we ask ourselves whether the emphasis on the missionary structure of the Christian faith is indeed allowed to function without restriction— whether the tensions between Christian community and universal community, between detailed observation and universal reference, between experience and crisis, or between history and eschatology, are really creative and dynamic tensions. To answer that question we take another look at the motives behind Niebuhr's insistence on *relativism*.

There are, actually, two kinds of relativism here that we must distinguish, one historical, the other eschatological. Historical relativism speaks of the relativity of cultural expression, the necessity of modesty as opposed to apologetic defense, and the reference to the one sovereign ground of being. Eschatological relativism refers to the glory, the presence, and the activity of the one sovereign God in total life; it sees all relative areas of being as workings of his creative, redemptive, and governing action. These two relativisms are not simply identical in Niebuhr's thought. They are separated and bridged by the dynamic presence of the Christian ·faith, which, as it were, transforms historical into eschatological relativism. Yet at several points at which we found Niebuhr's thought somewhat hesitant between hope and resignation, it is difficult to suppress the question of whether he does not tacitly identify the two relativisms. Such an identification can, of course, lead either to an enthusiastic negation or to a quiet acceptance of existing structures. Niebuhr seems on the whole to be inclined toward the second alternative, which in turn gives rise to the question of whether historical revelation is genuinely possible or even necessary.

The problem is partly traceable to Niebuhr's "theocentric correction" of Troeltsch. Troeltsch's relativism was not an accompanying motif of eschatology, and the effort to restore the relation between relativism and eschatology is precisely part of Niebuhr's correction. Yet though he does establish the relation, this does not alter or influence the basic view of history as a static panorama, inherent in Troeltsch's relativism; and this seems to paralyze the relation between history and eschatology, including the concept of hope, in Niebuhr's thought. Yet this is only part of it. The problem is more fundamentally theological: it is the problem of the situation of the self between being and new being, between *Sosein* and future, between relatedness and conversion, between determination and grace. And in the case of Niebuhr we have to say even more than this. For it is, we believe, precisely his consistent concern for the missionary structure of the Christian faith in the sense indicated before that makes a genuine perplexity out of this theological problem.

The paralysis of the relation between history and eschatology, which somehow affects his whole theology, originates in the fact that his missionary concern works backward, as it were, to influence the theological method itself. The starting point in the faith of the Christian community which refers to an "eschatological" view of being and history is itself continually *threatened* by the resistance to Christ- and church-centrism. This resistance is, in Niebuhr's thought, not merely theological; or better yet, the theological resistance, as we have seen repeatedly, is coupled to the analyzable relativity of the church in its society. In other words, the existing larger world in which the church lives becomes, by the very fact that it *is*, the judge of the church's isolation and closedness, and is thus more or less identified with the eschatological criticism directed against all closedness.

This identification is a result of the fact that Niebuhr takes the involvement of the church in society very seriously, and that the relativity of the church simply as *historical* phenomenon, like that of all other historical phenomena, has theological significance by virtue of its relation to the sovereign principle of being. It is obvious that this "backfiring" of his consistent attention to the missionary structure differs basically from a "dialectical" self-interpretation of the Christian community according to which the community differs in no way from the rest of the world except by virtue of the work of Christ and the Holy Spirit *in* the community, so that church-world relations are always characterized by *both* dependence *and* freedom. For in Niebuhr's case the community's self-interpretation is realistically connected to all that is; and this has the important consequence that the poles of *Sosein*, relatedness, and determination receive predominance in his thought and paralyze the eschatological dynamics. His attraction to Spinoza is indicative of this.

In pursuing this problem farther our question must be whether this paralyzing effect is really necessary and inevitable, and we must be very careful not to solve this question by weakening important components of Niebuhr's attention for the missionary structure, particularly the crisis motif and the involvement of the church in the world. We are then led to observe that there is, in Niebuhr's thought, a basic unclarity as to the relation between the system of being and the context of history. Both are reference points for an analysis of the self and its faith, and as such they both function in Niebuhr.

In searching for the ultimate meaning of things, man not only reaches *beyond* himself and *beyond* the many to the transcendent source of being, but he also reaches *ahead* in the ongoing process of communal interpretation. Increasingly, however, the latter is subsumed in the former and loses its distinct characteristics; in other words, *the eschatological nature of historical experience itself* disappears or is identified with the transcendental reference to meaning and unity of being. This is significantly illustrated by Niebuhr's statement—which testifies to his increasing indebtedness to Jonathan Edwards—that hope is directed toward the manifestation of God's rule in the *present.* The danger involved in such a development is, that ongoing historical experience is no longer allowed to impinge upon the interpretation of the "system of being" but can only illustrate a once-acquired interpretation. In this way, ultimately, the neighbor or the other becomes a *paradigm* of the one action behind all actions, rather than a revelation of new possibilities.

We believe it is necessary to insist that a historical event as such has a creative quality (the term is from H. N. Wieman), and that cosmic schemes are contingent upon such quality; in other words, that the structures of being as they arise in the interpretations of the self-in-community are a secondary result of historical experience. In reality, of course, the relations between historical experience and total interpretations of being are far more complex. Not only are there many events with greater or lesser "quality" which in constant rivalry influence and determine the interpretative framework of selves and communities, but also the schemes of interpretation themselves can and do lead separate lives which in turn influence and determine historical experience. Nevertheless, the specific nature of historical experience should not be allowed to dissolve. We should still be able to assert, for instance, that conflicts between *faiths* or communities of faith are basically not conflicts between absolutized fragments of the total system of being but rather conflicts between *events*, and between their respective determinative power or quality.

The revelatory significance of the Christ-event can be clarified against this background. It is an event which by its ongoing determinative power, manifested in and by the Christian community (the Holy Spirit), convinces men of the possibility of a consistent eschatological relativism; it relativizes all total interpretations, all cosmic schemes, by revealing that it is an aspect of man's lostness that he seeks to clutch self-designed centers of value rather than trust himself to the openness of eschatological relativity. Needless to say, the power or quality of the Christ-event does not possess an unambiguous "once for allness"; it has to prove its quality in an unceasing rivalry with other events with equal or lesser determinative power. This is precisely the missionary structure of the Christian faith, and relinquishing it would imply a denial of that to which the event refers.

Nevertheless, to the Christian community this is basically what is going on: the Christ-event "opens vistas of being beyond being"; it sets thought free for the future as "pure" future; it suspends all conclusive statements about being itself until, so to speak, there is no longer a future. For the basic problem of man's continuous interpretation of being is that it is anxiety-ridden; that to man, being is not "simply" present in a coherent, intelligible, and harmonious world; that he *must* therefore impose his schemes and wishes on the world around him. The awareness that *this* is the basic problem is thrust upon man precisely by the Christ-event, though perhaps also by other events; and it is given together with the awareness of a possibility of reconciliation. And reconciliation to being means that it will simply be there in all its "eschatological" variety, that its appearance will no longer force men to construct schemes and systems in which an all-inclusive—or a less-inclusive—power is the central focus of attention.

Here lies the basic reason and moving force behind the permanent *theocide*—or dethronement of the gods—that takes place from the standpoint of radically monotheistic faith. The gods must go; in other words, there is no longer a third possibility next to complete pessimism and a future-directedness which asserts itself from situation to situation. Time and again, however, man's inevitable idolatries pull him back into the atmosphere of the anxious relation with a so-called power of being; and eventually he may even be led to reinterpret the eschatological vision of the Christ-event in such a way that it becomes an illustrative addition to the "largest possible whole." What we imply here is that the notion of the one substance or of universal being *can become the most subtle of idolatries.*

Needless to say, we do not mean to accuse Niebuhr's theology of idolatrous tendencies; that would be beyond the scope of a theological critique. But we do mean to suggest that some attention to the relation of history, eschatology, and being can give a clearer picture of the possibilities, the significance, and the quality of historical revelation, to the advantage of the specifically Niebuhrian emphasis on the missionary structure of the Christian faith. It cannot eliminate "the problem of Niebuhr's theology" so far as it is a problem of *all* theology, which takes the element of crisis seriously. But it might be able to soften the impression now arising from Niebuhr's theology, that the ultimate role of the self is one of *passivity* in view of a solidified system of crisis which can be modified only by "grace" to the extent that it is no longer frightening.

In our designation of the problem of Niebuhr's theology we do not intend to go along with those tendencies in contemporary theology which seek to suppress all questions relating to the transcendent meaning and unity of being in favor of an exclusive concentration on history and (messianic) eschatology. For it is questionable whether these approaches can really maintain the notion of crisis to the extent that they do not "christologize" history in a semi-Barthian way. We suggest only that the answers to the questions relating to the transcendent meaning and unity of being, which in themselves can be a stringent reminder of the "human condition," not be conclusive and final. This is one way to retain the crisis motif meaningfully and yet guard effectively against its unnecessary side effects that we have described. "Crisis" then means that we do not and cannot *know* where history is leading us, that we have no right to paint a sunny picture of the future in which all notion of fate is erased beforehand, and that we will not be able to speak of a God who in his "coming" transcends and determines all historical reality. Yet we will be able to assess the movement of human faith as it originates and lives in the encounter with being, in its efforts to interpret and transcend the power of the persistent structures of being; and we will allow ourselves to be taken along by the quality of the Christ-event that reveals the possibility of an eschatological reality in which all being is reconciled and renewed.

3. WAYS AHEAD

In our assessment of the significance of Niebuhr's theology we suggested that a true description of the missionary structure of the Christian faith cannot do without a crisis motif; more specifically, a crisis motif which is not concentrated anew in one historical event or phenomenon but is made operative in the context of the general human problem of faith. In our analysis of the problem of Niebuhr's theology our purpose was to make clear that a theological method which intends to unite these concerns can be made more fruitful and flexible by specific attention to the eschatological nature of historical experience. We will now conclude our critique by sketching a few possible results of this "shift of emphasis," in three successive areas: the reflection on the moral life, the reflection on Christ and the church, and finally the reflection on God.

a. **The moral life.** Niebuhr's ethics manifests a great wealth of categories, approaches, and connections which not only exhibit the dimensions of the moral life in their radicality and inclusiveness but also offer significant ways to analyze and guide it. Yet it also shows the permanent danger of shifting the center of ethical reflection from the moral-historical activity to the "system" in which it takes place. It seems sometimes that for Niebuhr the major incentive for moral action or nonaction lies in the being of being and its revealed goodness, rather than in events or occurrences which direct and move the moral self to a further goal. The question here is whether the concept of being itself can really be said to have ethical potency, and whether we should not rather look to the event(s) in which the possibility of meaningful action is disclosed. This shift of emphasis, which is in a sense simply another way of stating what we meant in the preceding section, becomes significant at two points.

The first point is the problem of concrete choice or comparative judgment. In Niebuhr's reflections on the war one often gets the impression that for him there is no real significance in a choice between the conflicting issues because in the end all possible points of view are rolled together in a common share of guilt. The seriousness and the value of such a position cannot of course be denied, and yet one wonders whether it is not possible to combine a realistic notion of crisis with an acknowledgment of ultimate value in human decision and action. There is of course no question about the relativity and limitation of moral judgment; yet when Niebuhr immediately connects this insight with a heavy emphasis on the *one divine action* which restrains and judges us, the paralyzing effect of the latter can hardly be escaped.

The question arises as to whether it is *necessary* to contrast human relativity and divine totality *immediately* and *directly*. Does this not increase the danger of identifying historical and eschatological relativism? The alternative seems to us to be, that we rest content with basing our moral judgment on the historical quality of the events which determine both the situation and our faith, in the full awareness that our judgment is not final—if it were, there would not be anything left to do. We should not want to see "the whole" at the time of moral decisions, yet believe that our action can have its own quality-in-relativity. The possibility of real choice is thus given, not with the objectivity of norms but with the true meaning of historical development.

The second point is the problem of passivity and activity in the moral life. The will of God, Niebuhr says, is what he *does*, not what he requires; and with this the major problem for the responsible self is how to become patient of the will of God. Because of this emphasis on the action of God over against and upon the self, there is always the strong suggestion that "becoming a true self" means the alignment of the self with the persistent structures of being which are always larger than the self's own sinful ideals. Suggestions like this can lead to an attitude of passive acquiescence in the status quo and to an image of God as a stable structure which fences in the moral self, molds it into a determined machine, or keeps reminding it of its inadequacy. An appeal to self-denial in this context seems to stop short of the possibilities given with an event that is truly hope-eliciting. The freedom of redemption remains in Niebuhr's ethics definitely subordinated to the categories of acceptance and ordering in a context of createdness; and although it cannot, of course, completely be isolated from this context, its true possibility should cause postponement of the conclusive definition of the context of being in which it takes place, in favor of an active future-directedness.

With this statement we implicitly touch upon the definition of *sin* in Niebuhr's thought. At first sight it seems to be a very balanced definition: sin is inevitable because of relativity and finitude, it is truly sinful because of defensiveness and absolutizing of the relative, yet it is not tragic because God and the possibility of reconciliation are truly *in history*. (This last point is the basic issue between the two Niebuhr brothers.) Yet there is some truth to the charge that because Niebuhr seeks to unite both the totalitarian character of sin and the true possibility of reconciliation, his position must lead to complacency and passivity. Perhaps to him this is the only viable alternative to the Social Gospel; and indeed it is an alternative which introduces the crisis motif into Social Gospel thinking without destroying the basic structure of the latter by divorcing the ideal from the historically attainable. Yet, though it sets out to do full justice to history in the framework of creation and redemption, this alternative seems unable to eliminate the suggestion of paralysis in the moral life.

This sense of paralysis should not be countered by any feeling of certainty which would lose the notion of crisis and weaken the concept of sin, but rather by an emphasis on courage in the face of uncertainty, by an "evangelical skepticism" which can ally itself with the anthropological realism of Niebuhr's thought, and thus become an expression of the distance and tension between history and eschatology which we are seeking to rescue. In this connection we may also draw attention to the concept of *suffering* which, in Niebuhr's thought, indicates the consequences of sin and as such also the locus of reconciliation. In the light of a definition of sin against the background of a creative tension between history and eschatology, suffering can become an ultimate possibility of active, aggressive future-directedness which asserts itself, and the history by which it is inspired, in the face of all contrary evidence of the structures of being.

b. Christ and the church. One of the major difficulties in Niebuhr's theology lies in the relation between the particular revelation and the general human problem. His concern for the missionary structure limits the creative possibilities of the revelatory event from the standpoint of the general problem; more concretely, the role of the church as the bearer of the revelatory image of Christ is curtailed by the increasing fear of all henotheism, especially those kinds which are Christ- or church-centered. We have described the legitimate concerns behind this development, yet we also have to raise the question of whether the functioning of a revelation which is genuinely historical is not unnecessarily restricted in this way. We can remind ourselves of Niebuhr's tendency to incorporate the "effects" of the Christ-event into the general variety of response patterns related to the One beyond the many, and to weaken the work of the Holy Spirit by the nature of the disjunction between Jesus Christ and God that we observed in his thought. And with regard to the church we can establish that, for all the emphasis on the ministry of reconciliation to the unreconciled *oikoumene*, the relation between church and world tends to be one of stalemate, of static confessionalism.

The point here is the way in which the revelatory event is related to "total life." We are given *faith* in connection with this event, Niebuhr writes, and faith "involves us in a permanent revolution of the mind and of the heart, a continuous life which opens out infinitely into ever new possibilities"; in other words, it puts us on the road of *metanoia*, of a constant revision of our defective interpretations of and responses to being. For it is basically and originally *resurrection-faith*, which means that the history of Jesus Christ can stay with us as a revelatory image and a criterion for our responses in total life because we have been allowed to believe that "God kept faith with him." With this, very much has been said and implied, as we have made clear; and we certainly do not wish to depart from the basic pattern of this Christology or from the way in which it avoids many "christological pitfalls." Nevertheless, here, too, we feel that more advantage can be taken of the specific way in which an event—particularly *this* event—relates us to our world and our history. As we pointed out in the preceding section, any event that has revelatory character to a greater or lesser extent, causes to the same extent a certain eschatological tension in that it influences interpretative patterns and pulls those in the direction of the central image which it yields.

In a similar way, resurrection-faith suspends all interpretations of being by hope for genuine and total newness. Of course it will have to take up arms against many contrary experiences; the resurrection-faith cannot stand in the midst of total life as an unassailable rock of certainty, but it drives itself in the direction of complete verification. This is precisely its missionary structure (we may call it the work of the Holy Spirit), and we lose sight of its possibilities when we relate it *too soon* to a God who *is* and who is revealed as faithful. In other words, the tension between cross and resurrection is not solved by a miraculous gift of faith though this is, of course, part of it; the tension between cross and resurrection comprises the whole of history and becomes, for the Christian community, the distance and the bridge between being and new being. To put it differently, the Christian community eagerly awaits the confirmation of the uniqueness of Christ, which, as we have seen, is simultaneously the disappearance of his uniqueness. For the uniqueness of the Christ-event is not "provisional" in any static or paradoxical sense. It is provisional, rather, in the sense that it disappears in the missionary structure of the community in the world. At the end there will be no Christian community which points to itself as the center of truth; there will be a world of men who respond to one another in freedom and reconciliation. The verification of the resurrection, and the final "revelation" of Christ as simply a man among men, coincide with the advent of this new world.

With the above we have already indicated the possibilities for a definition of the position of the church in the world. Any serious effort to utilize the implications of the missionary structure which is so much the object of Niebuhr's concern, will avoid all kinds of pre- or post-critical church-centrism, even when it is disguised in concepts of mission that emphasize "presence" and "humanization." Yet it will also avoid any paralyzing stalemate between church and world, inasmuch as it allows for a creative, change-producing rivalry between the quality of the Christ-event and that of other events. In this sense the revival which is anticipated in Niebuhr's thought, and which is expected to be instigated by a resymbolized Christian message, can be future-directed and imply the possibility of concrete structural change, which refers to the newness that is expected. The church as such cannot become the pioneering agency in this process; the missionary structure of its presence in the world which is built on the notion of crisis prohibits this. At the same time, however, it must be said that the Christian faith has no existence and no right to exist apart from its total incarnation in this process, apart from its constant reference to what *can be.*

This implies two things. On the one hand, it implies that the creative quality of the Christ-event must necessarily be institutionalized; in other words, a certain *religious structure* has to be maintained, which interprets the ultimate questions of man and his world in the light of certain symbols derived from the Christ-event and its history. Such institutionalization is necessary because the "miraculous gift of resurrection-faith" does not allow man to step directly into redeemed, "eschatological" existence; and because this gift has to be given again and again in a situation in which it is lost to the power of other events and other interpretative images.

On the other hand, however, the necessity of institutionalization is not the final word to be said about the position of the Christian faith in the world. For "being a Christian," in the sense of adhering to the religious structure mentioned, is not identical with entering the process of creative, eschatological tension in total life on the basis of the Christ-event which refers to "vistas of being beyond being." These two things are not identical; more precisely, there is an asymmetric relation between them. For although the religious structure is necessary to preserve the possibility of redirecting, transforming, and inspiring the faith of men, or of instigating the "increase among men of the love of God and neighbor," it is bound to disappear "eschatologically," because and insofar as it necessarily relates the Christ-faith to a coherent scheme of interpretation of being that can never transcend the relation of anxiety which the Christ-faith itself seeks to relativize. That the term "missionary structure" which we have used in no sense refers to the effort to enlarge and propagate this "religious structure" is obvious both from Niebuhr's thought and from the shift of emphasis which we have sought to introduce. Here lies the most fundamental reason why the task of the church is to direct men toward God and neighbor, rather than to convert them to Christianity.

c. God. What we have done so far amounts to an effort to restore the emphasis on a dynamic relation between history and eschatology which is implied in consistent attention to the missionary structure of the Christian faith but remains somewhat obscured in the general tendencies of Niebuhr's thought. Since this effort could not be based on a weakening of the crisis motif, it actually consisted of a search for a new foundation of what "crisis" can possibly mean. Up to this point we have tried to neutralize the effect which crisis-thinking tends to have in Niebuhr's thought—turning the divine action into a solid structure to which all human efforts stand in the same relation—by considering the crisis motif represented in a dialectic between the creative quality of historical events on the one hand and an attitude of skepticism or uncertainty with regard to the whole of history and being—a "postpone-ment of final judgments"—on the other. A sense of lostness, in other words, is inevitable as the reverse of a historical faith which keeps incarnating itself and refusing to be "christologized."

Thus the missionary structuring of the Christian faith amounts to a narrow path between pessimism and idolatry, and mostly it will have to use a little bit of one to avoid the other. More specifically, the religious structure with its inevitable accents of idolatry is necessary to keep men from complete despair and resignation (assuming, of course, that they have lost confidence in the "lesser gods"); and reminders of the enigmatic ground of being are necessary to keep men from turning their creative historical faith into premature confidence in themselves or their own value centers. The "greatness of God"—so crucial in Niebuhr's thinking—is ultimately not an abyss before which man can only stand and wait; it is a permanent critical red signal on man's historical journey. It is indeed the relation to God which is the basis of man's faith or unfaith in total life, but it is the transformation and renewal of total life which is the final goal, rather than a clarified or reconciled relation to God *as such*.

For our reflection on God, this means that we will have to find a way between Spinozistic ways of thinking—which tend to include all being and all possibility in the "one substance"—and Barthian ways of thinking—which tend to know too much about God, man, history, and the position of the Christian community in the world on the basis of the Christ-event. The crucial temptation in such an effort is, of course, to drop the crisis motif and to seek refuge in pre- or post-critical varieties of immanentism, in which, to mention only one example, the will of God is identified either with the maintenance of the status quo or with its revolutionary reversal. The whole problem leads us to some reflection on the identification of "God" and "being," and even though in the context of these concluding remarks such reflection can only be very limited and superficial, it is a necessary part of the way which we have begun to indicate.

The problem of the identification of God and being, as it appears against the background of our considerations up to this point, seems to us to lie in the fact that we cannot stop short of such an identification but that, nevertheless, the identification is suspended or disturbed by the eschatological dynamics of the historical event—more particularly the Christ-event. The temptation, however, to separate theology from ontology, or to subsume the latter completely in the former, must be resisted, not only because it would deny or reverse a major part of the history of Western thought but also because the relation to *being itself* is the religious problem *par excellence*—as we have seen, this is Niebuhr's point. Indeed, religiously God is the *final* problem of man and·there seems to be nothing, therefore, which can keep us from calling him the principle of being itself.

Nevertheless, there are two things which deserve further consideration. The first is the significance of "external history," which continually, as it were, demands a wider perspective in its way of considering and investigating "being," and which is therefore also a form of judging and relativizing the "religious" points of view. The second is the fact that there are revelatory glimpses of a redeemed world in which all relations between man and his circumambient world will be freed from anxiety and from the need for self-defense, in which the relation between man and being will be totally "normalized." Judging from here, a too ready identification of God with being itself might leave too little room for unexpected and radical renewal. For how great is the difference between identifying God with the principle of being and making being itself, as it appears to us in its enigmatic, threatening, or gracious character, into God? We have seen what the negative effects of this can be in a consistently critical theology like Niebuhr's: it weakens or suppresses the eschatological nature of historical experience itself.

The obvious conclusion might seem to be that in order to "save" eschatology, we should suspend or arrest any identification of God with being, just as we should stop short of a straightforward atheism. God is either the principle of being itself or nothing at all; perhaps we should avoid both extremes and say nothing. For, leaving atheism out of consideration for the time being, we seem forced to conclude that a complete identification of God with being itself represents *either* a premature grasp of a "final revelation" which basically ignores the dimensions of the human problems of faith and religion, *or* an inclusion of faith and history in the framework of the "one substance," *or* a variety of faith absolutism—in sum, denies an open-ended view of history. However, as we have pointed out, this obvious conclusion has its own shortcomings; it would do less than justice to the dimensions of religious thought.

In all this, we are not doing anything but formulating the problem of Trinitarianism in the context of contemporary critical theology. How do we express the unity of God as the unity between the creative power, the truth of the glimpses caught in the revelatory image of the Christ-event, and the promise given with the ongoing incarnation of radical faith in total life? That God is one in all three is the only ground the Christian faith has to stand on. *Therefore* God must be one with the principle of being itself; and yet as soon as we start there, his true unity *in*—not above or behind—the three "modes of being" becomes questionable.

This basic quandary will probably remain with us till the final renewal of all being to which the Christian faith testifies. But it does make a difference, particularly for the missionary structure of the Christian faith, in what way the Christian community articulates its vision of this renewal. The question here is, it seems to us, whether the community, on the basis of the quality of the Christ-event, can allow itself to relativize—to "see through"—the fact that being is present to men as God, and God as being; that is to say, whether it can testify to the redemption, the normalization, of the relation between man and being, and to the disappearance of all anxiety and defensiveness, in terms of a *de-religionizing* of the relation between man and the principle of being. This would mean that any religious structure—central, inevitable, and necessary though it may be in the human life—is provisional; that any positing of *God* as the principle of being with all the quandaries it entails, though it may be the only way to articulate man's final problems in his unredeemed state, is provisional as well, in view of the possibilities which light up in events like the Christ-event.

Redemption, in other words, though we can only speak adequately about it as "action of the one God," would include redemption from the necessity to have a god, and thus it would include God's final disappearance in the total renewal of things and relations. It may be that this is the only possible way to speak adequately about God's unity without weakening the significance of his complete self-revelation in history. And it may be that this is the only way to speak adequately about the missionary structure of the Christian faith while avoiding all the dead alleys which consistent critical thinking at this point has exposed. Needless to say, eschatologically the final disappearance of God may be identical with his full unambiguous revelation; but the former may be more suitable as a perspectival point for the Christian community and as a guiding principle for the incarnation of faith in total life.

NOTES

CHAPTER 1—CHOICE OF DIRECTION

A. Persistent Patterns

1. "Theology must always be able to adopt the language of the man in the street, speaking to his need simply and persuasively, awakening faith, and winning conviction. It must be preachable." Winthrop S. Hudson, *The Great Tradition of the American Churches* (New York: Harper & Row Torchbook, 1963), p. 254. Cf. also one of Niebuhr's own remarks: "There is bound to be in this American Christianity a deep suspicion of any theology which is not rooted firmly in the great Christian convictions and in the Bible on the one hand and which is not germane to the life of the common people." From "The Nature of Protestant Christianity in America and the Problem of Educating Its Ministers" (an unpublished paper).

2. Cf. Henry Steele Commager, *The American Mind* (New Haven: Yale University Press, 1950), pp. 28 f., 42, 98, 164, 200, 410 f.

3. Perry Miller, "The Marrow of Puritan Divinity," *Errand into the Wilderness* (New York: Harper & Row Torchbook, 1964), pp. 48-98; and also *The New England Mind*, Vol. I: *The Seventeenth Century* (New York: Oxford University Press, 1953).

4. Cf. F. H. Foster, *A Genetic History of the New England Theology* (New York: Russell & Russell, 1963), chapter 1.

5. Cf. the section on Edwards below, chapter 2, part A.

6. Cf. Douglas J. Elwood, *The Philosophical Theology of Jonathan Edwards* (New York: Columbia University Press, 1960), p. 6.

7. H. Richard Niebuhr, "Introduction to Edwards," *Christian Ethics: Sources of the Living Tradition*, ed. with introduction by Waldo Beach and H. Richard Niebuhr (New York: Ronald Press, 1955), p. 384.

8. The word voluntarism designates the importance of voluntary church membership and freedom of religious association in America. It is not meant to characterize theories about the role of the human will in the event of conversion, though this is a related problem which plays its specific part in the transition from establishment to religious liberty.

9. Frederick J. Turner. *The Frontier in American History* (New York: H. Holt & Company, 1953); W. W. Sweet, *Religion in the Development of American Culture, 1765-1840* (New York: Charles Scribner's Sons, 1952).

10. Sidney E. Mead, "Denominationalism: The Shape of Protestantism in America," *Church History* 23-1954, pp. 291-320.

11. H. Richard Niebuhr, *The Kingdom of God in America* (New York: Harper & Bros. Torchbook, 1959), p. 177.

12. Sidney E. Mead, "American Protestantism Since the Civil War," I: From Denominationalism to Americanism, *Journal of Religion* 36-1956, pp. 1-16.

13. Cf. Sydney E. Ahlstrom, "Theology in America: A Historical Survey," *The Shaping of American Religion,* ed. by James W. Smith and Leland A. Jamison, "Religion in American Life Series" (Princeton: Princeton University Press, 1961), I, pp. 232-321; 255 f.: through the loophole of the permission of sin as necessary for the moral order, "Edwards' grandson Timothy Dwight marched the legions of 'human agency.' " Cf. in general: F. H. Foster, *op. cit.;* Ronald Bainton, *Yale and the Ministry* (New York: Harper & Bros., 1957); Sidney E. Mead, *Nathaniel William Taylor, 1786-1858: A Connecticut Liberal* (Chicago: University of Chicago Press, 1942).

14. Cf. Perry Miller, "From Edwards to Emerson," *Errand into the Wilderness,* pp. 184-203, who sees Emerson as "an Edwards in whom the concept of original sin has evaporated" (p. 185).

15. Cf. G. Hammar, *Christian Realism in Contemporary American Theology* (Uppsala: Appelberg, 1940), pp. 127 ff. For a recent study of Bushnell, cf. W. A. Johnson, *Nature and the Supernatural in the Theology of Horace Bushnell* (Lund: CWK Gleerup, 1963).

16. Horace Bushnell, *God in Christ—Three Discourses with a Preliminary Dissertation on Language* (New York: 1876), p. 127.

17. *Ibid.,* p. 301.

18. Horace Bushnell, "Christian Nurture," *American Philosophic Addresses 1700-1900,* ed. by Joseph L. Blau (New York: Columbia University Press, 1946), pp. 608-23; 613.

19. *Ibid.,* p. 616.

20. Cf. Alec R. Vidler, *The Theology of F. D. Maurice* (London: SCM Press, 1948), pp. 13-21, 73-81.

21. F. D. Maurice, *Theological Essays* (London: James Clarke & Co., Ltd., 1957), p. 276.

22. *Ibid.,* p. 221.

23. *Ibid.,* pp. 60, 67.

24. F. D. Maurice, *The Kingdom of Christ* (London: SCM Press, 1958), II, p. 347.

25. C. H. Hopkins, *The Rise of the Social Gospel in American Protestantism 1865-1915* (New Haven: Yale University Press, 1940), pp. 325 f.

26. Cf. Reinhold Niebuhr, "Intellectual Autobiography," *Reinhold Niebuhr—His Religious, Social and Political Thought,* ed. by Charles W. Kegley and Robert W. Bretall, The Library of Living Theology (New York: Macmillan, 1956), II, pp. 1-23 (paperback edition).

27. Kenneth Cauthen, *The Impact of American Religious Liberalism* (New York: Harper & Row, 1962), p. 212 (italics added).

28. D. D. Williams, "Tradition and Experience in American Theology," *The Shaping of American Religion,* pp. 443-95. Williams suggests that Americans in general are more inclined toward Platonism than toward Kantianism; *ibid.,* p. 462.

29. Cf. L. L. Bernard and J. Bernard, *Origins of American Sociology* (New York: Russell & Russell, 1943); Commager, *op. cit.,* pp. 199-226.

30. Cf. William L. Kolb, *Values, Positivism, and the Functional Theory of Religion: The Growth of a Moral Dilemma* (1953), reprinted in J. Milton Yinger, *Religion, Society, and the Individual: An Introduction to the Sociology of Religion* (New York: Macmillan, 1957), pp. 599-609.

31. Niebuhr was closely associated with Macintosh in the 1930's, but he never identified himself with his theology, although he mentions him sympathetically in "Theology and Psychology—A Sterile Union," *Christian Century* 44-1927, pp. 47-48; and in the Preface of *The Meaning of Revelation* (New York: Macmillan Paperback Edition, 1960), pp. ix-x. Wieman is mentioned only in the essay "Value Theory and Theology," *The Nature of Religious Experience: Essays in Honor of Douglas Clyde Macintosh* (New York:Harper & Bros., 1937), pp. 93-116.

32. "Revelation of the reality of God in the religious experience of moral salvation is as normal and natural as any other process of cognition. It is the discovery of reality through experience. A dependable religious experience is what we ought to expect of a dependable religious Reality, when we discover and practice the right religious adjustment." D. C. Macintosh, *The Reasonableness of Christianity* (New York: Charles Scribner's Sons, 1925), pp. 126 f. "Just what this right religious adjustment is, *is for experience to teach." Ibid.,* p. 227 (italics added).

33. "But why should we not believe—if, while remaining adequately critical, we can do so—that which we tend almost inevitably to believe when we are at our best, physically, mentally, and morally, that which it is most desirable for the highest ends that we should make the guide and basis of our active life? Religion has been described as 'an act of self-maintenance,' and moral optimism, this vital core of spiritual religion, this confidence that ultimately the universe is on the side of the highest values—moral optimism is one act of self-maintenance on the part

of the spiritual life of man. Is it not reasonable, then, to regard it as a morally justified hypothesis and to act upon the supposition that it is true?" *Ibid.*, p. 49. And then: "As in all empirical investigation, progress is made by elimination of unsuccessful adjustments; it is the trial and error method." *Ibid.*, p. 229. The basis of Macintosh's system is clearly a certain form of Pragmatism. Cf. p.e., p. 231.

34. H. N. Wieman, *The Source of Human Good* (Chicago: University of Chicago Press, 1946), p. 8. On the same grounds he opposes Barthianism and neoorthodoxy.

35. *Ibid.*, p. 69.

36. G. H. Mead, *Mind, Self and Society from the Standpoint of a Social Behavorist*, ed. and introd. by Charles W. Morris (Chicago: University of Chicago Press, 1934) p. 38.

37. "Where a vocal gesture uttered by one individual leads to a certain response in another, we may call it a symbol of that act; where it arouses in the man who makes it the tendency to the same response, we may call it a significant symbol." G. H. Mead, "The Genesis of the Self and Social Control," *The Philosophy of the Present*, ed. by Arthur E. Murphy (Chicago: Open Court, 1932), pp. 176-95, 189.

38. G. H. Mead, *Mind, Self and Society from the Standpoint of a Social Behaviorist*, p. 178.

39. G. H. Mead, "The Genesis of the Self and Social Control," p. 192.

40. Gabriel Marcel, quoted on the jacket of J. Royce's *The Religious Aspect of Philosophy* (1885) (New York: Harper & Bros., 1958).

41. Josiah Royce, *The Philosophy of Loyalty* (New York: Macmillan, 1924), p. 372.

42. Royce, *The Religious Aspect of Philosophy*, pp. 238-52.

43. Josiah Royce, *The Problem of Christianity*, Vol. II: *The Real World and the Christian Ideas* (New York: Macmillan, 1913), pp. 140-44.

44. *Ibid.*, p. 147.

45. *Ibid.*, pp. 208, 211.

46. *Ibid.*, p. 425.

47. Royce, *The Philosophy of Loyalty*, p. 17.

48. *Ibid.*, p. 52.

49. *Ibid.*, p. 310.

50. *Ibid.*, p. 357.

51. *Ibid.*, p. 196.

52. Ernst Troeltsch. *Die Soziallehren der Christlichen Kirchen und Gruppen*, Gesammelte Schriften Band I (Tübingen: J. C. B. Mohr, 1912). English: *The Social Teachings of the Christian Churches* (New York: Harper & Bros. Torchbook, 1960).

53. H. Richard Niebuhr, *Christ and Culture* (New York: Harper & Bros. Torchbook, 1956), pp. ix-x.

54. H. Richard Niebuhr, "Ernst Troeltsch's Philosophy of Religion" (Yale, 1924), p. 225 (unpublished doctoral dissertation).

55. Ernst Troeltsch, *Die Absolutheit des Christentums und die Religionsgeschichte* (Tübingen: J. C. B. Mohr, 1902), p. 72.

56. Cf. Ernst Troeltsch, *Der Historismus und seine Probleme*, I Buch: *Das Logische Problem der Geschichtsphilosophie*, Gesammelte Schriften Band III (Tübingen: J. C. B. Mohr, 1922), pp. 9, 110, 112 ff., 214.

57. Cf. *ibid.*, pp. 118, 169.

58. W. F. Kasch, *Die Sozialphilosophie von Ernst Troeltsch* (Tübingen: J. C. B. Mohr, 1963), p. 8.

59. Troeltsch, *Der Historismus und seine Probleme*, p. 96.

60. *Ibid.*, pp. 181, 185.

61. Ernst Troeltsch, *Der Historismus und seine Überwindung* (lectures) (Berlin: Pan Verlag Rolf Heise, 1924), p. 77.

62. Troeltsch, *Der Historismus und seine Probleme*, pp. 209, 675 ff.

63. *Ibid.*, p. 187.

64. R. G. Collingwood, *The Idea of History* (New York: Oxford University Press, 1964-3), p. 303.

65. The direct influence of Troeltsch's *Social Teachings* is most evident in *The Social Sources of Denominationalism* (New York: Meridian Books, 1958-2). Cf. Niebuhr's repeated insistence that doctrines live on, and change with, social structure (p. 17); his admiration for Weber with the same nuance that Troeltsch adds "we are dealing with interacting phases of a culture rather than with a relation of cause and effect, operating in one direction only" (p. 288, n. 9); and his location of religious movements in the lower strata (p. 29). An example of straightforward Troeltschean thinking is Niebuhr's lecture *Moral Relativism and the Christian Ethic* (New York: International Missionary Council, 1929). Cf. the following quotation: "The absolute within the relative comes to appearance at two points—in the absolute obligation of an individual or a society to follow its highest insights, and in the element of revelation of ultimate reality" (p. 9).

66. In the course of the following sections, it will become obvious that we have to distinguish between two kinds of *anthropocentricism:* as a methodological concentration on man and the human predicament, it is a permanent characteristic of Niebuhr's theology; but as a *faith* in which man is the center of *loyalty* and *hope*, it is rejected by Niebuhr from the beginning.

67. Niebuhr, *Christ and Culture*, p. x (italics added).

B. Post-liberal Consciousness

1. H. Richard Niebuhr, *The Social Sources of Denominationalism* (New York, Meridian Books, 1958-2), p. 16.

2. *Ibid.*, p. 21.

3. Culture is *"that total process of human activity and that total result of such activity* to which now the name culture now the name *civilization* is applied in common speech." H. Richard Niebuhr, *Christ and Culture* (New York: Harper & Bros. Torchbook, 1956), p. 32 (italics added).

4. *Ibid.*, pp. 69 ff.

5. *"The very essence of Christianity* lies in the tension which it presupposes or creates between the worlds of nature and of spirit, and its resolution of that conflict by means of justifying faith." Niebuhr, *The Social Sources of Denominationalism*, p. 4 (italics added).

6. H. Richard Niebuhr, "What Holds Churches Together?" *The Christian Century* 43-1926, pp. 346-48.

7. H. Richard Niebuhr, "Back to Benedict?" *The Christian Century* 42-1925, pp. 860-61.

8. At the Elmhurst Service Conference in 1927, of which a brief (unsigned) report can be found in *The Evangelical Herald* 26-1927, pp. 344-45. A report of a lecture given by Niebuhr on "Planetary Provincialism and Cosmic Faith" appears in the same issue.

9. Niebuhr, *The Social Sources of Denominationalism*, p. 21.

10. *Ibid.*, p. 5.

11. *Ibid.*, p. 265. Surrender: sc. to the world.

12. *Ibid.*, pp. 273 f.

13. *Ibid.*, p. 24.

14. *Ibid.*, p. 21.

15. *Ibid.*, pp. 278 f.

16. Cf. Niebuhr's own criticism in *The Kingdom of God in America* (New York: Harper & Bros. Torchbook, 1959), pp. ix f. Niebuhr's "way out," as we shall see, leads through the discovery of the creative force of the religious ideal itself in any cultural expression *and* of the qualitative difference between the divine and the human.

17. Cf. Henry Steele Commager, *The American Mind* (New Haven: Yale University Press, 1950), pp. 41-54 (the "watershed of the nineties").

18. Cf. Paul A. Carter, *The Decline and Revival of the Social Gospel* (Ithaca, N. Y.: Cornell University Press, 1956), pp. 141 ff.; Sydney E. Ahlstrom, "Continental Influences on American Christian Thought Since World War I," *Church History* 27-1958, pp. 256 ff.

19. Reinhold Niebuhr, *Moral Man and Immoral Society* (New York: Charles Scribner's Sons, 1932).

20. Especially in Reinhold Niebuhr's *The Nature and Destiny of Man: A Christian Interpretation* (New York: Charles Scribner's Sons, 1941, 1943), 2 vols.

21. In 1932 Niebuhr spent a year in Europe, which was of great importance for these things. He did not visit Europe again until 1960.

22. Sydney E. Ahlstrom, "Neo-orthodoxy Demythologized," *The Christian Century* 47-1957, pp. 649-51, p. 650.

23. Cf. Kenneth Cauthen, *The Impact of American Religious Liberalism* (New York: Harper & Row, 1962), p. 228. Also Charles C. Morrison, "The Liberalism of Neo-orthodoxy," *The Christian Century* 67-1950, pp. 697-99, 731-33, 760-63.

24. Cf. T. F. Torrance, *Karl Barth: An Introduction to His Early Theology 1910-1931* (London: SCM Press, 1962), p. 44.

25. Ahlstrom, "Continental Influences on American Christian Thought Since World War I," p. 4. On the influence of Kierkegaard in the United States, see Walter Lowrie, "Translators and Interpreters of Kierkegaard," *Theology Today* 12-1955, pp. 312-27.

26. H. Richard Niebuhr, "Sören Kierkegaard," *Christianity and the Existentialists*, ed. by Carl D. Michalson (New York: Charles Scribner's Sons, 1956), pp. 23-42. Cf. for both elements Niebuhr's "Evangelical and Protestant Ethics," *The Heritage of the Reformation*, ed. by E. J. F. Arndt (New York: Richard R. Smith, 1950), pp. 211-29.

27. Cf., next to the *Epistle to the Romans* in general, for this point especially Karl Barth, "Das Wort Gottes als Aufgabe der Theologie" (1922), *Anfänge der Dialektischen Theologie*, J. Moltmann Hrsg. (München: Chr. Kaiser Verlag, 1962), I, pp. 197-218.

28. See especially Karl Barth, "Schicksal und Idee in der Theologie" (1929), *Theologische Fragen und Antworten*, Gesammelte Vorträge 3. Band (Zürich, 1957), pp. 54-92; and *Fides Quaerens Intellectum— Anselms Beweis der Existenz Gottes im Zusammenhang Seines Theologischen Programms* (München, 1931). English: *Anselm's Proof of the Existence of God in the Context of His Theological Scheme*, trans. by Ian W. Robertson (Richmond, Va.: John Knox Press, 1960).

29. T. F. Torrance contends that the shift in Barth makes it impossible to regard the *Dogmatik* as dialectical theology: "It would now be a misnomer to speak of his theology as 'dialectical,' for the emphasis is no longer upon *diastasis* but upon *analogy*; i.e., it is no longer a movement of thought setting men apart from God, but a movement referring man back to his source in the grace of God the creator and redeemer." *Op. cit.*, p. 89. Torrance, however, regards this as a positive

development; cf. his remark that Barth's "scholastic realism" needs no balance of dialectical thinking because it is grounded in the incarnation. *Ibid.*, p. 194.

30. Cf. especially H. Richard Niebuhr, "Can German and American Christians Understand Each Other?" *The Christian Century* 47-1930, pp. 914-16; "Religious Realism and the Twentieth Century," *Religious Realism*, ed. by D. C. Macintosh (New York: Macmillan, 1931), pp. 413-28; and Niebuhr's preface to his translation of Tillich's *The Religious Situation* (New York: Henry Holt & Co., 1932), pp. vii-xxii.

31. Cf. Paul Tillich, "Autobiographical Reflections," *The Theology of Paul Tillich*, ed. by Charles W. Kegley and Robert W. Bretall, The Library of Living Theology (New York: Macmillan, 1964-2), I, pp. 1-21.

32. Cf. the following summary of the "early" Tillich: *Offenbarung—VA: Religionsphilosophisch*, in the 2d ed. of *Religion in Geschichte und Gegenwart*, Hermann Gunkel and Leopold Zscharnack Hrsg. (Tübingen, 1929-32), Vol. IV, pp. 664-69; *Religiöse Verwirklichung*. (Berlin, 1930); *Der Widerstreit von Raum und Zeit—Schriften zur Geschichtsphilosophie, Gesammelte Werke* Band VI, (Stuttgart, 1963); and *Der Protestantismus als Kritisches und Gestaltendes Prinzip*, in P. Tillich Hrsg., *Kritik und Gestaltung* (Darmstadt, 1929), pp. 3-37.

33. With the term "beliefful realism" Niebuhr himself translates Tillich's term "Gläubiger Realismus," which indicates an attitude in which reality is approached and encountered under the aspect of the Eternal.

34. New York: Henry Holt & Co., 1932; trans. of *Die Religiöse Lage der Gegenwart*, Berlin, Verlag Ullstein, 1926.

35. *The Religious Situation* is a consistent attack on a civilization that has sealed itself off in its own finitude against the creative presence of the Eternal. Capitalism becomes the symbol of this attitude. Cf. Niebuhr's articles about these problems in the early thirties: "The Irreligion of Communist and Capitalist." *The Christian Century*, 47-1930, pp. 1306-7; "Faith, Works and Social Salvation," *Religion in Life*, 1-1932, pp. 426-30; "Nationalism, Socialism and Christianity." *World Tomorrow*, 16-1933, pp. 469-70, and his contributions to *The Church Against the World* (Chicago: Willett Clark & Co., 1935).

36. "The result is a theological method as clearly distinguished from the psychological and historical method of the nineteenth century as from the dogmatic method of the Reformation and the theology of crisis." Niebuhr, "Religious Realism and the Twentieth Century," p. 423. (The term "theology of crisis" in this quotation is obviously restricted to Barthianism.)

37. Cf. Tillich, "Autobiographical Reflections," pp. 8, 14, 20.

38. Tillich opposes the "dialectical system" that is based on the

single and exclusive fact of Jesus Christ; such a system will inevitably entail *Heteronomie, Gesetz, und absolute Religion.* Paul Tillich, "Kritisches und Positives Paradox—Eine Auseinandersetzung mit Karl Barth und Friedrich Gogarten" (1923), *Anfänge der dialektischen Theologie,* I, pp. 165-74, p. 173.

39. Reinhold Niebuhr, *Essays in Applied Christianity,* sel. and ed. by D. B. Robertson (New York: Meridian Books, 1959), pp. 149, 151, 172.

40. Niebuhr, *The Social Sources of Denominationalism,* pp. 275-78.

41. Niebuhr, "Religious Realism and the Twentieth Century," p. 420.

42. Cf. Donald B. Meyer, *The Protestant Search for Political Realism 1919-1941* (Berkeley: University of California Press, 1960), p. 249.

43. Cf. in this respect also Wilhelm Pauck, *Karl Barth—Prophet of a New Christianity?* (New York: Harper & Bros., 1931).

44. The question of whether any effort to introduce Barthian elements into a way of thought which Barth himself emphatically rejects is bound to fail or to lead to contrary results, would belong in a more elaborate essay on the effects of Barthianism in contemporary theology, though it is obviously a related problem. Cf. Hans W. Frei, "Niebuhr's Theological Background," *Faith and Ethics: The Theology of H. Richard Niebuhr,* ed. by Paul Ramsey (New York: Harper & Bros., 1957), pp. 9-64, esp. pp. 40-44.

45. Niebuhr, "Religious Realism and the Twentieth Century," p. 414.

46. Cf. H. Richard Niebuhr, "Theology and Psychology: A Sterile Union," *The Christian Century* 44-1927, pp. 47-48, in which Niebuhr places Schleiermacher and D. C. Macintosh over against each other.

47. Niebuhr, "Religious Realism and the Twentieth Century," p. 419.

48. *Ibid.,* p. 424.

49. Niebuhr, "Can German and American Christians Understand Each Other?" pp. 914-16.

50. *Ibid.,* p. 916.

51. Niebuhr, "Religious Realism and the Twentieth Century," p. 427.

52. *Ibid.,* p. 428.

53. H. Richard Niebuhr, "The Grace of Doing Nothing," *The Christian Century* 49-1932, pp. 378-80. The debate was published again in *The Christian Century Reader,* ed. by H. Fey and M. Frakes (New York: Association Press, 1962), pp. 216-31.

54. *Ibid.*, p. 380 (italics added).

55. Reinhold Niebuhr, "Must We Do Nothing?" *The Christian Century* 49-1932, pp. 415-17.

56. H. Richard Niebuhr, "A Communication: The Only Way into the Kingdom of God," *The Christian Century* 49-1932, p. 447 (italics added).

57. H. Richard Niebuhr, "Man the Sinner," *Journal of Religion* 15-1935, pp. 272-80.

58. D. C. Macintosh, *The Reasonableness of Christianity* (New York: Charles Scribner's Sons, 1925), pp. 127 f.

59. H. Richard Niebuhr, "Value Theory and Theology," *The Nature of Religious Experience: Essays in Honor of Douglas Clyde Macintosh* (New York:Harper & Bros., 1937) (italics added).

60. *Ibid.*, p. 116.

61. H. Richard Niebuhr, *The Meaning of Revelation* (New York: Macmillan Paperback Edition, 1960), p. 153.

62. Macintosh, in his answer to Niebuhr's essay, does not discern or understand this particular concern: he does not see why theology should not be *both* existential (thus he labels Niebuhr's position) *and* valuational. D. C. Macintosh, "Theology, Valuational or Existential?" *Review of Religion* 4-1939, pp. 23-44.

63. Cf. Hans W. Frei, "The Theology of H. Richard Niebuhr," *Faith and Ethics: The Theology of H. Richard Niebuhr*, ed. by Paul Ramsey (New York: Harper & Bros.; 1957), pp. 65-116, esp. p. 74.

64. H. Richard Niebuhr, "The Question of the Church," "Toward the Independence of the Church," *The Church Against the World* (Chicago: Willett Clark & Co., 1935), pp. 1-13, 123-56.

65. H. Richard Niebuhr, "Toward the Emancipation of the Church," abbreviated version of the above-mentioned chapter "Toward the Independence of the Church," *Christendom* 1-1935, pp. 133-45.

66. H. Richard Niebuhr, "Nationalism, Socialism, and Christianity," *World Tomorrow* 16-1933, p. 470.

67. Niebuhr, "The Question of the Church," p. 11.

68. Niebuhr, "Toward the Independence of the Church," p. 154.

69. Cf. H. Richard Niebuhr, "The Irreligion of Communist and Capitalist," *The Christian Century* 47-1930, pp. 1306-7. This is Niebuhr's main objection to the Social Gospel: it did not use direct but indirect means against the social ills and thus gave evidence that it did not see how *false faith* is the source of evil. Cf. H. Richard Niebuhr, "The Attack upon the Social Gospel," *Religion in Life* 5-1936, pp. 176-81.

CHAPTER 2 — DEVELOPMENT OF POSITION

A. *The Structure of Niebuhr's Theology*

1. The renewed attention to Edwards is reflected in an increasing amount of biographies and academic studies (cf. Nelson R. Burr, *A Critical Bibliography of Religion in America*, Religion in American Life Series [Princeton: Princeton University Press, 1961], III, especially pp. 985-87). We draw attention especially to the new edition of Edwards' works begun under supervision of Perry Miller (New Haven: Yale University Press, 1957 ff.); to such editions as C. H. Faust and T. H. Johnson, eds., *Representative Selections*, rev. ed. (New York: Hill & Wang, 1962, 1963-2); and Harvey G. Townsend, ed., *The Philosophy of Jonathan Edwards from His Private Notebooks* (Eugene: University of Oregon Press, 1955); and to such widely known works as Perry Miller, *Jonathan Edwards* (New York: Meridian Books, 1949); and Douglas J. Elwood, *The Philosophical Theology of Jonathan Edwards* (New York: Columbia University Press, 1960).

2. Jonathan Edwards, "Personal Narrative," *Representative Selections*, p. 67.

3. "God understands himself and all other things by the actual and immediate presence of an idea of the things understood." Jonathan Edwards, "Miscellanies," No. 782, *The Philosophy of Jonathan Edwards from His Private Notebooks*, p. 118.

4. "It follows that the constant exercise of the infinite power of God is necessary to preserve bodies in being . . . all body is nothing but what immediately results from the exercise of divine power in such a particular manner." Edwards, "Of Being," *The Philosophy of Jonathan Edwards from His Private Notebooks*, p. 16.

5. *Ibid.*, p. 18.

6. The distinction appears in Edwards' sermon "God Glorified in Man's Dependence" (1731), *The Works of President Edwards* (New York: R. Carter, 1881), IV, pp. 169-78; cf. p. 174.

7. Miller, *Jonathan Edwards*, p. 81.

8. Elwood, *op. cit.*, p. 111.

9. Jonathan Edwards, "A Treatise Concerning Religious Affections" (1746), *The Works of Jonathan Edwards*, Perry Miller, gen. ed. (New Haven: Yale University Press, 1959), II, p. 95.

10. *Ibid.*, p. 101.

11. *Ibid.*, p. 124.

12. *Ibid.*, pp. 272, 283, 201.

13. Jonathan Edwards, *The Nature of True Virtue* (1755) (Ann Arbor: University of Michigan, 1960, Ann Arbor Paperback).

14. H. Richard Niebuhr, "Ex Libris," *The Christian Century* 79-1962, p. 754, a book list submitted in response to the query: "What books did most to shape your vocational attitude and your philosophy of life?"

15. H. Richard Niebuhr, "Introduction to Edwards," *Christian Ethics: Sources of the Living Tradition*, ed. with introd. by Waldo Beach and H. Richard Niebuhr (New York: Ronald Press, 1955), p. 389.

16. Jonathan Edwards, "The Freedom of the Will," *The Works of Jonathan Edwards*, Perry Miller, gen. ed. (New Haven: Yale University Press, 1957, 1962-2), I, p. 141.

17. "Moral necessity implies the very ground and reason, why men's actions are to be ascribed to them as their own. . . . It establishes the moral system of the universe, and God's moral government, in every respect." Jonathan Edwards "Remarks on the Essays on the Principles of Morality and Natural Religion," *Representative Selections*, p. 314. Cf. also "The Freedom of the Will," p. 431.

18. Edwards, "The Freedom of the Will," pp. 172 ff.

19. *Ibid.*, p. 278.

20. Edwards, "A Treatise Concerning Religious Affections," p. 257.

21. H. Richard Niebuhr, "The Anachronism of Jonathan Edwards," 1958 (unpublished lecture).

22. H. Richard Niebuhr, *The Kingdom of God in America* (New York: Harper & Bros. Torchbook, 1959), p. 1.

23. *Ibid.*, p. x.

24. "Such considerations urge upon us the desirability of seeking to understand the relation of American Christianity to American culture by making *the former rather than the latter* our starting point. After we have done this we may compare the results with those yielded by *the opposite approach.*" *Ibid.*, p. 14 (italics added).

25. *Ibid.*, p. 14.

26. "We need to take our stand within the movement so that its objects may come into view. . . . No movement can be understood until its presuppositions, the fundamental faith upon which it rests, have been at least provisionally adopted." *Ibid.*, pp. 12 f.

27. Hans W. Frei, "Niebuhr's Theological Background," *Faith and Ethics: The Theology of H. Richard Niebuhr*, ed. by Paul Ramsey (New York: Harper & Bros., 1957), pp. 30 f.

28. Niebuhr, *The Kingdom of God in America*, p. xvi.

29. *Ibid.*, p. xvi.

30. *Ibid.*, p. xiv.

31. Cf. *ibid.*, pp. xii, 1-15 passim.

32. *Ibid.*, p. xii.

33. *Ibid.*, p. 44.

34. *Ibid.*, p. 193.

35. H. Richard Niebuhr, "War as the Judgment of God," *The Christian Century* 59-1942, pp. 630-33; "Is God in the War?" *The Christian Century* 59-1942, pp. 953-55; "War as Crucifixion," *The Christian Century* 60-1943, pp. 513-15.

36. Niebuhr, "Is God in the War?" p. 954.

37. Niebuhr, "War as the Judgment of God," p. 633.

38. H. Richard Niebuhr, *Radical Monotheism and Western Culture* (New York: Harper & Bros., 1960). The term "radical monotheism" was used for the first time in the articles on the war. "Radical monotheism must meet everything that happens with the faith that God is one and universal. . . . To look for God's judgment is to affirm as radical monotheists that there is no person, no situation, no event in which the opportunity to serve God is not present." "Is God in the War?" p. 954.

39. Niebuhr, *Radical Monotheism and Western Culture*, p. 31 (italics added).

40. See esp. Niebuhr, *ibid.*, pp. 59 f. and H. Richard Niebuhr, *The Responsible Self: An Essay in Christian Moral Philosophy* (New York: Harper & Row, 1963), p. 45.

41. Niebuhr, *Radical Monotheism and Western Culture*, p. 60.

42. H. Richard Niebuhr in collaboration with Daniel Day Williams and James M. Gustafson, *The Purpose of the Church and Its Ministry: Reflections on the Aims of Theological Education* (New York: Harper & Bros., 1956), p. 37.

43. Niebuhr, *Radical Monotheism and Western Culture*, p. 16.

44. *Ibid.*, p. 56 (italics added); cf. pp. 64 f.

45. H. Richard Niebuhr, "Toward the Independence of the Church," *The Church Against the World* (Chicago: Willett Clark & Co., 1935), p. 126.

46. Cf. especially H. Richard Niebuhr, "The Idea of Covenant and American Democracy," *Church History* 23-1954, pp. 126-35. "One of the great common patterns that guided men in the period when American democracy was formed, that was present both in their understanding and in their action, and *was used in psychology, sociology, and metaphysics as in ethics, politics, and religion*, was the pattern of the covenant or of federal society" (p. 129 [italics added]).

47. H. Richard Niebuhr, "On the Nature of Faith," *Religious Experience and Truth*, ed. by Sidney Hook (New York: New York University Press, 1961), pp. 93-102.

48. Cf. Niebuhr, *The Responsible Self*, p. 121.

49. *Ibid.*, p. 141.

50. H. Richard Niebuhr, "The Gift of the Catholic Vision,"

Theology Today 4-1948, p. 520 (italics added).

51. H. Richard Niebuhr, "The Norm of the Church," *Journal of Religious Thought* 4-1946, p. 10.

52. Cf. Frei, "The Theology of H. Richard Niebuhr," pp. 76-78. Also Kenneth Cauthen, "An Introduction to the Theology of H. Richard Niebuhr," *Canadian Journal of Theology* 10-1964, No. 1, pp. 4-14, who speaks rather puzzlingly of "a shift from sociological toward more theological modes of analysis" (p. 7), but rightly continues to emphasize that the combination of "sociological, historical, and theological analyses into a unified framework of interpretation which explores from various angles the situation of the self in the totality of its personal and social relationships before God" (p. 8), is a permanent feature of Niebuhr's thought.

53. Cf. Niebuhr, *The Responsible Self,* pp. 42-46.

54. H. Richard Niebuhr, *Christ and Culture* (New York: Harper & Bros. Torchbook, 1956), p. x. It should be remembered that, in speaking of relativism, Niebuhr always has in mind *both* the relativity of the object *and* that of the subject. Relativism is inescapable not only in the judgment of historical events, facts, objects, faiths, but also in the judgment of the standpoint from which judgment is made. "All knowledge is conditioned by the standpoint of the knower . . . though we regard the universal, the image of the universal in our mind is not a universal image." H. Richard Niebuhr, *The Meaning of Revelation* (New York: Macmillan Paperback Edition, 1960), pp. 7, 10.

55. Frei, "The Theology of H. Richard Niebuhr," p. 88.

56. L. D. Kliever, "Methodology and Christology in H. Richard Niebuhr" (Durham, N. C.: Duke University, 1963), p. 60 (unpublished doctoral dissertation).

57. In the American tradition there is always some given combination of relativism (pluralism) with some kind of faith in a providential and sovereign God. The development toward "radical monotheism," viewed from here, means that gradually all premature "halting points," *all* localizations of the universal in the particular, are abandoned. This clears the road for a profound and detailed analysis of the phenomenon of faith in human life. In contrast to this, Troeltsch, who stands in the German academic tradition in which the problem of man is primarily the formal problem of the noumenal over against the phenomenal self, would find it impossible ever to combine complete relativism and radical faithfulness.

58. Cf. his contribution to the *Faith and Ethics* volume: *The Transformation of Ethics* (New York: Harper & Bros., 1957), pp. 140-72, and chapter 6 of his book *Nine Modern Moralists* (Englewood Cliffs, N. J.: Prentice-Hall, Inc., 1962), pp. 149-79. The latter essay

contains a reiteration of the criticism developed in the former.

59. Paul Ramsey, *The Transformation of Ethics*, p. 164.

60. *Ibid.*, p. 171. "Nothing in the nature of radical monotheism or the conversionist motif itself, but only a certain philosophical conception of human historical reason, seems to require that large concessions be made to relativism" (p. 162).

61. *Ibid.*, p. 159.

62. *Ibid.*, pp. 165 f.

63. Cf. especially H. Richard Niebuhr, "How My Mind Has Changed," *How My Mind Has Changed*, ed. by Harold E. Fey (New York: Meridian Books, 1961), pp. 69-80.

64. Niebuhr, *Radical Monotheism and Western Culture*, pp. 52 f.

65. H. Richard Niebuhr, "Faith in Gods and in God," reprint of an article written in 1943 as supplementary essay in *Radical Monotheism and Western Culture*, pp. 114-26, pp. 125 f.

B. The Temper of Niebuhr's Theology

1. Cf. H. Richard Niebuhr, *Radical Monotheism and Western Culture* (New York: Harper & Bros., 1960), p. 38.

2. Cf. H. Richard Niebuhr's addition in the reprint of his essay "The Center of Value," *Radical Monotheism and Western Culture*, p. 105, n. 1; also James M. Gustafson's introduction to *The Responsible Self* by H. Richard Niebuhr (New York: Harper & Row, 1963), p. 26.

3. Paul Tillich, *Systematic Theology* II (Chicago: University of Chicago Press, 1959-3), p. 11.

4. H. Richard Niebuhr, Review of Tillich's *Systematic Theology* I, *Union Seminary Quarterly Review* 7-1951, pp. 45-49 (italics added).

5. Cf. Niebuhr, *Radical Monotheism and Western Culture*, p. 32.

6. This is the reason also why Niebuhr prefers to speak more precisely of God as *principle* of being and *principle* of value, rather than as being and value "in the primary sense." Cf. *ibid.*, p. 33, n. 7.

7. H. Richard Niebuhr, *The Meaning of Revelation* (New York: Macmillan Paperback Edition, 1960), p. 35. Niebuhr combines this with the necessity of a *disinterested approach* to God (cf. H. Richard Niebuhr, "Value Theory and Theology," *The Nature of Religious Experience: Essays in Honor of Douglas Clyde Macintosh* (New York, London: Harper & Bros., 1937, 93-116). This seeming contradiction clearly points to the basic dilemma of his method: God is to be approached and loved only for *his own sake*; his right to be prior and superior to man in his creative and judging actions must be fully respected; yet our approach is a *valuing* approach—it is full of ultimate concern, because *we depend on God for existence.*

8. H. Richard Niebuhr, "Faith in Gods and in God," reprint of an article written in 1943 as supplementary essay in *Radical Monotheism and Western Culture*, p. 116.

9. H. Richard Niebuhr, "Reflections on Faith, Hope and Love," p. 4 (unpublished paper).

10. Niebuhr, "Faith in Gods and in God," p. 122.

11. *Ibid.*, p. 123.

12. Cf. for the following especially Spinoza's *Ethics*, English edition.

13. H. Richard Niebuhr, "The Anachronism of Jonathan Edwards," 1958 (unpublished paper).

14. George Santayana, Introduction to Spinoza's *Ethics*, Everyman's Edition (New York: E. P. Dutton & Co., 1910), p. xxii; cf. Niebuhr's use of the quotation in *Radical Monotheism and Western Culture*, p. 89.

15. H. Richard Niebuhr, "How My Mind Has Changed," *How My Mind Has Changed*, ed. by Harold E. Fey (Cleveland, New York: Meridian Books, 1961), p. 72.

16. H. Richard Niebuhr, *Christ and Culture* (New York: Harper & Bros. Torchbook, 1956), p. 254.

17. Niebuhr, *Radical Monotheism and Western Culture*, p. 42.

18. Niebuhr, "Faith in Gods and in God," p. 125 (italics added).

19. Niebuhr, *The Meaning of Revelation*, p. 154.

20. Cf. especially Barth's earlier quoted essay "Schicksal und Idee in der Theologie" (1922).

21. Cf. Niebuhr, *The Responsible Self*, pp. 149-78.

22. H. Richard Niebuhr, "A Communication: The Only Way into the Kingdom of God," *The Christian Century* 49-1932, p. 447 (cf. chapter 1, part B).

23. Niebuhr, "Faith in Gods and in God," p. 126.

24. Gustafson, *op. cit.*, p. 8.

25. *Ibid.*, p. 18.

26. Cf. especially his essay "The Center of Value," *Moral Principles of Action: Man's Ethical Imperative*, ed. by Ruth Nanda Anshen (New York: Harper & Bros., 1952), pp. 162-75, published again as supplementary essay in *Radical Monotheism and Western Culture*, pp. 100-13.

27. The chronological localization of the two schemes—though it cannot be carried through with precision (both schemes overlap each other considerably)—may be seen in connection with Niebuhr's tendency to move from value-theoretical to existentialist modes of thought (see chapter 2, part A).

28. Niebuhr, *The Responsible Self*, p. 46.

29. Cf. E. T. Culver's report of the "Earl Lectures" given by Niebuhr, *The Christian Century* 79-1962, pp. 403-5.

30. I found the term only in Niebuhr's notes for his "Ethics Lectures" (1961); though it expresses concisely what he means, it does not—to my knowledge—appear in anything that has been published.

31. H. Richard Niebuhr, "On the Nature of Faith," *Religious Experience and Truth*, ed. by Sidney Hook (New York: New York University Press, 1961), p. 102.

32. See chapter 4.

33. Niebuhr, *The Meaning of Revelation*, pp. 29-33.

34. *Ibid.*, p. 33.

35. Gustafson, *op. cit.*, p. 15.

36. Niebuhr, *The Responsible Self*, p. 86.

37. *Ibid.*, pp. 44 f.

38. The remark is taken from my own notes of Niebuhr's classroom lectures in 1959.

39. Niebuhr, *The Meaning of Revelation*, pp. 177 ff.

40. Kenneth Cauthen, "An Introduction to the Theology of H. Richard Niebuhr," *Canadian Journal of Theology* 10-1964, p. 6.

41. *Ibid.*, p. 10 (italics added).

42. Niebuhr, *The Responsible Self*, p. 150.

CHAPTER 3 — THE SCOPE OF RESPONSIBILITY

A. The Triad of Faith

1. H. Richard Niebuhr, *The Responsible Self* (New York: Harper & Row, 1963), p. 71.

2. Cf. H. Richard Niebuhr, "Science in Conflict with Morality," a supplementary essay in *Radical Monotheism and Western Culture* (New York: Harper & Bros., 1960).

3. H. Richard Niebuhr, *The Meaning of Revelation* (New York: Macmillan Paperback Edition, 1960), p. 104 (italics added).

4. Niebuhr, *Radical Monotheism and Western Culture*, p. 86.

5. Cf. Niebuhr, *The Meaning of Revelation*, pp. 145 f.

6. H. Richard Niebuhr, *Christ and Culture* (New York: Harper & Bros. Torchbook, 1956), pp. 243-46.

7. Cf. especially Niebuhr, *The Meaning of Revelation*, pp. x, 65, 146.

8. Cf. for a comparative study of G. H. Mead and Martin Buber:

Paul Pfuetze, *The Social Self* (New York: Bookman Associates, 1954).

9. H. Richard Niebuhr, "Towards New Symbols" (unpublished lecture).

10. Niebuhr, *The Meaning of Revelation*, p. 141.

11. Niebuhr, *The Responsible Self*, p. 65.

12. G. H. Mead, "The Genesis of the Self and Social Control," *The Philosophy of the Present*, ed. by Arthur E. Murphy (Chicago: Open Court, 1932), pp. 181, 184 f.

13. Niebuhr, *The Responsible Self*, p. 78.

14. *Ibid.*, pp. 63 ff., 85. Cf. Niebuhr's interpretation of *conscience* in "The Ego-Alter Dialectic and the Conscience," *Journal of Philosophy* 42-1945, pp. 352-59.

15. Niebuhr, *The Meaning of Revelation*, p. 13.

16. Mead, *op. cit.*, p. 177.

17. *Ibid.*, p. 190.

18. Niebuhr, *The Responsible Self*, p. 98.

19. *Ibid.*, p. 109.

20. Niebuhr, *The Meaning of Revelation*, p. 13.

21. Niebuhr, *The Responsible Self*, pp. 80 f.

22. H. Richard Niebuhr, "The Triad of Faith," *Andover Newton Bulletin* 47-1954, pp. 3-12, esp. p. 6.

23. H. Richard Niebuhr, "Faith in Gods and in God," reprint of an article written in 1943 as supplementary essay in *Radical Monotheism and Western Culture*, p. 118.

24. Niebuhr, *The Meaning of Revelation*, p. 80 (italics added).

25. Niebuhr explains the dual meaning of faith in many places; of special significance is *Christ and Culture*, pp. 252-56, and *Radical Monotheism and Western Culture*, pp. 16-23.

26. Niebuhr, *Radical Monotheism and Western Culture*, p. 42.

27. Niebuhr, *The Responsible Self*, p. 110.

28. *Ibid.*, pp. 86 f.

29. *Ibid.*, p. 118 (italics added).

30. *Ibid.*, p. 175.

31. H. Richard Niebuhr, "On the Nature of Faith," *Religious Experience and Truth*, ed. by Sidney Hook (New York: New York University Press, 1961), p. 101.

32. The following is taken from Niebuhr's own notes of his "Ethics Lectures" (1961).

33. Niebuhr, "The Triad of Faith," p. 10.

34. H. Richard Niebuhr, "The Center of Value," *Radical Monotheism and Western Culture*, p. 107.

35. *Ibid.*, p. 110.

36. *Ibid.*, p. 111.

37. *Ibid.*, p. 112 (italics added).

38. George Schrader, "Value and Valuation," *Faith and Ethics*, ed. by Paul Ramsey (New York: Harper & Bros., 1957), pp. 173-204; cf. Niebuhr's added footnote in the second publication of "The Center of Value," p. 105.

39. Schrader, *op. cit.*, p. 190.

40. Niebuhr, "The Center of Value," p. 105, n. 1.

41. Schrader, *op. cit.*, p. 200.

42. Niebuhr, "The Center of Value," p. 105, n. 1.

43. Niebuhr, *The Responsible Self*, pp. 122 f.

44. Niebuhr, *Radical Monotheism and Western Culture*, p. 33.

45. Niebuhr, *The Responsible Self*, pp. 123 f.

46. *Ibid.*, pp. 115 f.

47. Niebuhr, *Radical Monotheism and Western Culture*, p. 44.

48. Cf. in general F. Schleiermacher, *The Christian Faith* (Edinburgh: T & T Clark, 1960), esp. pp. 12-26, 137-40.

49. H. Richard Niebuhr, in collaboration with Daniel Day Williams and James M. Gustafson, *The Purpose of the Church and Its Ministry* (New York: Harper & Bros., 1956), p. 34.

50. "Schleiermacher's realm of feeling I call the symbolic layer, where we are related to totalities, ultimate contents—to the circumambient; it modifies all thinking and doing." Niebuhr's notes of his "Ethics Lectures" (1961). Thus as Niebuhr once remarked in a seminar on Theology and Language (1960), the Christian community seeks to apply the *symbolic pattern of Jesus Christ* to its interpretation of encountered reality. With this remark Niebuhr simply restated the problem of *The Meaning of Revelation*. He thought it necessary that theology should engage in reflections on language. Even *Christ and Culture* "might be written today from the standpoint of language" (remark in the same seminar).

51. Niebuhr, *The Meaning of Revelation*, p. 23.

52. Conversely, of course, it is precisely the association with *religious* relativism that keeps *historical* relativism from becoming skepticism.

53. Niebuhr, *The Meaning of Revelation*, p. 27: "Though he (Schleiermacher) acknowledged the togetherness of God and the feeling of absolute dependence so that one could not speak of the former save from the point of view of the latter, *yet he did not really take this standpoint in his theology but made the feeling of absolute dependence his object*" (italics added).

54. *Ibid.*, pp. viii, x.

55. Cf. Hans W. Frei, *Faith and Ethics: The Theology of H. Richard Niebuhr*, ed. by Paul Ramsey (New York: Harper & Bros., 1957), pp. 71 f., n. 15.

56. H. Richard Niebuhr, "How My Mind Has Changed," *How My Mind Has Changed*, ed. by Harold E. Fey (Cleveland, New York: Meridian Books, 1961), p. 76.

57. Niebuhr, *The Meaning of Revelation*, p. 34.

58. *Ibid.*, p. 35.

B. The Moral Life

1. H. Richard Niebuhr, *Radical Monotheism and Western Culture* (New York: Harper & Bros., 1960), p. 32.

2. H. Richard Niebuhr, *The Responsible Self* (New York: Harper & Row, 1963), pp. 165 ff.

3. Dannhorst certainly overstates the case when he says that in Niebuhr there is no such thing as biblical ethics, but "only a viewing of changing moral problems in the light of an unchanging God." Donald E. Dannhorst, "Social Norms and Protestant Ethics: The Ethical Views of Reinhold Niebuhr and H. Richard Niebuhr" (St. Louis, 1963), p. 134 (unpublished doctoral dissertation). Dannhorst likewise oversimplifies Niebuhr's method in ethics when he says that it is indicative and inductive, whereas the method of Reinhold Niebuhr is imperative and deductive. *Ibid.*, p. 40.

4. Niebuhr, *The Responsible Self*, p. 100.

5. H. Richard Niebuhr, "Faith in Gods and in God," reprint of an article written in 1943 as supplementary essay in *Radical Monotheism and Western Culture*, p. 120.

6. Cf. Niebuhr, *The Responsible Self*, pp. 139, 142, 143 f.

7. This is the theme of Jonathan Edwards' *The Nature of True Virtue* (Ann Arbor: University of Michigan, 1960, Ann Arbor Paperback). "Disinterested benevolence" toward God is a condition for true virtue; without it man remains caught in "private affection" though this may be extended to the largest possible number.

8. Niebuhr, *The Responsible Self*, p. 138.

9. H. Richard Niebuhr, *The Kingdom of God in America* (New York: Harper & Bros. Torchbook, 1959), p. 115.

10. H. Richard Niebuhr, "An Attempt at a Theological Analysis of Missionary Motivation," *Occasional Bulletin* from the Missionary Research Library (New York, 1963), p. 3.

11. H. Richard Niebuhr, "Man the Sinner," *Journal of Religion* 15-1935 and "The Attack upon the Social Gospel," *Religion in Life* 5-1936.

12. Niebuhr's notes of his "Ethics Lectures" (1961).

13. Niebuhr, *The Responsible Self*, p. 107.

14. Niebuhr, "Faith in Gods and in God," p. 126.

15. Cf. Niebuhr, *Radical Monotheism and Western Culture*, p. 63.

16. H. Richard Niebuhr, "A Communication: The Only Way into the Kingdom of God," *The Christian Century* 49-1932, p. 447.

17. Niebuhr, *The Responsible Self*, p. 167.

18. H. Richard Niebuhr, "Reflections on Faith, Hope and Love" (unpublished paper).

19. Jonathan Edwards, "A Treatise Concerning Religious Affections," *The Works of Jonathan Edwards*, Perry Miller, gen. ed. (New Haven: Yale University Press, 1959) II, pp. 311 ff.

20. Niebuhr, "An Attempt at a Theological Analysis of Missionary Motivation," p. 5.

21. Niebuhr, *The Responsible Self*, p. 142 (italics added).

22. *Ibid.*, p. 121.

23. *Ibid.*, p. 125.

24. H. Richard Niebuhr, *Christ and Culture* (New York: Harper & Bros. Torchbook, 1956), p. 11 (italics added).

25. The first time Niebuhr uses these terms is in the article "The Ego-Alter Dialectic and the Conscience," *Journal of Philosophy* 42-1945; they are fully elaborated in *Radical Monotheism and Western Culture.*

26. Niebuhr, "Faith in Gods and in God," p. 121.

27. Niebuhr, *Radical Monotheism and Western Culture*, p. 35. "Nothing human is alien to the believer in humanity and he is alien to no other human; but mankind for him remains alien in a world that contains so many powers besides itself."

28. *Ibid.*, p. 88.

29. *Ibid.*, p. 74.

30. Cf. especially Niebuhr, "How My Mind Has Changed," pp. 77 f.

CHAPTER 4 — THE REVELATION OF GOD IN CHRIST

A. The Possibility of Historical Revelation

1. R. G. Collingwood, *The Idea of History* (New York: Oxford University Press, 1964-3), p. 84; cf. Richard R. Niebuhr, *Resurrection and Historical Reason* (New York: Charles Scribner's Sons, 1957), pp. 74 ff., 90 f.

2. R. Bultmann, *History and Eschatology* (New York: Harper & Row Torchbook, 1962), esp. chapter 6.

3. Cf. H. Richard Niebuhr, *The Meaning of Revelation* (New York: Macmillan Paperback Edition, 1960), pp. 65 ff.

4. *Ibid.*, pp. 7, 10.

5. *Ibid.*, p. 17.

6. *Ibid.*, p. 48.

7. H. Richard Niebuhr, *Christ and Culture* (New York: Harper & Bros. Torchbook, 1956), p. x.

8. Cf. *ibid.*, p. 234.

9. Niebuhr, *The Meaning of Revelation*, pp. 61, 63; in general, pp. 59-73.

10. *Ibid.*, p. 78.

11. Cf. H. Richard Niebuhr, *The Responsible Self* (New York: Harper & Row, 1963), pp. 151 ff.

12. Cf. Niebuhr, *The Meaning of Revelation*, pp. 65-67.

13. Niebuhr, *The Responsible Self*, p. 83.

14. Cf. Niebuhr, *The Meaning of Revelation*, p. 109.

15. *Ibid.*, pp. 102, 173.

16. *Ibid.*, p. 131.

17. Jonathan Edwards, "A Treatise Concerning Religious Affections," *The Works of Jonathan Edwards*, Perry Miller, gen. ed. (New Haven: Yale University Press, 1959), II, p. 288 (italics added).

18. Niebuhr, *The Meaning of Revelation*, p. 121.

19. *Ibid.*, p. 137.

20. *Ibid.*, pp. 84-90.

21. Niebuhr, *The Responsible Self*, p. 126.

22. Cf. Niebuhr, *The Meaning of Revelation*, pp. 127 ff.

23. *Ibid.*, p. 90.

24. *Ibid.*, p. 74.

25. *Ibid.*, p. 177.

26. *Ibid.*, p. 84.

27. *Ibid.*, p. 37.

28. Cf. James M. Gustafson, "Time and Community: A Discussion," appendix to *Treasure in Earthen Vessels: The Church as a Human Community* (New York: Harper & Row, 1961), pp. 113-37.

29. Niebuhr, *The Meaning of Revelation*, p. 118.

30. H. Richard Niebuhr, "The Seminary in the Ecumenical Age," *Theology Today* 17-1960, pp. 300-10.

31. Niebuhr presents these points in his notes of the "Ethics Lectures" (1961).

32. Cf. Niebuhr, *The Meaning of Revelation*, p. 115.

33. *Ibid.*, p. 116.

B. *The Unity of God and the Work of Christ*

1. For this point and the following, cf. H. Richard Niebuhr, "The Doctrine of the Trinity and the Unity of the Church," *Theology Today* 3-1946, pp. 371-84.

2. Cf. H. Richard Niebuhr, *Christ and Culture* (New York: Harper & Bros. Torchbook, 1956), p. 115.

3. Niebuhr, "The Doctrine of the Trinity and the Unity of the Church," p. 379.

4. H. Richard Niebuhr, *The Kingdom of God in America* (New York: Harper & Bros. Torchbook, 1959), pp. 197 f.

5. Niebuhr, *Christ and Culture*, p. 81.

6. H. Richard Niebuhr in collaboration with Daniel Day Williams and James M. Gustafson, *The Purpose of the Church and Its Ministry: Reflections of the Aims of Theological Education* (New York: Harper & Bros., 1956), pp. 36 f.

7. Cf. Hans W. Frei, *Faith and Ethics: The Theology of H. Richard Niebuhr*, ed. by Paul Ramsey (New York: Harper & Bros., 1957), p. 97.

8. *Ibid.*, pp. 98-100.

9. Niebuhr's notes of his "Ethics Lectures" (1961). Cf. his articles on the war, the first elaboration of the theme of *radical monotheism*.

10. H. Richard Niebuhr, "An Attempt at a Theological Analysis of Missionary Motivation," *Occasional Bulletin* from the Missionary Research Library (New York: 1963), p. 1; also Niebuhr, *Christ and Culture*, p. 108.

11. Niebuhr, *Christ and Culture*, p. 108; cf. Niebuhr, *The Responsible Self*, p. 155.

12. Niebuhr, "The Doctrine of the Trinity and the Unity of the Church," p. 382.

13. H. Richard Niebuhr, "Participation in the Present Passion" (unpublished sermon).

14. Cf. J. Royce, *The Problem of Christianity* (New York: Macmillan, 1913), I, pp. 263, 294 ff., p. 322.

15. Cf. Niebuhr's articles on the war (see chapter 2, part A).

16. H. Richard Niebuhr, "A Christian Interpretation of War" (unpublished paper); cf. H. Richard Niebuhr, "War as Crucifixion," *The Christian Century* 60-1943, p. 514.

17. Niebuhr, *The Responsible Self* (New York: Harper & Row, 1963), p. 177.

18. Cf. Niebuhr, *The Purpose of the Church and Its Ministry*, p. 33.

19. Niebuhr, *Christ and Culture*, p. 255.

20. *Ibid.*, p. 29; cf. Niebuhr, *The Responsible Self,* p. 163.

21. H. Richard Niebuhr, *Radical Monotheism and Western Culture* (New York: Harper & Bros., 1960), p. 42.

22. Niebuhr, *Christ and Culture*, p. 28.

23. *Ibid.*, p. 25.

24. "They are not habits somehow established in the constitution of the agent, but relations which depend for their duration on the constancy with which the objective good, to which the self is related in these ways, is given. This is true not only of faith, hope, and love, but of all other good human conduct as seen in the perspective of faith. . . . That is to say, the idea of virtue itself has no real place in Christian ethics. . . . Insofar as the distinction between moral or achieved, habitual virtues and theological virtues may be maintained, the line must be drawn elsewhere than Thomas and his followers draw it. It lies between the habits which put one in the way of receiving the gifts and the gifts themselves." H. Richard Niebuhr, "Reflections on Faith, Hope and Love" (unpublished paper).

25. Cf. also Jonathan Edwards, "A Treatise Concerning Religious Affections," *The Works of Jonathan Edwards*, Perry Miller, gen. ed. (New Haven: Yale University Press, 1959), II, p. 273, who connects the mediatorship of Jesus with his moral perfection.

26. Niebuhr, *Christ and Culture*, p. 27.

27. *Ibid.*, p. 255.

28. Frei, *op. cit.*, pp. 106 ff.

29. Niebuhr, *The Purpose of the Church and Its Ministry*, p. 34.

30. Niebuhr, *Christ and Culture*, p. 255.

31. Martin Kähler, *The so-called Historical Jesus and the Historic, Biblical Christ* ("Der sogennante historische Jesus und der geschichtliche, biblische Christus"), trans., ed., and introd. by Carl E. Braaten (Philadelphia: Fortress Press, 1964).

32. Cf. Niebuhr, *The Meaning of Revelation* (New York: Macmillan Paperback Edition, 1960), p. 177.

33. Gerhard Ebeling, *Das Wesen des Christlichen Glaubens* (Tübingen: J. C. B. Mohr, 1960-4) and especially *Theologie und Verkündigung* (Tübingen: J. C. B. Mohr, 1962).

34. Cf. especially the essays of Amos N. Wilder and J. B. Cobb, *New Frontiers in Theology*, Vol. II, ed. by J. M. Robinson and J. B. Cobb, Jr., *The New Hermeneutic* (New York: Harper & Row, 1964), pp. 198-231.

35. John Knox, *The Church and the Reality of Christ* (New York: Harper & Row, 1962), pp. 22, 77.

36. Richard R. Niebuhr, *Resurrection and Historical Reason* (New York: Charles Scribner's Sons, 1957).

37. Niebuhr, *The Responsible Self*, pp. 161-78.

38. H. Richard Niebuhr, "The Church Defines Itself in the World" (unpublished paper).

39. Niebuhr, *The Purpose of the Church and Its Ministry*, pp. 44 f.

40. This must be maintained against Carl Michalson, "The Real Presence of the Hidden God," *Faith and Ethics: The Theology of H. Richard Niebuhr*, ed. by Paul Ramsey (New York: Harper & Bros., 1957), pp. 245-67, p. 248, and also against M. M. Thomas' review of Niebuhr's *Radical Monotheism and Western Culture, International Review of Missions* 52-1963, pp. 471-74, p. 473.

41. Cf. Niebuhr, *Christ and Culture*, pp. 21 f.

42. Notably in the essay "Faith in Gods and in God," reprint of an article written in 1943, as supplementary essay in *Radical Monotheism and Western Culture.*

CHAPTER 5 — THE CHURCH

A. The Christian Community

1. Cf. H. Richard Niebuhr, "How My Mind Has Changed," *How My Mind Has Changed*, ed. by Harold E. Fey (Cleveland, New York: Meridian Books, 1961), pp. 74 f.

2. H. Richard Niebuhr, *The Meaning of Revelation* (New York: Macmillan Paperback Edition, 1960), p. 38.

3. H. Richard Niebuhr, *The Responsible Self* (New York: Harper & Row, 1963), p. 150.

4. *Ibid.*, pp. 43 ff.

5. Niebuhr, *The Meaning of Revelation*, p. 40.

6. *Ibid.*, p. 88.

7. *Ibid.*, p. 41.

8. *Ibid.*, pp. 38 f.

9. *Ibid.*, pp. 31, 34.

10. H. Richard Niebuhr in collaboration with Daniel Day Williams and James M. Gustafson, *The Purpose of the Church and Its Ministry: Reflections on the Aims of Theological Education* (New York: Harper & Bros., 1956), p. 42.

11. Cf. Nels F. S. Ferré, "The Revelatory Moment Within the Historic Faith" (review of *The Meaning of Revelation), Christendom* 6-1941, pp. 439-41, p. 440; George F. Thomas, "Critical Review of H. Richard Niebuhr, *The Meaning of Revelation,"* *Journal of Religion* 21-1941, pp. 455-60, p. 456.

12. This is stated specifically in the unpublished paper "The Church Defines Itself in the World."

13. John B. Cobb, Jr., *Living Options in Protestant Theology* (Philadelphia: Westminster Press, 1962), p. 288.

14. Kenneth M. Hamilton, "Trinitarianism Disregarded," *Encounter* 23-1962, pp. 343-52, p. 345.

15. Kenneth Cauthen, "An Introduction to the Theology of H. Richard Niebuhr," *Canadian Journal of Theology* 10-1964, p. 10.

16. L. D. Kliever, "Methodology and Christology in H. Richard Niebuhr" (Durham, N. C.: Duke University, 1963), p. 80, n. 1, p. 83 (unpublished doctoral dissertation).

17. Niebuhr, *The Responsible Self*, pp. 86 f.

18. Cf. the section on the interpretation of moral existence.

19. Cf. J. B. Cobb, *op. cit.*, p. 297, who criticizes Niebuhr for holding more than one conception of God to be partially true; e.g., God as personal self or as impersonal being.

20. Niebuhr, *The Purpose of the Church and Its Ministry*, pp. 43 f.

21. Niebuhr, *The Responsible Self*, p. 46.

22. Niebuhr, *The Purpose of the Church and Its Ministry*, pp. 86 ff.

23. Niebuhr, *The Meaning of Revelation*, p. 50.

24. Cf. Niebuhr, *The Purpose of the Church and Its Ministry*, p. 120.

25. My notes from Niebuhr's "Ethics Lectures" (1959).

26. Niebuhr, *The Purpose of the Church and Its Ministry*, p. 88.

27. Cf. Niebuhr, "How My Mind Has Changed," p. 78.

28. "The scriptures point to God and through scriptures God points to men when they are read by those who share the same background which the community that produced the letter possessed, or by those who participate in the common life of which the scriptures contain the record." *The Meaning of Revelation*, pp. 50 f.

29. Niebuhr, *The Purpose of the Church and Its Ministry*, p. 45.

30. H. Richard Niebuhr, "The Norm of the Church," *Journal of Religious Thought* 4-1946, pp. 11 f.

31. H. Richard Niebuhr, *Radical Monotheism and Western Culture* (New York: Harper & Bros., 1960), p. 41.

32. Niebuhr, *The Meaning of Revelation*, p. 133.

33. Niebuhr, *The Responsible Self*, p. 170.

34. H. Richard Niebuhr, "Towards New Symbols" (unpublished lecture).

35. H. Richard Niebuhr, "Martin Luther and the Renewal of Human Confidence" (unpublished lecture).

36. Cf. esp. Jonathan Edwards, "Miscellanies," particularly those brought together in *The Philosophy of Jonathan Edwards from His*

Notebooks, ed. by Harvey G. Townsend (Eugene: University of Oregon Press, 1955), under the heading "Common Illuminations," pp. 109-26.

37. John E. Smith, Introduction to "A Treatise Concerning Religious Affections," *The Works of Jonathan Edwards*, Perry Miller, gen. ed. (New Haven: Yale University Press, 1959), II, p. 9. The connection between this view and the preaching of Revivalism can easily be discerned.

38. Horace Bushnell, *God in Christ—Three Discourses with a Preliminary Dissertation on Language* (New York: 1876), p. 33.

39. Niebuhr's notes of his "Ethics Lectures" (1961).

40. Cf. Niebuhr, *The Responsible Self*, pp. 119 f.

41. Niebuhr, "How My Mind Has Changed," pp. 79 f.

42. H. Richard Niebuhr, "The Main Issues in Theological Education," *Theology Today* 11-1955, pp. 512-27.

43. Cf. Niebuhr, "How My Mind Has Changed," p. 77.

44. Niebuhr, "Towards New Symbols."

B. The Church in the World

1. H. Richard Niebuhr, "The Idea of the Church in Theological Education" (unpublished paper, italics added).

2. Cf. H. Richard Niebuhr in collaboration with Daniel Day Williams and James M. Gustafson, *The Purpose of the Church and Its Ministry: Reflections on the Aims of Theological Education* (New York: Harper & Bros., 1956), p. 21.

3. H. Richard Niebuhr, "The Hidden Church and the Churches in Sight," *Religion in Life* 15-1945, pp. 106-16; "The Responsibility of the Church for Society," *The Gospel, the Church and the World*, ed. by Kenneth Scott Latourette (New York, London: Harper & Bros., 1946), pp. 111-33; "The Doctrine of the Trinity and the Unity of the Church," *Theology Today* 3-1946, pp. 371-84; "The Norm of the Church," *Journal of Religious Thought* 4-1946-47, pp. 5-15; "The Gift of the Catholic Vision," *Theology Today* 4-1948, p. 507-21; and "The Disorder of Man in the Church of God," *Man's Disorder and God's Design*, "The Amsterdam Assembly Series" (New York: Harper & Bros., 1949), I, pp. 78-88.

4. Niebuhr, "The Responsibility of the Church for Society," esp. p. 132.

5. Niebuhr, *The Purpose of the Church and Its Ministry*, pp. 30 f.

6. H. Richard Niebuhr, unpublished paper, 1957. Cf. in addition "The Seminary in the Ecumenical Age," *Theology Today* 17-1960, pp. 300-10.

7. Niebuhr, *The Purpose of the Church and Its Ministry*, p. 31.

8. Cf. Niebuhr, "The Seminary in the Ecumenical Age," p. 310, and Niebuhr's concept of the minister as pastoral director, *The Purpose*

of the Church and Its Ministry, pp. 75-95.

9. H. Richard Niebuhr, *The Meaning of Revelation* (New York: Macmillan Paperback Edition, 1960), p. 21.

10. H. Richard Niebuhr, "Theology in the University," supplementary essay to *Radical Monotheism and Western Culture* (New York: Harper & Bros., 1960), p. 95.

11. Niebuhr, *The Purpose of the Church and Its Ministry*, p. 113.

12. H. Richard Niebuhr, "Isolation and Cooperation in Theological Education," Theological Education in America (mimeographed bulletin of the staff of the inquiry into theological education in America, 1954-56), No. 3, 1955, pp. 1-6, esp. p. 2.

13. Niebuhr, *The Purpose of the Church and Its Ministry*, pp. 105, 112, 109.

14. Niebuhr, "Theology in the University," p. 98.

15. Niebuhr, *The Purpose of the Church and Its Ministry*, p. 34 (italics added).

16. Cf. *ibid.*, pp. 21 f.

17. H. Richard Niebuhr, *Der Gedanke des Gottesreiches im Amerikanischen Christentum* (German translation of *The Kingdom of God in America)*, trans. by R. M. Honig (New York: Church World Service, 1948). The word we refer to is *Verdinglichung;* cf. the translation of the Preface, and also p. 118 ("Verdinglichung der kirchlichen Gemeinschaft"). Cf. also pp. 72 and 120 in which the translator speaks of *Formverfestigung* as equivalent to institutionalization.

In general, the German translation of the book tends to obscure specific "Niebuhrian" accents which play such a significant role in his thought. "Experiment in constructive Protestantism" *(The Kingdom of God,* p. 43) is translated with "Arbeit am Aufbau des Protestantismus" *(Der Gedanke,* p. 32); "dialectic movement" *(The Kingdom of God,* p. 73) is translated with "zwiefache Richtung" *(Der Gedanke,* p. 58).

18. Especially in the essay H. Richard Niebuhr, "The Protestant Movement and Democracy in the United States," *The Shaping of American Religion,* ed. by James W. Smith and Leland A. Jamison, "Religion in American Life Series" (Princeton: Princeton University Press, 1961), pp. 20-71.

19. Cf. H. Richard Niebuhr, *The Churches and the Body of Christ* (Philadelphia: Young Friends Movement of the Philadelphia Yearly Meeting of Friends, 1953), pp. 13 ff.

20. Niebuhr, *The Purpose of the Church and Its Ministry*, p. 25.

21. Cf. *ibid.*, p. 21; *The Churches and the Body of Christ,* p. 8; "The Gift of the Catholic Vision"; "The Seminary in the Ecumenical Age."

22. H. Richard Niebuhr, "The Norm of the Church," *Journal of Religious Thought* 4-1946-47, p. 10.

23. H. Richard Niebuhr, *The Social Sources of Denominationalism* (New York: Meridian Books, 1958-2), p. 21.

24. Niebuhr, *The Meaning of Revelation*, p. 118; cf. "Th⸗ Seminary in the Ecumenical Age." p. 304.

25. Cf. Niebuhr, "The Gift of the Catholic Vision," pp. 507 ff.

26. H. Richard Niebuhr, *The Kingdom of God in America* (New York: Harper & Bros. Torchbook, 1959), pp. xv f. Cf. also "The Doctrine of the Trinity and the Unity of the Church."

27. Niebuhr, *The Meaning of Revelation*, p. 116.

28. Niebuhr, "The Church Defines Itself in the World" (unpublished paper).

29. Cf. Niebuhr, *The Meaning of Revelation*, p. 184.

30. Niebuhr, "The Seminary in the Ecumenical Age," p. 308.

BIBLIOGRAPHY OF THE WRITINGS
OF H. RICHARD NIEBUHR

Compiled by Jane E. McFarland

BOOKS AND PAMPHLETS

The Advancement of Theological Education by H. Richard Niebuhr, Daniel Day Williams, and James M. Gustafson. New York: Harper & Bros., 1957.

Christ and Culture. New York: Harper & Bros., 1951. (Also: London: Faber & Faber, 1952; New York: Harper Torchbooks, 1956.)

Christian Ethics: Sources of the Living Tradition, ed. with introduction by Waldo Beach and H. Richard Niebuhr. New York: Ronald Press, 1955.

> Professor Niebuhr undertook the special responsibility for the selection of material and the introduction for chapters 1, 8, 9, and 13.

The Church Against the World by H. Richard Niebuhr, Wilhelm Pauck, and Francis P. Miller. Chicago: Willett Clark & Co., 1935.

> Professor Niebuhr did: "The Question of the Church," 1-13, and "Toward the Independence of the Church," 123-56.

The Churches and the Body of Christ. Philadelphia: The Young Friends Movement of the Philadelphia Yearly Meeting, 1953.

> "The William Penn Lecture," 1953.

Ernst Troeltsch's Philosophy of Religion. Yale University Ph.D. thesis, 1924. Available on microfilm from University Microfilms, Ann Arbor, Mich.

The Gospel for a Time of Fears: Three Lectures: I. Our Eschatological Time, II. The Eternal Now, III. The Gospel of the Last Time. Washington, D.C.: Henderson Services, 1950.

> The Washington Federation of Churches and The School of Religion, Howard University, Sixth Annual Lecture Series, 1950.

The Kingdom of God in America. Chicago: Willet Clark & Co., 1937. (Also: Hamden, Conn.: Shoe String Press, 1956; New York: Harper Torchbooks, 1959; translated into German by Richard Honig as *Der Gedanke des Gottesreiches im Amerikanischen Christentum.* New York, Church World Service, 1948.)

> In substance these chapters were given in the form of

lectures at the tercentenary summer session of the Harvard Divinity School in July 1936, and on the Alden-Tuthill Foundation Lectureship at Chicago Theological Seminary in January 1937.

The Meaning of Revelation. New York: Macmillan, 1941. (Also: Macmillan Paperbacks Edition, 1960.)

Contains, with some additions and revisions, the "Nathanael W. Taylor Lectures" given at the Divinity School of Yale University in April 1940.

The Ministry in Historical Perspectives, ed. by H. Richard Niebuhr and Daniel Day Williams. New York: Harper & Bros., 1956.

Moral Relativism and the Christian Ethic. New York: International Missionary Council, 1929.

The Purpose of the Church and Its Ministry: Reflections on the Aims of Theological Education by H. Richard Niebuhr in collaboration with Daniel Day Williams and James M. Gustafson. New York: Harper & Bros., 1956.

Radical Monotheism and Western Civilization. Lincoln: University of Nebraska Press, 1960.

Montgomery Lectureship on Contemporary Civilization, 1957, University of Nebraska.

Radical Monotheism and Western Culture, with Supplementary Essays. New York: Harper & Bros., 1960. (Also: London: Faber & Faber, 1960.) Translated into German by F. Weidner as *Radikaler Monotheismus: Theologie des Glaubens in einer pluralistischen Welt.* Gütersloh, 1965.

Revised and expanded form of the "Montgomery Lectures on Contemporary Civilization," 1957, University of Nebraska.

The Responsible Self: An Essay in Christian Moral Philosophy, with an introduction by James M. Gustafson. New York: Harper & Row, 1963.

The Social Sources of Denominationalism. New York: Henry Holt, 1929. (Also: Hamden, Conn.: Shoe String Press, 1954; New York: Living Age Books; Meridian Books, 1957.)

ARTICLES IN BOOKS

"The Center of Value," *Moral Principles of Action: Man's Ethical Imperative,* ed. Ruth Nanda Anshen. New York: Harper & Bros., 1952, 162-75. Reprinted in *Radical Monotheism and Western Culture, with Supplementary Essays,* 100-113. Translated into German by Pastor E. Fischer as *Die Wertmitte,* in *Zeitschrift für Evangelische Ethik,* IV (1960), 148-59.

"Christ Against Culture" (from *Christ and Culture*), *Religion, Culture, and Society: A Reader in the Sociology of Religion*, ed. Louis Schneider. New York: John Wiley & Sons, 1964, 203-19.

"Christ and Culture: Five Types of Interpretation" (from *Christ and Culture*), *Religion and Contemporary Western Culture: Selected Readings*, comp. Edward C. Cell. Nashville, Tenn.: Abingdon Press, 1967, 47-64.

"Christ and the Kingdom of Caesar" (from *Christ and Culture*), *Dimensions of Faith: Contemporary Prophetic Protestant Theology*, ed. William Kimmel and Geoffrey Clive. New York: Twayne Publishers, 1960, 341-84.

"The Churches of the Disinherited: I-II (from *The Social Sources of Denominationalism*), *Religion, Culture, and Society: A Reader in the Sociology of Religion*, ed. Louis Schneider. New York: John Wiley & Sons, 1964, 466-71.

"The Churches of the Immigrants" (from *The Social Sources of Denominationalism*), *Church and State in American History*, ed. John F. Wilson. Boston: D. C. Heath & Co., 1965, 42-45.

"The Churches of the Middle Class" (from *The Social Sources of Denominationalism*), *Religion, Society, and the Individual: An Introduction to the Sociology of Religion*, ed. John Milton Yinger. New York: Macmillan, 1957, 455-58.

"The Disorder of Man in the Church of God," *Man's Disorder and God's Design*, Vol. I: *The Universal Church in God's Design*. New York: Harper & Bros., 1949, 78-88.

An Encyclopedia of Religion, ed. Vergilius Ferm. New York: The Philosophical Library, 1945. Articles: "Church: Conceptions of the Church in Historic Christianity," 169-70; "Ethics: Christian Ethics," 259-60; "Inspiration," 374; "Revelation," 660-61; "Troeltsch, Ernst," 795-96.

Encyclopaedia of the Social Sciences, ed. E. R. A. Seligman. New York: Macmillan, 1931. Articles: "Dogma," Vol. V, 189-91; "Sectarian Education," Vol. V, 421-25; "Fundamentalism," Vol. VI, 526-27; "Higher Criticism," Vol. VII, 347-49; "Protestantism," Vol. XII, 571-75; "Reformation: Non-Lutheran," Vol. XIII, 190-93; "Religious Institutions, Christian: Protestant," Vol. XIII, 267-72; "Schaff, Philip," Vol. XIII, 562; "Sects," Vol. XIII, 624-31.

"Evangelical and Protestant Ethics," in *The Heritage of the Reformation: Essays Commemorating the Centennial of Eden Theological Seminary*, ed. E. J. F. Arndt. New York: Richard R. Smith, 1950, 211-29.

Foreword to *The Essence of Christianity* by Ludwig Feuerbach, trans. George Eliot. New York: Harper & Bros., 1957, vii-ix.

Foreword to *In His Likeness* by G. McLeod Bryan. Richmond, Virginia: John Knox Press, 1959, 5-6.

Introduction to *The Social Teaching of the Christian Churches,* Ernst Troeltsch. New York: Harper Torchbooks; The Cloister Library; Harper & Row, 1960, 7-12.

"The Meaning of Responsibility" (from *The Responsible Self), On Being Responsible: Issues in Personal Ethics* by James M. Gustafson and James T. Laney. New York: Harper & Row, 1968, 19-38.

"Modifications of Calvinism" (from *The Social Sources of Denominationalism), Religion, Society, and the Individual: An Introduction to the Sociology of Religion,* ed. John Milton Yinger. New York: Macmillan, 1957, 524-28.

"On the Nature of Faith," *Religious Experience and Truth: A Symposium,* ed. Sidney Hook. New York: New York University Press, 1961, 93-102.

"The Protestant Movement and Democracy in the United States," *Religion in American Life,* Vol. I: *The Shaping of American Religion,* ed. James Ward Smith and A. Leland Jamison. Princeton: Princeton University Press, 1961, 20-71.

"Religion and Socialism" (from *The Social Sources of Denominationalism),* in *Religion, Culture, and Society; A Reader in the Sociology of Religion,* ed. Louis Schneider. New York: John Wiley & Sons, 1964, 178-80.

Die Religion in Geschichte und Gegenwart. Dritte, völlig neu bearbeitete Auflage in Gemeinschaft mit Hans Frhr. von Campenhausen, Erich Dinkler . . . 1958. Articles: "Emerson, Ralph Waldo (1803-82)," Vol. II, 454-55; "Individual- und Sozialethik," Vol. III, 715-20.

"Religious Realism and the Twentieth Century," *Religious Realism,* ed. D. C. Macintosh. New York: Macmillan, 1931, 413-28.

"The Responsibility of the Church for Society," *The Gospel, the Church and the World,* ed. Kenneth Scott Latourette. New York, London: Harper & Bros., 1946, 111-33.

"Sören Kierkegaard," *Christianity and the Existentialists,* ed. Carl Michalson. New York: Charles Scribner's Sons, 1956, 23-42.

"The Sovereignty of God" (from *The Kingdom of God in America), Church and State in American History,* ed. John F. Wilson. Boston: D. C. Heath & Co., 1965, 20-25.

"The Story of Our Life" (from *The Meaning of Revelation), Interpreting Religion* by Donald Walhout. Englewood Cliffs, N.J.: Prentice-Hall, 1963, 305-14.

Translator's Preface to *The Religious Situation* by Paul Tillich, trans. by H. Richard Niebuhr. New York: Holt, Rinehart & Winston, 1932, vii-xxii.

Reprinted as "The Religious Situation," *Contemporary Religious Thought*, ed. T. S. Kepler. New York: Abingdon-Cokesbury, 1941, 83-88.

"Value Theory and Theology," *The Nature of Religious Experience: Essays in Honor of Douglas Clyde Macintosh*; editorial committee: Julius Seelye Bixler, Robert Lowry Calhoun, H. Richard Niebuhr. New York, London: Harper & Bros., 1937, 93-116.

"Who Are the Unbelievers and What Do They Believe?" Report Submitted to the Secretariat for Evangelism, World Council of Churches, Second Assembly, *The Christian Hope and the Task of the Church: Six Ecumenical Surveys and the Report of the Assembly Prepared by the Advisory Commission on the Main Theme, 1954*. New York: Harper & Bros., 1954, 35-37.

ARTICLES IN PERIODICALS

"The Alliance Between Labor and Religion" *Theological Magazine of the Evangelical Synod of North America*, XLIX (1921), 197-203.

"An Aspect of the Idea of God in Recent Thought" *Theological Magazine of the Evangelical Synod of North America*, XLVIII (1920), 39-44.

"The Attack upon the Social Gospel" *Religion in Life*, V (1936), 176-81.

"An Attempt at a Theological Analysis of Missionary Motivation" *Missionary Research Library* (New York City) *Occasional Bulletin*, XIV (1963), 1-6.

"Back to Benedict?" *The Christian Century*, XLII (1925), 860-61.

"Can German and American Christians Understand Each Other?" *The Christian Century*, XLVII (1930), 914-16.

"The Christian Church in the World's Crisis" *Christianity and Society*, VI (1941), 11-17.

"The Christian Evangel and Social Culture" *Religion in Life*, VIII (1939), 44-48.

"Christianity and the Industrial Classes" *Theological Magazine of the Evangelical Synod of North America*, LVII (1929), 12-18.

"Christianity and the Social Problem" *Theological Magazine of the Evangelical Synod of North America*, L (1922), 278-91.

"The Churches and the Body of Christ" (reprint of the concluding section of *The Churches and the Body of Christ) Friends' Intelligencer*, CX (1953), 621-23.

"Churches That Might Unite" *The Christian Century*, XLVI (1929), 259-61.

"A Communication: The Only Way into the Kingdom of God" *The Christian Century*, XLIX (1932), 447.

> Reprinted as: "The Only Way into the Kingdom of God" *Religion and Contemporary Western Culture: Selected Readings*, comp. Edward Cell. Nashville, Tenn.: Abingdon Press, 1967, 382-84.

"The Doctrine of the Trinity and the Unity of the Church" *Theology Today*, III (1946), 371-84.

"The Ego-Alter Dialectic and the Conscience" *Journal of Philosophy*, XLII (1945), 352-59.

"Ex Libris" *The Christian Century*, LXXIX (1962), 754. (A booklist submitted in response to the query: What books did most to shape your vocational attitude and your philosophy of life?)

"Faith, Works and Social Salvation" *Religion in Life*, I (1932), 426-30.

"The Gift of the Catholic Vision" *Theology Today*, IV (1948), 507-21.

"The Grace of Doing Nothing" *The Christian Century*, XLIX (1932), 378-80.

> Reprinted as: "The Grace of Doing Nothing" *The Christian Century Reader: Representative Articles, Editorials, and Poems Selected from More than Fifty Years of The Christian Century*, ed. Harold E. Fey and Margaret Frakes. New York: Association Press, 1962, 216-21. "The Grace of Doing Nothing" *Religion and Contemporary Western Culture: Selected Readings*, comp. Edward Cell. Nashville, Tenn.: Abingdon Press, 1967, 375-78.

"The Hidden Church and the Churches in Sight" *Religion in Life*, XV (1945-46), 106-17.

"The Idea of Covenant and American Democracy" *Church History*, XXIII (1954), 126-35.

"The Illusions of Power" *The Pulpit*, XXXIII (1962), 4(100)-7(103).

"Inconsistency of the Majority" *World Tomorrow*, XVII (1934), 43-44.

"The Irreligion of Communist and Capitalist" *The Christian Century*, XLVII (1930), 1306-07.

"Is God in the War?" *The Christian Century*, LIX (1942), 953-55.

"Issues Between Catholics and Protestants" *Religion in Life*, XXIII (1954), 199-205.

"Jesus Christ, Intercessor" *International Journal of Religious Education*, III: 4 (1927), 6-8.

"Life Is Worth Living" *Intercollegian and Far Horizons*, LVII (1939), 3-4, 22.

"The Main Issues in Theological Education" (with Daniel Day Williams and James M. Gustafson), *Theology Today*, XI (1955), 512-27.

"Man the Sinner" *Journal of Religion*, XV (1935), 272-80.

"Nationalism, Socialism and Christianity" *World Tomorrow*, XVI (1933), 469-70.

"The Nature and Existence of God: A Protestant's View" *Motive*, IV (1943), 13-15, 43-46.

Reprinted as: "Faith in Gods and in God" *Radical Monotheism and Western Culture, with Supplementary Essays*, 114-26.

"The Norm of the Church" *Journal of Religious Thought*, IV (1946-47), 5-15.

"Reformation: Continuing Imperative" *The Christian Century*, LXXVII (1960), 248-51; in the series "How My Mind Has Changed."

Reprinted as: H. Richard Niebuhr,' *How My Mind Has Changed*, ed. Harold E. Fey. Cleveland, New York: Living Age Books; Meridian Books, 69-80.

"Religion and Ethics" *World Tomorrow*, XIII (1930), 443-46.

"Reply to Professor Willem F. Zuurdeeg," in "Critic's Corner," *Theology Today*, XVIII (1961), 359-60.

"Science and Religion" *Yale Divinity News* (January 1960), 3-21.

"A dialogue between scientists and theologians as it took place at a recent Yale Divinity School convocation . . . telescoped version."

"The Seminary in the Ecumenical Age" (an address delivered at the inauguration of James I. McCord as president of Princeton Theological Seminary) *Princeton Seminary Bulletin*, LIV (July 1960), 38-45. Reprinted in *Theology Today*, XVII (1960), 300-310.

"Theology and Psychology: A Sterile Union" *The Christian Century*, XLIV (1927), 47-48.

"Theology—Not Queen but Servant" *Journal of Religion*, XXXV (1955), 1-5.

Reprinted as "Theology in the University" *Radical Monotheism and Western Culture, with Supplementary Essays*, 93-99.

"Toward the Emancipation of the Church" *Christendom*, I (1935-36), 133-45.

"Towards a New Otherworldliness" *Theology Today*, I (1944), 78-87.

"Training a Preacher" *Presbyterian Survey* (September 1956), 24-25.

"The Triad of Faith" *Andover Newton Bulletin*, XLVII (October 1954), 3-12.

First part of the Stephen Greene Lecture, October 1954.

Two Lenten Meditations ("Tired Christians" and "Preparation for Maladjustment") *Yale Divinity News*, XXXV (March 1939), 3-4.

"Utilitarian Christianity" *Christianity and Crisis*, VI (1946), 3-5.

Reprinted in *Witness to a Generation: Significant Writings from Christianity and Crisis (1941-66)*, ed. Wayne H. Cowan. Indianapolis: Bobbs-Merrill, 1966, 240-45.

"War as Crucifixion" *The Christian Century*, LX (1943), 513-15.

"War as the Judgment of God" *The Christian Century*, LIX (1942), 630-33.

"What Holds Churches Together?" *The Christian Century*, XLIII (1926), 346-48.

"What Then Must We Do?" *Christian Century Pulpit*, V (1934), 145-47.

"Why Restudy Theological Education?" *The Christian Century*, LXXI (1954), 516-17, 527.

SELECTED UNPUBLISHED MATERIALS

"The Anachronism of Jonathan Edwards," 1958.

"Bulletins of the Staff of the Inquiry into Theological Education in America, 1954-56," H. Richard Niebuhr, director; Daniel Day Williams, associate director; James M. Gustafson, assistant director.

No. 1. April 1954. "A Study of Theological Education in the United States and Canada," 4 pp.

No. 2. September 1954. "What Are the Main Issues in Theological Education?" 12 pp. (Reprinted as: "The Main Issues in Theological Education," *Theology Today*, XI [1955], 512-27.)

No. 3. January 1955. "Isolation and Cooperation in Theological Education," 6 pp.

No. 4. September 1955. "Memorandum on the Theological Education of Negro Ministers," 8 pp.

No. 5. April 1956. "Toward the Reorganization of Theological Education," 11 pp.

"A Christian Interpretation of War," n.d.

"The Church Defines Itself in the World," 1957.

"Classroom Lectures on Christian Ethics" (Niebuhr's notes), 1961.

"The Idea of the Church in Theological Education," n.d.

"Man's Work and God's," n.d.

"Martin Luther and the Renewal of Human Confidence," 1959.

"The Nature of Protestant Christianity in America and the Problem of Educating Its Ministers," n.d.

"Participation in the Present Passion," n.d.

"Reflections on Faith, Hope, and Love," n.d.

"Reflections on a 'Protestant Theory of Higher Education,' " 1959.

"The Relativities of Religion," n.d.
"Religion and the Ethical Crisis of Our Time," 1961.
"Theological Frontiers": 1. "The Position of Theology Today," 2.
    "Towards New Symbols"; Cole Lectures at Vanderbilt University.
"Types of Christian Ethics," n.d.